**Break**

# Break Clauses

**Mark Warwick, LL.B.**
*Barrister, Selborne Chambers*

**Nicholas Trompeter, M.A. (Oxon)**
*Barrister, Selborne Chambers*

SWEET & MAXWELL    THOMSON REUTERS

First Edition 2011 by Mark Warwick and Nicholas Trompeter

Published in 2011 by Sweet & Maxwell, 100 Avenue Road, London NW3 3PF part of Thomson Reuters (Professional) UK Limited (Registered in England & Wales, Company No 1679046.

Registered Office and address for service: Aldgate House, 33 Aldgate High Street, London EC3N 1DL)

For further information on our products and services, visit www.sweetandamaxwell.co.uk

Typeset by LBJ Typesetting Ltd of Kingsclere

Printed and bound by CPI Group (UK) Ltd, Croydon, CR0 4YY.

No natural forests were destroyed to make this product; only farmed timber was used and re-planted.

A CIP catalogue record of this book is available for the British Library.
ISBN: 978-0-41404-815-7

Thomson Reuters and the Thomson Reuters logo are trademarks of Thomson Reuters.

Sweet & Maxwell ® is a registered trademark of Thomson Reuters (Professional) UK Limited.

Crown copyright material is reproduced with the permission of the Controller of HMSO and the Queen's Printer for Scotland.

All rights reserved. No part of this publication may be reproduced or transmitted in any form or by any means, or stored in any retrieval system of any nature without prior written permission, except for permitted fair dealing under the Copyright, Designs and Patents Act 1988, or in accordance with the terms of a licence issued by the Copyright Licensing Agency in respect of photocopying and/or reprographic reproduction. Application for permission for other use of copyright material including permission to reproduce extracts in other published works shall be made to the publishers. Full acknowledgement of author, publisher and source must be given.

© 2011 Thomson Reuters (Legal) Limited

# FOREWORD

In recent years break clauses have been one of the most litigated areas of the law of landlord and tenant. Most of the cases have concerned attempts to exercise tenants' rights to break.

The inclusion of a tenant's right to break in a commercial lease in some ways gives the tenant the best of both worlds. He can terminate the lease if he chooses to exercise the break; or stay for the remainder of the term if he chooses not to. Why would the landlord agree to the inclusion of a clause which gave the tenant the best of both worlds? The answer, I suspect, is that in most cases the quid pro quo for the break clause is the tenant's agreement to an upward only rent review clause. If the tenant took a shorter term without the break, and had the right to renew the lease under the Landlord and Tenant Act 1954, then the rent could go down on renewal. So from the landlord's perspective a longer term with a break clause is a limited form of guaranteeing the income stream.

At the drafting stage the landlord will try to make the break difficult to exercise. He will try to hedge it about with conditions to be fulfilled. The tenant, for his part, will try to excise or dilute the conditions. Many of the cases concern both the interpretation of such conditions, and also the factual question whether they have been fulfilled.

If the tenant tries to exercise the break, the chances are that he does so because the market has changed. He is paying more than the rental value of the leased property and wants cheaper accommodation elsewhere. The consequence of failure will be expensive. But the change in economic conditions will be precisely the reason why the landlord will fiercely resist the tenant's attempt to break the lease. He will pick over the tenant's notice exercising the break looking for any possible error; and he will examine minutely whether the tenant has fulfilled any conditions on which the validity of the break notice depends. Does it specify the right date? Was it served by the right person? Was it given to the right person? Was it given in accordance with any stipulated timetable? Did the tenant comply sufficiently with his obligations under the lease? Has the tenant given vacant possession? If any one of these questions elicits even a plausible negative answer the stage is set for a full scale battle.

Landlords' break clauses are products of different economic circumstances. The most common form of landlord's break clause is a redevelopment break clause. Naturally enough, when the market is slow break clauses of this kind are less common. Here the principal battleground has been lease renewals under the Landlord and Tenant Act 1954. Ever since Mr David Neuberger (unadorned as he then was) won the unwinnable appeal in *Adams v Green* the courts have been trying to repair the damage. The story is told in Chapter 9 of this book.

Mark Warwick and Nicholas Trompeter have produced a comprehensive guide to the many questions that arise when drafting, exercising and litigating break clauses. It is both scholarly and practical. It will be invaluable to all those involved in the property industry. A guide through the complexities and pitfalls on the path to breaking a lease is a necessity; because as WC Fields memorably said: "Never give a sucker an even break".

Kim Lewison<br>
Royal Courts of Justice<br>
London WC2A 2LL

# PREFACE

Break clauses are of huge significance to landlords and tenants alike, from both a financial and practical (i.e. estate management and business planning) perspective. This significance is reflected in the recent figures published by the British Property Federation in its Annual Lease Review 2011, which show that, in 2010/2011, the proportion of new leases containing a break clause stood at 31.1 per cent.

It is, perhaps, a sign of current economic conditions that one finds an increasing number of reported cases which touch upon break clauses. Indeed, a search of legal databases reveals that, in the last three or so years, a decision concerning the subject matter of this book has been handed down, on average, about once every three months. In many ways, this is unsurprising given that, in a falling or turbulent property market, tenants will be keen to extricate themselves from leases under which they are liable to pay to their landlords a passing rent which is above the market rent; which, of course, is something that landlords are equally keen to prevent.

Given the spate of recent litigation concerning break clauses, it is thought that it is a timely moment for a book devoted to the subject to be produced. At all times, we have sought to make this book as practical as possible, by offering advice from both the landlord's and the tenant's perspective.

We are both extremely grateful to Lord Justice Lewison for writing a foreword to this book. Not only does he refer to the volume of litigation involving break clauses, but lucidly explains many of the reasons behind it.

Since this is a new book we are conscious that it may suffer from many blemishes, or worse. It goes without saying that any errors are ours alone. We welcome any comments that readers may have.

The law is stated as at October 14, 2011.

**Mark Warwick**
**Nicholas Trompeter**
Selborne Chambers
10 Essex Street
London
WC2R 3AA

# Contents

| | |
|---|---|
| *Foreword* | v |
| *Preface* | vii |
| *Table of Cases* | xvii |
| *Table of Statutes* | xxvii |
| *Table of Statutory Instruments* | xxxi |

**Chapter 1: The Nature of a Break Clause in a Lease**     1

1. A definition     1
2. A break notice is not a notice to quit     1
3. The right to terminate is unilateral     2
4. Forfeiture/acceptance of repudiatory breach distinguished     2
5. A break clause is a type of option     3
6. Break clauses can appear in all types of tenancies and in many different forms     4

**Chapter 2: Formalities and Registration**     5

1. Formalities     5
2. Registration     6

**Chapter 3: Assignment**     7

1. The common law position relating to assignment     7
2. Section 63 of the Law of Property Act 1925     8
3. Section 142 of the Law of Property Act 1925     9
4. Section 3 of the Landlord and Tenant (Covenants) Act 1995     10
5. The position where the tenant assigns the term     11
6. The position where the landlord assigns the reversion     13
7. Equitable assignees     15
8. The position where the option is not contained in the lease     16
9. General good practice     17

## Chapter 4: Contents of a Break Clause — 19

1. Introduction — 19
2. The date of termination—general observations — 19
3. Notices—length and termination dates — 20
4. The language of the break notice and mistakes—the general approach — 22
5. Mistakes as to the date of termination — 24
6. Mistakes in the identity of the landlord or the tenant — 25
7. Mistakes in the description of the premises — 27
8. The relevance of the reaction of the party receiving the break notice — 28
9. Break notices that incorporate the phrases "without prejudice" and "subject to contract" — 29
10. Sequential break notices — 31
11. Invalid notices and estoppels — 31

## Chapter 5: Who May Exercise the Break Clause — 33

1. General observations — 33
2. Where the break clause is personal to the original tenant — 36
3. Where the lease is silent/ambiguous — 39
4. Assignees — 40
5. Joint lessees — 40
6. Joint lessors — 41
7. The survivor of joint lessees/joint lessors — 41
8. Trustees in bankruptcy — 41
9. Administrators — 42
10. Liquidators — 42
11. The use of agents — 42

## Chapter 6: Service (and Withdrawal) of the Break Notice — 47

1. Who may serve the break notice — 47
2. On whom a break notice must be served — 47
3. Method of service — 50
4. When a break notice should be served — 53
5. Estoppel and waiver — 58
6. Withdrawal of a break notice — 58
7. Professional liability in connection with invalid break notices — 60

## Chapter 7: Conditions in a Break Clause — 63

1. The principle of strict compliance — 63
2. Subjectivity and motive — 64
3. Spent breaches — 65
4. The time for compliance with any conditions — 66
5. Words qualifying the principle of strict compliance — 68

## CONTENTS

| | |
|---|---|
| 6. "Reasonable" or "reasonably"? | 69 |
| 7. "Material" | 70 |
| 8. "Substantial" | 71 |
| 9. Vacant possession | 72 |
| 10. Reinstatement obligations | 74 |
| 11. Paying the rent | 75 |
| 12. Waiver of or estoppel in relation to conditions in a tenant's break clause—the tenant's position | 76 |
| 13. Waiver of conditions in a tenant's break clause—the landlord's position | 78 |
| 14. Conditions in a landlord's break clause | 79 |
| 15. The server of a notice cannot rely upon its own wrong | 80 |

### Chapter 8: The Effect of Exercising a Break Clause — 83

1. As between landlord and tenant — 83
2. As regards an underlessee — 89

### Chapter 9: Business Tenancies — 91

1. Introduction — 91
2. A landlord's break notice and the 1954 Act — 91
3. The inclusion of a landlord's break notice in a new lease — 93
4. The inclusion of a tenant's break clause in a new lease — 96
5. A tenant cannot break a lease and then seek a new lease under the 1954 Act — 96
6. The position of sub-tenants — 97

### Chapter 10: Agricultural Tenancies — 99

1. Termination of contracts for agricultural tenancies — 99
2. Termination of a farm business tenancy — 104

### Chapter 11: Residential Tenancies — 107

1. Termination of Rent Act protected tenancies — 107
2. Termination of assured tenancies — 108
3. Termination of assured shorthold tenancies — 110
4. Termination of contractual tenancies without any statutory security of tenure — 111

### Chapter 12: Drafting Break Clauses — 113

1. General remarks — 113
2. Matters to address when drafting a break clause — 114

### Chapter 13: Practical Advice as to the Exercise of Break Clauses and Disputes as to Their Exercise — 117

1. Points for the tenant when exercising a break clause — 117

## CONTENTS

2. Points for the landlord on receiving a tenant's break notice — 118
3. Points for the landlord when exercising a break clause — 119
4. Points for the tenant on receiving a landlord's break notice — 120
5. Litigation tactics—the tenant's exercise of a break clause — 121
6. Litigation tactics—the landlord's exercise of a break clause — 121

**Appendix 1: Break Clause for the Landlord—On One or More Specified Dates — 123**

Break clause for the landlord—on one or more specified dates — 123
The schedule—the form of the landlord's break notice — 123

**Appendix 2: Break Clause for the Landlord—Incorporating a Rolling Break — 125**

Break clause for the landlord—incorporating a rolling break — 125
The schedule—the form of the landlord's break notice — 125

**Appendix 3: Break Clause for the Tenant—On One or More Specified Dates — 127**

Break clause for the tenant—on one or more specified dates — 127
The schedule—the form of the tenant's break notice — 128

**Appendix 4: Break Clause for the Tenant—Incorporating a Rolling Break — 129**

Break clause for the tenant—incorporating a rolling break — 129
The schedule—the form of the tenant's break notice — 130

**Appendix 5: Particulars of Claim: Landlord's Claim for Declaration, Etc — 131**

**Appendix 6: Defence and Counterclaim: In Response to Landlord's Claim for Declaration, Etc — 135**

**Appendix 7: Relevant Provisions of the Landlord and Tenant Act 1730 — 139**

Section I—Persons holding over Lands, &c. After Expiration of Leases, to pay double the yearly Value. — 139

## CONTENTS xiii

**Appendix 8: Relevant Provisions of the Distress for Rent Act 1737**    141

    Section 18—Tenants holding after the time they notify for quitting, to pay double rent.    141

**Appendix 9: Relevant Provisions of the Law of Property Act 1925**    143

    Section 63—All estate clause implied.    143
    Section 140—Apportionment of conditions on severance.    143
    Section 142—Obligation of lessor's covenants to run with reversion.    144
    Section 196—Regulations respecting notices.    145
    Section 205—General definitions.    146

**Appendix 10: Relevant Provisions of the Landlord and Tenant Act 1954**    147

    Section 24—Continuation of tenancies to which Part II applies and grant of new tenancies.    147
    Section 25—Termination of tenancy by the landlord.    147
    Section 26—Tenant's request for new tenancy.    148
    Section 30—Opposition by landlord to application for new tenancy.    149
    Section 33—Duration of new tenancy.    149
    Section 35—Other terms of new tenancy.    150
    Section 69—Interpretation.    150

**Appendix 11: Relevant Provisions of the Recorded Delivery Service Act 1962**    151

    Section 1—Recorded delivery service to be an alternative to registered post.    151

**Appendix 12: Relevant Provisions of the Rent Act 1977**    153

    Section 1—Protected tenants and tenancies.    153
    Section 2—Statutory tenants and tenancies.    153
    Section 3—Terms and conditions of statutory tenancies.    154
    Section 98—Grounds for possession of certain dwelling-houses.    154

**Appendix 13: Relevant Provisions of the Protection from Eviction Act 1977**    155

    Section 5—Validity of notices to quit.    155

**Appendix 14: Relevant Provisions of the Agricultural Holdings Act 1986**    157

    Section 1—Principal definitions.    157

| | |
|---|---|
| Section 2—Restriction on letting agricultural land for less than from year to year. | 158 |
| Section 3—Tenancies for two years or more to continue from year to year unless terminated by notice. | 158 |
| Section 25—Length of notice to quit. | 159 |
| Section 26—Restriction on operation of notices to quit. | 160 |
| Section 27—Tribunal's consent to operation of notice to quit. | 160 |
| Section 60—Right to, and measure of, compensation for disturbance. | 162 |
| Section 96—Interpretation. | 162 |

**Appendix 15: Relevant Provisions of the Housing Act 1988** — **163**

| | |
|---|---|
| Section 5—Security of tenure. | 163 |
| Section 21—Recovery of possession on expiry or termination of assured shorthold tenancy. | 165 |

**Appendix 16: Relevant Provisions of the Landlord and Tenant (Covenants) Act 1995** — **167**

| | |
|---|---|
| Section 3—Transmission of benefit and burden of covenants. | 167 |
| Section 28—Interpretation. | 168 |

**Appendix 17: Relevant Provisions of the Agricultural Tenancies Act 1995** — **171**

| | |
|---|---|
| Section 1—Meaning of "farm business tenancy". | 171 |
| Section 5—Tenancies for more than two years to continue from year to year unless terminated by notice. | 172 |
| Section 6—Length of notice to quit. | 172 |
| Section 7—Notice required for exercise of option to terminate tenancy or resume possession of part. | 173 |
| Section 16—Tenant's right to compensation for tenant's improvement. | 173 |
| Section 36—Service of notices. | 174 |
| Section 38—Interpretation. | 175 |

**Appendix 18:** *Finch v Underwood* **(1875–1876) L.R. 2 Ch.D. 310 at 314—316** — **177**

**Appendix 19:** *United Scientific Holdings Ltd v Burnley Borough Council* **[1978] A.C. 904 at 928—929, 945—946, and 951** — **179**

**Appendix 20:** *Bass Holdings Ltd v Morton Music Ltd* **[1988] 1 Ch. 493 at 517—520** — **183**

# CONTENTS

**Appendix 21:** *Hounslow London Borough Council v Pilling* [1993] 1 W.L.R. 1242 at 1246—1247 — 187

**Appendix 22:** *Union Eagle Ltd v Golden Achievement Ltd* [1997] A.C. 514 at 523 — 189

**Appendix 23:** *Mannai Investment Co Ltd v Eagle Star Life Assurance Co Ltd* [1997] A.C. 749 at 767—769, 773—775, and 780—782 — 191

**Appendix 24:** *Barrett v Morgan* [2000] 2 A.C. 264 at 270—271 — 199

**Appendix 25:** *PW & Co v Milton Gate Investments Ltd* [2004] Ch. 142 at 164 — 201

**Appendix 26:** *Davy's Of London (Wine Merchants) Ltd v City Of London Corporation* [2004] EWHC 2224 (Ch) at 22—25 — 203

**Appendix 27:** *Fitzroy House Epworth Street (No.1) Ltd v Financial Times Ltd* [2006] 1 W.L.R. 2207 at 24 and 35—36 — 205

**Appendix 28:** Extracts From 'The Code for Leasing Business Premises in England and Wales 2007' — 207

*Index* — 209

# Table of Cases

Aberdeen Steak Houses Group Plc v Crown Estate Commissioners [1997] 2
E.G.L.R. 107; [1997] 31 E.G. 101; [1997] E.G. 14 (C.S.); [1997] N.P.C.
12, CA (Civ Div) .......................................... 6–024, 7–061
Adams v Green [1978] 2 E.G.L.R. 46; (1978) 247 E.G. 49, CA (Civ Div) ..... 9–009,
A26–001
Agbaje v Agbaje [2010] UKSC 13; [2010] 1 A.C. 628; [2010] 2 W.L.R. 709;
[2010] 2 All E.R. 877; [2010] 1 F.L.R. 1813; [2010] 2 F.C.R. 1; [2010]
Fam. Law 573; (2010) 107(12) L.S.G. 20; (2010) 154(11) S.J.L.B. 29,
SC .......................................................... 7–034
Al-Saloom v Shirley James Travel Services Ltd (1981) 42 P. & C.R. 181;
(1981) 259 E.G. 420; (1981) 125 S.J. 397, Ch D ...................... 8–007
Amika Motors v Colebrook Holdings (1981) 259 E.G. 243, CA (Civ Div) ...... 9–009

BDW Trading Ltd (t/a Barratt North London) v JM Rowe (Investments) Ltd
[2011] EWCA Civ 548; [2011] 20 E.G. 113 (C.S.), CA (Civ Div) ... 1–010, 7–007
BP Oil UK Ltd v Lloyds TSB Bank Plc; Mobil Exploration & Production UK
Ltd v Lloyds TSB Bank Ltd [2004] EWCA Civ 1710; [2005] 1 E.G.L.R.
61; [2005] 10 E.G. 156; [2005] 3 E.G. 116 (C.S.); (2005) 102(9) L.S.G.
29, CA (Civ Div) ................................................. 5–015
Bairstow Eves (Securities) Ltd v Ripley (1993) 65 P. & C.R. 220; [1992] 32
E.G. 52; [1992] 2 E.G.L.R. 47; [1992] E.G. 83 (C.S.); [1992] N.P.C. 78,
CA (Civ Div) ............................................ 7–005, 7–006
Baker Tilly Management Ltd v Computer Associates UK Ltd, Unreported
December 11, 2009 Ch D ................................. 4–029, 5–006
Ballard (Kent) Ltd v Oliver Ashworth (Holdings) Ltd; sub nom. Oliver
Ashworth (Holdings) Ltd v Ballard (Kent) Ltd [2000] Ch. 12; [1999] 3
W.L.R. 57; [1999] 2 All E.R. 791; [1999] L. & T.R. 400; [1999] 2 E.G.L.R.
23; [1999] 19 E.G. 161; (1999) 96(16) L.S.G. 36; (1999) 149 N.L.J. 521;
[1999] N.P.C. 36, CA (Civ Div); ................................... 8–014
Barrett v Morgan [2000] 2 A.C. 264; [2000] 2 W.L.R. 284; [2000] 1 All E.R.
481; (2001) 81 P. & C.R. 1; [2000] L. & T.R. 209; [2000] 1 E.G.L.R. 8;
[2000] 06 E.G. 165; (2000) 97(6) L.S.G. 36; (2000) 144 S.J.L.B. 84;
(2000) 79 P. & C.R. D23, HL .... 1–006, 1–007, 8–018, 9–014,A24–001,A25–001
Bass Holdings Ltd v Morton Music Ltd [1988] Ch. 493; [1987] 3 W.L.R. 543;
[1987] 2 All E.R. 1001; (1987) 54 P. & C.R. 135; [1987] 1 E.G.L.R. 214;
(1987) 84 L.S.G. 1414; (1987) 131 S.J. 473, CA (Civ Div) ....... 7–004, 7–010,
7–021, 7–032, A20–001
Bassett v Whiteley (1983) 45 P. & C.R. 80 ...................... 7–027, A20–001
Bastin v Bidwell (1880–81) L.R. 18 Ch. D. 238, Ch D .......... 7–016, 7–017, 7–050
Beanby Estates Ltd v Egg Stores (Stamford Hill) Ltd; sub nom. Egg Stores
(Stamford Hill) Ltd v Beanby Estates Ltd [2003] EWHC 1252 (Ch);
[2003] 1 W.L.R. 2064; [2004] 3 All E.R. 184; [2003] 3 E.G.L.R. 85;
[2003] 21 E.G. 190 (C.S.); (2003) 100(26) L.S.G. 37; [2003] N.P.C. 65;
[2003] 2 P. & C.R. DG15, Ch D ................................... 6–018

# TABLE OF CASES

Bebington's Tenancy, Re; Bebington v Wildman [1921] 1 Ch. 559, Ch D ...... 3–019, 4–050
Becker v Hill Street Properties [1990] 38 E.G. 107; (1990) 2 E.G.L.R. 78; [1990] E.G. 31 (C.S.), CA (Civ Div) .............................. 9–009
Bennett v Fowler (1840) 2 Beav. 302 ................................... 7–057
Betty's Cafes Ltd v Phillips Furnishing Stores Ltd (No.1) [1959] A.C. 20; [1958] 2 W.L.R. 513; [1958] 1 All E.R. 607; (1958) 102 S.J. 228, HL ..... 7–060
Biondi v Kirklington and Piccadilly Estates Ltd [1947] 2 All E.R. 59; [1947] L.J.R. 884; 177 L.T. 101; (1947) 91 S.J. 599, Ch D ................... 6–026
Blore v Giulini [1903] 1 K.B. 356, KBD ................................ 8–003
Blunden v Frogmore Investments Ltd [2002] EWCA Civ 573; [2003] 2 P. & C.R. 6; [2002] L. & T.R. 31; [2002] 2 E.G.L.R. 29; [2002] 29 E.G. 153; [2002] 20 E.G. 223 (C.S.); [2002] N.P.C. 62; [2002] 2 P. & C.R. DG11, CA (Civ Div) ........................................... 6–018, 9–004
Brown & Root Technology Ltd v Sun Alliance and London Assurance Co Ltd [2001] Ch. 733; [2000] 2 W.L.R. 566; (1998) 75 P. & C.R. 223; [1997] 1 E.G.L.R. 39; [1997] 18 E.G. 123; (1997) 94(7) L.S.G. 29; (1997) 141 S.J.L.B. 38; [1996] N.P.C. 183; (1997) 73 P. & C.R. D33, CA (Civ Div) .... 3–028, 3–029
Brutus v Cozens [1973] A.C. 854; [1972] 3 W.L.R. 521; [1972] 2 All E.R. 1297; (1972) 56 Cr. App. R. 799; [1973] Crim. L.R. 56; (1972) 116 S.J. 647, QBD ....................................................... A27–001
Business Environment Bow Lane Ltd v Deanwater Estates Ltd [2007] EWCA Civ 622; [2007] L. & T.R. 26; [2007] 2 E.G.L.R. 51; [2007] 32 E.G. 90; [2007] 27 E.G. 303 (C.S.); [2007] N.P.C. 79, CA (Civ Div) ............. 2–002

CBS United Kingdom Ltd v London Scottish Properties [1985] 2 E.G.L.R. 125; (1985) 275 E.G. 718 ............................................. 9–011
Cadby v Martinez, 11 A. & E. 720 ................................... A23–002
Cannon Brewery Co v Signal Press Ltd (1929) 139 L.T. 384 ................ 6–016
Capital and City Holdings Ltd v Dean Warburg Ltd (1989) 58 P. & C.R. 346; [1989] 25 E.G. 97; [1988] E.G. 174 (C.S.); (1989) 1 E.G.L.R. 90, CA (Civ Div) ...................................................... 7–047
Carradine Properties Ltd v Aslam [1976] 1 W.L.R. 442; [1976] 1 All E.R. 573; (1976) 32 P. & C.R. 12; (1976) 120 S.J. 166, Ch D ....... 4–019, 4–020, 4–022, 4–023, 4–024, 4–027, 4–039, A23–001, A23–002, A23–003
Central Estates Ltd v Secretary of State for the Environment (1996) 72 P. & C.R. 482; [1997] 1 E.G.L.R. 239; [1995] E.G. 110 (C.S.); [1995] N.P.C. 106; (1996) 71 P. & C.R. D1, CA (Civ Div) ......................... 8–007
Chapman v Honig [1963] 2 Q.B. 502; [1963] 3 W.L.R. 19; [1963] 2 All E.R. 513; (1963) 107 S.J. 374, CA ..................................... 7–007
Cheall v Association of Professional, Executive, Clerical and Computer Staff (APEX) [1983] 2 A.C. 180; [1983] 2 W.L.R. 679; [1983] 1 All E.R. 1130; [1983] I.C.R. 398; [1983] I.R.L.R. 215; (1983) 133 N.L.J. 538, HL ....... 7–063
City of London Corp v Fell; Herbert Duncan Ltd v Cluttons [1994] 1 A.C. 458; [1993] 3 W.L.R. 1164; [1993] 4 All E.R. 968; 92 L.G.R. 1; (1995) 69 P. & C.R. 461; [1993] 49 E.G. 113; (1994) 91(4) L.S.G. 44; (1993) 143 N.L.J. 1747; (1994) 138 S.J.L.B. 13; [1993] N.P.C. 162, HL ........... 3–001, 3–002, 5–009
City Offices (Regents Street) Ltd v Europa Acceptance Group Plc (1990) 1 E.G.L.R. 63 ................................................ 7–062
Coates v Diment [1951] 1 All E.R. 890, Assizes (Dorset) ....... 6–025, 7–062, 10–014
Commercial Union Life Insurance Co Ltd v Label Ink Ltd (2001) L. & T.R. 380 ............................................ 7–006, 7–007, 13–007
Company (No.0005945 of 2006), Re; sub nom. A Company, Re [2006] EWHC 3436 (Ch); [2007] B.P.I.R. 1; (2006) 150 S.J.L.B. 1153, Ch D ........... 7–047

# TABLE OF CASES

Cordon Bleu Freezer Food Centres Ltd v Marbleace Ltd (1987) 2 E.G.L.R.
143 .................................................. 4–049
Coventry City Council v J Hepworth & Sons (1983) 46 P. & C.R. 170; (1983)
265 E.G. 608, CA (Civ Div) ............................. 8–007, 8–008
Cowan v Wrayford [1953] 1 W.L.R. 1340; [1953] 2 All E.R. 1138; 51 L.G.R.
659; (1953) 97 S.J. 780, CA ................................. 10–010
Cozens v Brutus. *See* Brutus v Cozens
Cumberland Consolidated Holdings Ltd v Ireland [1946] K.B. 264, CA ....... 7–037,
7–038, 7–041
Cunliffe v Goodman [1950] 2 K.B. 237; [1950] 1 All E.R. 720; (1950) 66
T.L.R. (Pt. 2) 109; (1950) 94 S.J. 179, CA ..................... 6–023, 7–060

Davy's of London (Wine Merchants) Ltd v City of London Corp; Davy's of
London (Wine Merchants) Ltd v Saxon Land BV [2004] EWHC 2224
(Ch); [2004] 3 E.G.L.R. 39; [2004] 49 E.G. 136; [2004] 42 E.G. 161
(C.S.); [2004] N.P.C. 144; [2005] 1 P. & C.R. DG8, Ch D ...... 9–009, A26–001
Delta Vale Properties Ltd v Mills [1990] 1 W.L.R. 445; [1990] 2 All E.R. 176;
[1989] E.G. 171 (C.S.); (1990) 87(9) L.S.G. 44; (1990) 140 N.L.J. 290;
(1990) 134 S.J. 316, CA (Civ Div) .......... 4–019, 4–023, A23–001, A23–003
Denham Bros Ltd v W Freestone Leasing Pty Ltd [2003] Q.C.A. 376 .......... 3–034
Dickinson v St Aubyn [1944] K.B. 454, CA ............................. 8–002
Disraeli Agreement, Re; sub nom. Agricultural Holdings Act 1923, Re; Cleasby
v Park Estate (Hughenden) Ltd [1939] Ch. 382, Ch D ................. 10 014
Divall v Harrison [1992] 38 E.G. 147; [1991] 14 E.G. 108; [1992] N.P.C. 25,
CA (Civ Div) ................................................... 5–029
Dodds v Walker [1981] 1 W.L.R. 1027; [1981] 2 All E.R. 609; (1981) 42 P. &
C.R. 131; (1981) 125 S.J. 463, HL ................................. 4–013
Dun & Bradstreet Software Services (England) Ltd v Provident Mutual Life
Assurance Association [1998] 2 E.G.L.R. 175; [1997] E.G. 89 (C.S.);
[1997] N.P.C. 91, CA (Civ Div) ................. 4–052, 5–036, 7–048, 7–049

East v Pantiles (Plant Hire) [1982] 2 E.G.L.R. 111; (1982) 263 E.G. 61, CA
(Civ Div) ..................................................... 4–011
Edell v Dulieu [1924] A.C. 38, HL ............................ 10–006, 11–020
Edwin Woodhouse Trustee Co v Sheffield Brick Co [1984] 1 E.G.L.R. 130 ..... 8–011
Ellis v Rowbotham [1900] 1 Q.B. 740, CA ............................. 7–047
Elsden v Pick [1980] 1 W.L.R. 898; [1980] 3 All E.R. 235; (1980) 40 P. & C.R.
550; (1980) 254 E.G. 503; (1980) 124 S.J. 312, CA (Civ Div) .... 6–034, 10–007
Enfield LBC v Devonish 1997) 29 H.L.R. 691; (1997) 74 P. & C.R. 288; [1996]
E.G. 194 (C.S.); [1996] N.P.C. 171, CA (Civ Div) ..................... 6–014
Equinox Industrial (GP2) Ltd v Sketchley Ltd [2003] EWHC 2 (Ch); [2003]
N.P.C. 13, Ch D .......................................... 5–012, 5–015
Extra MSA Services Cobham v Accor UK [2011] EWHC 775 (Ch), Ch D ...... 7–063

Fairweather v St Marylebone Property Co Ltd; sub nom. St Marylebone
Property Co Ltd v Fairweather [1963] A.C. 510; [1962] 2 W.L.R. 1020;
[1962] 2 All E.R. 288; (1962) 106 S.J. 368, HL ....................... 8–016
Fawaz v Aylward; sub nom. Aylward v Fawaz (1997) 29 H.L.R. 408; [1996]
E.G. 199 (C.S.); [1996] N.P.C. 109, CA (Civ Div) ...... 11–015, 11–016, 11–017
Finch v Underwood (1875–76) L.R. 2 Ch. D. 310, CA ... 7–002, 7–003, 7–004, 7–015,
7–023, 7–050, A18–001, A19–001
Fitzroy House Epworth Street (No.1) Ltd v Financial Times Ltd [2006] EWCA
Civ 329; [2006] 1 W.L.R. 2207; [2006] 2 All E.R. 776; [2006] 2 P. & C.R.
21; [2006] L. & T.R. 20; [2006] 2 E.G.L.R. 13; [2006] 19 E.G. 174;
[2006] 14 E.G. 175 (C.S.); [2006] N.P.C. 40, CA (Civ Div) ...... 7–007, 7–024,
7–032, 7–033, 7–034,
7–035, 13–007, A27–001

## TABLE OF CASES

Flather v Hood (1928) 44 T.L.R. 698 .................................... 10–005
Fortman Holdings Ltd v Modem Holdings Ltd [2001] EWCA Civ 1235, CA
  (Civ Div) ................................................ A27–001
Foster v Robinson [1951] 1 K.B. 149; [1950] 2 All E.R. 342; 66 T.L.R. (Pt. 2)
  120; (1950) 94 S.J. 474, CA .................................... 11–004
Freeman v Evans [1922] 1 Ch. 36, CA ..................... 6–035, 6–036, 6–037

Galinski v McHugh (1989) 21 H.L.R. 47; (1989) 57 P. & C.R. 359; [1989]
  1 E.G.L.R. 109; [1989] 05 E.G. 89; [1988] E.G. 127 (C.S.); (1988) 138
  N.L.J. Rep. 303, CA (Civ Div) .................................... 6–009
Ganton House Investments v Crossman Investments (1995) 1 E.G.L.R. 239;
  (1988) 1 E.G.L.R. 69 ........................................ 9–012, 7–057
Gardner v Blaxill [1960] 1 W.L.R. 752; [1960] 2 All E.R. 457; (1960) 104 S.J.
  585, QBD ....................................................... 7–026
Garston v Scottish Widows Fund & Life Assurance Society [1998] 1 W.L.R.
  1583; [1998] 3 All E.R. 596; [1998] L. & T.R. 230; [1998] 2 E.G.L.R. 73;
  [1998] 32 E.G. 88; [1998] E.G. 101 (C.S.); (1998) 95(26) L.S.G. 32;
  (1998) 142 S.J.L.B. 199; [1998] N.P.C. 109, CA (Civ Div) ....... 4–027, 9–013,
                                                                A23–003
Gentle v Faulkner [1990] 2 QB 267 ................................... 3–029
Germax Securities Ltd v Spiegal (1979) 37 P. & C.R. 204; (1978) 250 E.G. 449;
  (1979) 123 S.J. 164, CA (Civ Div) ............................. A23–002
Gladstone v Bower [1960] 2 Q.B. 384; [1960] 3 W.L.R. 575; [1960] 3 All E.R.
  353; 58 L.G.R. 313; (1960) 104 S.J. 763, CA .......... 10–005, 10–006, 11–020
Goodright on the demise of Hall v Richardson (1789) 3 Term Reports 462 ...... 6–030
Grant v Edmondson [1931] 1 Ch. 1, CA ................................ 3–004
Gregson v Cyril Lord Ltd [1963] 1 W.L.R. 41; [1962] 3 All E.R. 907; [1962]
  R.V.R. 730; (1962) 106 S.J. 899, CA ............................. 6–022
Grey v Friar, 10 E.R. 583; (1854) 4 H.L. Cas. 565, QB .................. A20–001

Hammersmith and Fulham LBC v Monk; Barnet LBC v Smith [1992] 1 A.C.
  478; [1991] 3 W.L.R. 1144; [1992] 1 All E.R. 1; [1992] 1 F.L.R. 465;
  (1992) 24 H.L.R. 206; 90 L.G.R. 38; (1992) 63 P. & C.R. 373; [1992] 1
  E.G.L.R. 65; [1992] 09 E.G. 135; [1992] Fam. Law 292; (1992) 156 L.G.
  Rev. 481; [1991] E.G. 130 (C.S.); (1992) 89(3) L.S.G. 32; (1991) 141
  N.L.J. 1697; (1992) 136 S.J.L.B. 10; [1991] N.P.C. 132, HL ....... 1–002, 5–023
Hankey v Clavering [1942] 2 K.B. 326, CA ..................... 4–020, 8–001,
                                                                A23–002
Harbour Estates Ltd v HSBC Bank Plc; sub nom. HSBC Bank Plc v Harbour
  Estates Ltd [2004] EWHC 1714 (Ch); [2005] Ch. 194; [2005] 2 W.L.R.
  67; [2004] 3 All E.R. 1057; [2005] 1 E.G.L.R. 107; [2004] 32 E.G. 62
  (C.S.), Ch D ......................................... 3–006, 3–018, 5–009
Harmond Properties v Gajdzis [1968] 1 W.L.R. 1858; [1968] 3 All E.R. 263;
  (1968) 19 P. & C.R. 718; (1968) 112 S.J. 762, CA (Civ Div) ........... 5–033
Havant International Holdings Ltd v Lionsgate (H) Investment Ltd [2000] L. &
  T.R. 297; [1999] E.G. 144 (C.S.); (1999) 96(47) L.S.G. 34, Ch D ........ 4–030,
                                                        4–036, 5–001, 5–003
Hawtrey v Beaufront Ltd [1946] K.B. 280, KBD ........................ 6–009
Heron Garage Properties Ltd v Moss [1974] 1 W.L.R. 148; [1974] 1 All E.R.
  421; (1974) 28 P. & C.R. 54; (1973) 117 S.J. 697, Ch D ................ 7–057
Hexstone Holdings Ltd v AHC Westlink Ltd [2010] EWHC 1280 (Ch); [2010]
  L. & T.R. 22; [2010] 2 E.G.L.R. 13; [2010] 32 E.G. 62, Ch D
  (Manchester) ............................................ 5–037, 5–039
Hinds v Randall (1961) 177 E.G. 733 .................................. 6–031
Hogg v Brooks (1884–85) L.R. 15 Q.B.D. 256, CA ...................... 6–018
Holwell Securities Ltd v Hughes [1974] 1 W.L.R. 155; [1974] 1 All E.R. 161;
  (1973) 26 P. & C.R. 544; (1973) 117 S.J. 912, CA (Civ Div) ...... 6–018, 6–039

Hotgroup Plc v Royal Bank of Scotland Plc [2010] EWHC 1241 (Ch); [2010]
  23 E.G. 107 (C.S.); [2010] 2 P. & C.R. DG23, Ch D .................. 6–008
Hounslow LBC v Pilling [1993] 1 W.L.R. 1242; [1994] 1 All E.R. 432; [1993]
  2 F.L.R. 49; (1993) 25 H.L.R. 305; 91 L.G.R. 573; (1993) 66 P. & C.R.
  22; [1993] 26 E.G. 123; [1993] Fam. Law 522; [1993] E.G. 36 (C.S.);
  (1993) 137 S.J.L.B. 187; [1993] N.P.C. 35, CA (Civ Div) ........ 5–022, 5–023,
    A21–001
Hussein v Mehlman 1992] 2 E.G.L.R. 287; [1992] 32 E.G. 59 ............... 1–009
Hynes v Vaughan (1985) 50 P. & C.R. 444, DC .......................... 7–042

Inland Revenue Commissioners v Southend on Sea Estates Co Ltd; sub nom.
  Southend On Sea Estates Co Ltd v Inland Revenue Commissioners [1915]
  A.C. 428, HL .................................................. 6–022

JH Edwards & Sons v Central London Commercial Estates; Eastern Bazaar v
  Central London Commercial Estates [1984] 2 E.G.L.R. 103; (1984) 271
  E.G. 697, CA (Civ Div) ............................... 9–009, A26–001
James v Heim Gallery (London) Ltd (1981) 41 P. & C.R. 269; (1980) 256 E.G.
  819; [1980] 2 E.G.L.R. 119, CA (Civ Div) .......................... 7–051
Jelley v Buckman; subv nom. Jelly v Buckman [1974] Q.B. 488; [1973] 3
  W.L.R. 585; [1973] 3 All E.R. 853; (1973) 26 P. & C.R. 215; (1973) 117
  S.J. 728, CA (Civ Div) ........................................... 3–025
John Laing Construction Ltd v Amber Pass Ltd [2005] L. & T.R. 12; [2004]
  2 E.G.L.R. 128; [2004] 17 E.G. 128 (C.S.); (2004) 101(16) L.S.G. 29,
  Ch D ....................................................... 7–043
Jones v Merton LBC; sub nom. Merton LBC v Jones [2008] EWCA Civ 660;
  [2009] 1 W.L.R. 1269; [2008] 4 All E.R. 287; [2009] H.L.R. 7; [2009] 1
  P. & C.R. 3; [2008] 2 E.G.L.R. 37; [2008] 33 E.G. 74; [2008] 25 E.G. 173
  (C.S.); [2008] N.P.C. 68; [2008] 2 P. & C.R. DG10, CA (Civ Div) ........ 7–043
Jones v Phipps (1867–68) L.R. 3 Q.B. 567, QB ..................... 5–031, 5–038

Kaiser Engineers & Constructors Inc v E R Squibb & Sons Ltd, Unreported
  November 12, 1971 ............................................. 3–019
Kammins Ballrooms Co Ltd v Zenith Investments (Torquay) Ltd (No.1) [1971]
  A.C. 850; [1970] 3 W.L.R. 287; [1970] 2 All E.R. 871; (1971) 22 P. &
  C.R. 74; (1970) 114 S.J. 590, HL ................................ 1–010
Keith Bayley Rogers & Co (A Firm) v Cubes, Ltd (1976) 31 P. & C.R. 412,
  Ch D ................................................. 4–043, 9–005
Kelly v Rogers [1892] 1 Q.B. 910, CA ................................. 8–022
Kinch v Bullard [1999] 1 W.L.R. 423; [1998] 4 All E.R. 650; [1999] 1 F.L.R.
  66; [1998] 3 E.G.L.R. 112; [1998] 47 E.G. 140; [1998] Fam. Law 738;
  [1998] E.G. 126 (C.S.); [1998] N.P.C. 137; (1999) 77 P. & C.R. D1,
  Ch D ....................................................... 6–039
Knight and Hubbard's Underlease, Re; sub nom. [1923] 1 Ch. 130, Ch D ....... 5–032
Kushner v Law Society [1952] 1 K.B. 264; [1952] 1 All E.R. 404; [1952]
  1 T.L.R. 424; (1952) 116 J.P. 132, DC ............................. 2–004

Lancecrest Ltd v Asiwaju [2005] EWCA Civ 117; [2005] L. & T.R. 22; [2005]
  1 E.G.L.R. 40; [2005] 16 E.G. 146; [2005] N.P.C. 21, CA (Civ Div) ... 4–041, 4–042
Land Settlement Association Ltd v Carr [1944] K.B. 657.CA ............... 10–019
Legal & General Assurance (Pension Management) Ltd v Cheshire CC (1984)
  269 E.G. 40, CA (Civ Div) ....................................... 8–006
Legal & General Assurance Society Ltd v Expeditors International (UK) Ltd
  [2007] EWCA Civ 7; [2007] 2 P. & C.R. 10; [2007] L. & T.R. 16; [2007]
  5 E.G. 307 (C.S.); (2007) 104(6) L.S.G. 32; (2007) 151 S.J.L.B. 163;
  [2007] N.P.C. 10, CA (Civ Div) ..................... 7–037, 7–038, 7–040,
    7–041, 7–053

## TABLE OF CASES

Lemmerbell Ltd v Britannia LAS Direct Ltd [1999] L. & T.R. 102; [1998] 3 E.G.L.R. 67; [1998] 48 E.G. 188; [1998] E.G. 138 (C.S.); [1998] N.P.C. 135, CA (Civ Div) .......................... 4–030, 4–031, 4–035, 4–036, 5–002, 5–004, 5–030, 5–038
Lemon v Lardeur [1946] K.B. 613, CA ................................. 5–029
Lester v Garland 33 E.R. 748; (1808) 15 Ves. Jr. 248, Ct of Chancery .......... 4–014
Linpac Mouldings Ltd v Aviva Life and Pensions UK Ltd. See Norwich Union Life & Pensions v Linpac Mouldings Ltd
Lord Inchiquin v Lyons (1887) L.R. 20 Ir. 474 ........................... 6–035
Lower v Sorrell [1963] 1 Q.B. 959; [1963] 2 W.L.R. 1; [1962] 3 All E.R. 1074; (1962) 233 L.T. 731, CA ............................ 6–035, 6–037, 6–038

MW Trustees Ltd v Telular Corp [2011] EWHC 104 (Ch); [2011] L. & T.R. 19, Ch D ...................................................... 7–055
Manchester Diocesan Council of Education v Commercial & General Investments, Ltd [1970] 1 W.L.R. 241; [1969] 3 All E.R. 1593; (1970) 21 P. & C.R. 38; (1970) 114 S.J. 70, Ch D ............................. 6–021
Mannai Investment Co Ltd v Eagle Star Life Assurance Co Ltd [1997] A.C. 749; [1997] 2 W.L.R. 945; [1997] 3 All E.R. 352; [1997] C.L.C. 1124; [1997] 1 E.G.L.R. 57; [1997] 24 E.G. 122; [1997] 25 E.G. 138; (1997) 16 Tr. L.R. 432; [1997] E.G. 82 (C.S.); (1997) 94(30) L.S.G. 30; (1997) 147 N.L.J. 846; (1997) 141 S.J.L.B. 130; [1997] N.P.C. 81, HL ....... 4–016, 4–017, 4–018, 4–019, 4–020, 4–021, 4–022, 4–023, 4–024, 4–025, 4–027, 4–028, 4–032, 4–033, 4–034, 4–035, 4–036, 4–037, 4–040, 4–041, 4–046, 4–048, 5–001, A23–001
Manorlike Ltd v Le Vitas Travel Agency and Consultative Services [1986] 1 All E.R. 573; [1986] 1 E.G.L.R. 79; (1986) 278 E.G. 412, CA (Civ Div) ...... 6–027
Marseille Fret SA v D Oltmann Schiffahrts GmbH & Co KG (The Trado) [1982] 1 Lloyd's Rep. 157; [1981] Com. L.R. 277, QBD (Comm) ........ 4–046
Max Factor Ltd v Wesleyan Assurance Society (1997) 74 P. & C.R. 8; [1996] 2 E.G.L.R. 210; [1996] E.G. 82 (C.S.); [1996] N.P.C. 70; (1997) 73 P. & C.R. D12, CA (Civ Div) ................................. 5–011, 5–015
May v Borup [1915] 1 K.B. 830, KBD ................................. 6–035
Metrolands Investments Ltd v JH Dewhurst Ltd [1986] 3 All E.R. 659; (1986) 52 P. & C.R. 232; [1986] 1 E.G.L.R. 125; (1986) 277 E.G. 1343, CA (Civ Div) ................................................ 8–009, 8–010
Micrografix v Woking 8 Ltd (1996) 71 P. & C.R. 43; [1995] 2 E.G.L.R. 32; [1995] 37 E.G. 179, Ch D .......................... A23–002, A23–003
Mourant Property Trust Ltd v Fusion Electronic (UK) Ltd [2009] EWHC 3659 (Ch), Ch D ................................................... 7–033

NYK Logistics (UK) Ltd v Ibrend Estates BV [2011] EWCA Civ 683; [2011] N.P.C. 61, CA (Civ Div) ...................................... 7–041
Newborough (Lord) v Jones [1975] Ch. 90; [1974] 3 W.L.R. 52; [1974] 3 All E.R. 17; (1974) 28 P. & C.R. 215; (1974) 118 S.J. 479, CA (Civ Div) ..... 6–016
Newlon Housing Trust v Al-Sulaimen; sub nom. Newlon Housing Trust v Alsulaimen [1999] 1 A.C. 313; [1998] 3 W.L.R. 451; [1998] 4 All E.R. 1; [1998] 2 F.L.R. 690; [1998] 3 F.C.R. 183; (1998) 30 H.L.R. 1132; [1999] L. & T.R. 38; [1998] Fam. Law 589; (1998) 95(35) L.S.G. 35; (1998) 148 N.L.J. 1303; (1998) 142 S.J.L.B. 247, HL ........................ A24–001
Norwegian American Cruises A/S v Paul Mundy Ltd (The Vistafjord) [1988] 2 Lloyd's Rep. 343, CA (Civ Div) ............................. A23–001
Norwich Union Life & Pensions v Linpac Mouldings Ltd; sub nom. Aviva Life & Pensions UK Ltd v Linpac Mouldings Ltd [2010] EWCA Civ 395; [2010] L. & T.R. 10; [2010] 17 E.G. 95 (C.S.); [2010] N.P.C. 48; [2010] 2 P. & C.R. DG16, CA (Civ Div) ............... 3–003, 5–013, 5–014, 5–016

## TABLE OF CASES xxiii

Oliver Ashworth (Holdings) Ltd v Ballard (Kent) Ltd. See Ballard (Kent) Ltd v Oliver Ashworth (Holdings) Ltd
Olympia & York Canary Wharf Ltd v Oil Property Investment Ltd; sub nom. Oil Property Investment Ltd v Olympia & York Canary Wharf Ltd (1995) 69 P. & C.R. 43; [1994] 2 E.G.L.R. 48; [1994] 29 E.G. 121; [1994] E.G. 36 (C.S.); [1994] N.P.C. 22, CA (Civ Div) ............................ 5–016
Orchard (Developments) Holdings Plc v Reuters Ltd [2009] EWCA Civ 6; [2009] 1 E.G.L.R. 13; [2009] 16 E.G. 140; [2009] 1 P. & C.R. DG21, CA (Civ Div) ...................................................... 6–020

P&A Swift Investments v Combined English Stores Group Plc [1989] A.C. 632; [1988] 3 W.L.R. 313; [1988] 2 All E.R. 885; (1989) 57 P. & C.R. 42; [1988] 43 E.G. 73; [1988] E.G. 104 (C.S.); (1988) 138 N.L.J. Rep. 202, HL ........................................................... 3–004
PW & Co v Milton Gate Investments Ltd [2003] EWHC 1994 (Ch); [2004] Ch. 142; [2004] 2 W.L.R. 443; [2004] L. & T.R. 8; [2004] 3 E.G.L.R. 103; (2003) 100(38) L.S.G. 36; (2003) 153 N.L.J. 1347, Ch D ........ 1–008, 8–019, A25–001
Packington Street (No.120), Islington, Re; sub nom. Balls Bros v Islington LBC 91966) 110 S.J. 672 .............................................. 3–017
Paddock Investments v Lory [1975] 2 E.G.L.R. 5; (1975) 236 E.G. 803, CA (Civ Div) ...................................................... 10–009
Parkinson v Barclays Bank Ltd [1951] 1 K.B. 368; [1950] 2 All E.R. 936; 66 T.L.R. (Pt. 2) 783; (1950) 94 S.J. 724, CA .......................... 7–062
Parry v 1,000,000 Pigs Ltd [1980] 260 E.G. 281 ......................... 10–014
Patel v Keles [2009] EWCA Civ 1187; [2010] Ch. 332; [2010] 2 W.L.R. 1159; [2010] 1 P. & C.R. 24; [2010] L. & T.R. 27; [2009] N.P.C. 128, CA (Civ Div) ......................................................... 6–023
Peel Developments (South) Ltd v Siemens Plc [1992] 47 E.G. 103; [1992] 2 E.G.L.R. 85; [1992] N.P.C. 18 .................................. 5–035
Peeling v Guidice (1963) 186 E.G. 113, CA ..................... 6–031, 6–032, 8–019, 8–020
Pennell v Payne [1995] Q.B. 192; [1995] 2 W.L.R. 261; [1995] 2 All E.R. 592; [1995] 1 E.G.L.R. 6; [1995] 06 E.G. 152; [1994] E.G. 196 (C.S.); (1995) 139 S.J.L.B. 17; [1994] N.P.C. 151; (1995) 69 P. & C.R. D1, CA (Civ Div) ......................................................... 8–015, A25–001
Porter v Shephard (1796) 6 Durn. & E. 665 ........................... A20–001
Procter & Gamble Technical Centres Ltd v Brixton Estates Plc; sub nom. Proctor & Gamble Technical Centres Ltd v Brixton Estates Plc [2002] EWHC 2835 (Ch); [2003] 2 E.G.L.R. 24; [2003] 32 E.G. 69, Ch D ...... 4–030, 4–034, 4–036, 5–004
Prudential Assurance Co Ltd v Exel UK Ltd; Hannah Close, Brent Park, Neasden, Re [2009] EWHC 1350 (Ch); [2010] 1 P. & C.R. 7; [2010] L. & T.R. 7, Ch D ..................................... 4–055, 5–007, 5–008

Reardon Smith Line Ltd v Hansen-Tangen (The Diana Prosperity); Hansen-Tangen v Sanko Steamship Co Ltd [1976] 1 W.L.R. 989; [1976] 3 All E.R. 570; [1976] 2 Lloyd's Rep. 621; (1976) 120 S.J. 719, HL ............. A23–001
Reed Personnel Services Plc v American Express Ltd [1997] 1 E.G.L.R. 229; [1996] N.P.C. 7, Ch D ............................................. 7–028
Reid v Blagrave (1831) 9 L.J. (OS) (Ch) 245 ............................ 6–031
Robinson v Thames Mead Park Estate Ltd [1947] Ch. 334; [1947] 1 All E.R. 366; [1947] L.J.R. 545; 176 L.T. 295, Ch D .......................... 7–017
Rose (Deceased), Re; sub nopm. Rose v Inland Revenue Commissioners [1952] Ch. 499; [1952] 1 All E.R. 1217; [1952] 1 T.L.R. 1577; (1952) 31 A.T.C. 138; [1952] T.R. 175, CA ......................................... 3–029

## TABLE OF CASES

Rose, Re; sub nom. Midland Bank Executor & Trustee Co Ltd v Rose [1949] Ch. 78; [1948] 2 All E.R. 971; [1949] L.J.R. 208; (1948) 92 S.J. 661, Ch D ..................................................... 3–029
Royal Bank of Canada v Secretary of State for Defence [2003] EWHC 1479 (Ch); [2004] 1 P. & C.R. 28; [2003] 2 P. & C.R. DG17, Ch D ...... 4–044, 7–041
Rye v Rye [1962] A.C. 496; [1962] 2 W.L.R. 361; [1962] 1 All E.R. 146; (1962) 106 S.J. 94, HL .............................................. A24–001

St Marylebone Property Co Ltd v Fairweather. See Fairweather v St Marylebone Property Co Ltd
Samuel Properties (Developments) v Hayek [1972] 1 W.L.R. 1296; [1972] 3 All E.R. 473; (1972) 24 P. & C.R. 223; (1972) 116 S.J. 764, CA (Civ Div) .............................................. 6–031, 6–032, 8–004, A19–002
Scholl Mfg Co v Clifton (Slim-line) [1967] Ch. 41; [1966] 3 W.L.R. 575; [1966] 3 All E.R. 16; (1966) 110 S.J. 687, CA ........................ 9–004
Seaward v Drew (1898) 67 LJ Q.B. 322 ................................. 3–027
Secretary of State for the Environment, Transport and Regions v Unicorn Consultancy Services Ltd, Unreported October 19, 2000 ............... 6–041
Shirlcar Properties v Heinitz (1983) 268 E.G. 362, CA (Civ Div) ............. 4–046
Shuter v Hersh [1922] 1 K.B. 438, KBD ................................ 11–004
Simons v Associated Furnishers Ltd [1931] 1 Ch. 379; [1930] All E.R. Rep. 427, Ch D ...................................................... A20–001
Smith v Kinsey [1936] 3 All E.R. 73 ..................................... 3–024
Southport Old Links v Naylor [1985] 1 E.G.L.R. 66; (1985) 273 E.G. 767 ...... 9–007
Spencer's Case (1583) 5 Co.Rep.16a .................................... 3–001
Stait v Fenner [1912] 2 Ch. 504, Ch D .................................. 3–027
Standard Life Investments Property Holdings Ltd v W&J Linney Ltd [2010] EWHC 480 (Ch); [2011] L. & T.R. 9, Ch D ................... 1–013, 2–001, 6–005, 6–006
Sudbrook Trading Estate Ltd v Eggleton [1983] 1 A.C. 444; [1982] 3 W.L.R. 315; [1982] 3 All E.R. 1; (1982) 44 P. & C.R. 153; (1983) 265 E.G. 215; (1982) 79 L.S.G. 1175; (1982) 126 S.J. 512, HL .................... A23–002
Sunrose Ltd v Gould [1962] 1 W.L.R. 20; [1961] 3 All E.R. 1142; (1961) 105 S.J. 988, CA ................................................. A23–001
System Floors Ltd v Ruralpride Ltd [1995] 1 E.G.L.R. 48; [1995] 07 E.G. 125; [1994] E.G. 162 (C.S.); [1994] N.P.C. 127; (1995) 69 P. & C.R. D18, CA (Civ Div) ........................................ 2–001, 3–031, 3–033

Taita Hotel v Spelman [1963] N.Z.L.R. 206 ............................. 5–017
Tayleur v Wildin (1867–68) L.R. 3 Ex. 303, Ex Ct .................... 6–035, 6–036
Topfell Ltd v Galley Properties Ltd [1979] 1 W.L.R. 446; [1979] 2 All E.R. 388; (1979) 38 P. & C.R. 70; (1978) 249 E.G. 341; (1979) 1 E.G.L.R. 161; (1979) 123 S.J. 81, Ch D ........................................ 7–042
Townsend Carriers Ltd v Pfizer Ltd (1977) 33 P. & C.R. 361; (1977) 242 E.G. 813; (1977) 121 S.J. 375, Ch D ............................................. 5–034
Trador, The. See Marseille Fret SA v D Oltmann Schiffahrts GmbH & Co KG (The Trado)
Trow v Ind Coope (West Midlands) Ltd [1967] 2 Q.B. 899; [1967] 3 W.L.R. 633; [1967] 2 All E.R. 900; (1967) 111 S.J. 375, CA (Civ Div); ... 4–014, 4–015, 6–027
Tulk v Moxhay, 41 E.R. 1143; (1848) 2 Ph. 774; (1848) 18 L.J. Ch. 83, Ch D ... 3–001

Union Eagle Ltd v Golden Achievement Ltd [1997] A.C. 514; [1997] 2 W.L.R. 341; [1997] 2 All E.R. 215; (1997) 141 S.J.L.B. 56; [1997] N.P.C. 16, PC (HK) ................................................. 6–030, A22–001

United Dominions Trust (Commercial) v Eagle Aircraft Services; sub nom.
United Dominions Trust (Commercial) v Eagle Aviation [1968] 1 W.L.R.
74; [1968] 1 All E.R. 104; (1967) 111 S.J. 849, CA (Civ Div) ... 1–012, A19–001,
A19–002, A19–003
United Scientific Holdings Ltd v Burnley BC; Cheapside Land Development
Co Ltd v Messels Service Co [1978] A.C. 904; [1977] 2 W.L.R. 806;
[1977] 2 All E.R. 62; 75 L.G.R. 407; (1977) 33 P. & C.R. 220; (1977) 243
E.G. 43; (1977) 121 S.J. 223, HL ............... 1–012, 6–029, 8–004, 8–006,
8–007, A19–001, A19–002, A19–003

Viola's Indenture of Lease, Re; sub nom. Humphrey v Stenbury [1909] 1 Ch.
244, Ch D ..................................... 5–020, 5–022, A21–001

Walker v Hatton (1842) 10 M. & W. 249 ................................. 6–036
Wandsworth LBC v Atwell (1995) 27 H.L.R. 536; 94 L.G.R. 419; [1996] 1
E.G.L.R. 57; [1996] 01 E.G. 100; [1995] E.G. 68 (C.S.); [1995] N.P.C. 67,
CA (Civ Div) ..................................................... 6–014
Webb v Russell (1789) 3 Durn. & E. 393 ........................... A24–001
Weg Motors v Hales [1962] Ch. 49; [1961] 3 W.L.R. 558; [1961] 3 All E.R.
181; (1961) 105 S.J. 610, CA .............................. 3–009, 3–032
Weinbergs Weatherproofs v Radcliffe Paper Mill Co; sub nom. Bleachers
Association's Leases, Re [1958] Ch. 437; [1958] 2 W.L.R. 1; [1957] 3 All
E.R. 663; (1958) 102 S.J. 15, Ch D ................................. 9–004
West Country Cleaners (Falmouth) Ltd v Saly [1966] 1 W.L.R. 1485; [1966]
3 All E.R. 210; 119 E.G. 563; (1966) 110 S.J. 634, CA ..... 7–018, 7–019, 7–052
Weston v Collins (1865) 12 L.T. 4; (1865) 5 New Rep. 345 ............... A19–001
Westway Homes Ltd v Moores (1992) 63 P. & C.R. 480; [1991] 2 E.G.L.R.
193; [1991] 31 E.G. 57, CA (Civ Div) ............................. 4–046
William Hill (Southern) Ltd v Govier [1984] 1 E.G.L.R. 121 ................. 8–007
Wingfield v Clapton Construction & Investment Co (1967) 201 E.G. 769 ....... 5–018
Wordsley Brewery v Halford (1903) 90 L.T. 89 .................... 3–003, 5–009

Yager v Fishman & Co [1944] 1 All E.R. 552; (1944) 77 Ll. L. Rep. 268, CA ... 6–040
Yates Building Co Ltd v RJ Pulleyn & Sons (York) Ltd (1975) 237 E.G. 183;
[1976] 1 E.G.L.R. 157; (1975) 119 S.J. 370, Ch D .................... 6–018

Zarvos v Pradhan [2003] EWCA Civ 208; [2003] 2 P. & C.R. 9; [2003]
L. & T.R. 30; [2003] 2 E.G.L.R. 37; [2003] 26 E.G. 180; [2003] 13 E.G.
114 (C.S.); (2003) 100(18) L.S.G. 35; (2003) 153 N.L.J. 404; (2003)
147 S.J.L.B. 301; [2003] N.P.C. 33; [2003] 2 P. & C.R. DG5, CA
(Civ Div) ..................................................... 6–023

# Table of Statutes

| | | | |
|---|---|---|---|
| 1730 | Landlord and Tenant Act (4 Geo.2, c.28) ....... 8–014 | | s.149(6) ...... 10–008, 10–020 |
| | s.1 .............. 8–012, A7 | | s.150 ............. A24–001 |
| | s.6 ............... A24–001 | | s.161 ................. 4–012 |
| 1737 | Distress for Rent Act (11 Geo.2, c.19) | | s.196 ......... 6–013, 6–014, 6–015, 6–017, 6–018, A9–004 |
| | s.18 .......... 8–012, 8–014, A8–001 | | (3) ......... 6–015, 6–016, 6–039 |
| 1845 | Real Property Act (8 & 9 Vict. c. 106) | | (4) .......... 6–015, 6–017 |
| | s.9 ............... A24–001 | | (5) ................ 6–014 |
| 1870 | Apportionment Act (33 & 34 Vict. c.35) ........... 7–047 | | s.205 .............. A9–005 |
| 1910 | Finance (1909–1910) Act (10 Edw. 7 & 1 Geo.5 c.8) ............... 6–022 | 1947 | (1)(ii) ............. 3–006 |
| | | | Agriculture Act (c.48).... 10–002 |
| 1920 | Increase of Rent and Mortgage Interest (Restrictions) Act (10 & 11 Geo.5 c.17) ................ 11–004 | 1948 | Agricultural Holdings Act (c.63) ... 10–002, 10–009 |
| | | | s.23(1) ............... 6–033 |
| | | | s.24 ................ 10–010 |
| | Agriculture Act (10 & 11 Geo.5 c.76) | | s.92 ................. 6–016 |
| | s.20 ................ 10–006 | 1954 | Agricultural (Miscellaneous Provisions) Act (2 & 3 Eliz.2 c.39) ........ 10–002 |
| | s.28 ................ 11–020 | | Landlord and Tenant Act (2 & 3 Eliz.2 c.56) ... 5–013, 9–001, 9–004, 9–008, 9–009, 9–011, A28–001 |
| 1923 | Agricultural Holdings Act (13 & 14 Geo.5 c.9) ... 10–014, 10–020 | | |
| | s.25(1) ....... 10–005, 11–020 | | Pt II ........... 7–062, 9–001 |
| 1925 | Law of Property Act (15 & 16 Geo.5 c.5) | | s.24 .............. A10–001 |
| | s.1 .................... 3–001 | | (1) ................ 9–002 |
| | s.62 ......... 3–014, A9–001 | | s.25 .......... 4–013, 9–002, 9–004, 9–005, 9–007, 12–005, A10–002 |
| | s.63 .... 3–006, 3–007, 3–009, 3–018, 3–020 | | |
| | (1)–(3) ............. 3–005 | | s.26 .......... 9–013, 9–014, A10–003 |
| | s.139 ....... 8–016, A24–001 | | |
| | s.140 .............. A9–002 | | s.30 .............. A10–004 |
| | (1) ................. 3–023 | | (1)(f) ....... 6–023, 7–060, 13–012 |
| | (2) ......... 3–023, 3–024, 10–019, 10–020 | | |
| | | | (g) ............. 6–023 |
| | s.142 ......... 3–009, 3–014, 3–015, 3–020, A9–003 | | s.33 ........ 9–009, A10–005 |
| | | | s.35 ........ 9–009, A10–006 |
| | (1) .......... 3–008, 3–032 | | s.37 ................ 12–005 |
| | (2) ................ 3–008 | | s.44 ................. 9–006 |
| | | | s.69 .............. A10–007 |
| | | | (1) ................ 9–003 |

## TABLE OF STATUTES

| 1962 | Recorded Delivery Service Act (10 & 11 Eliz.2 c.27) |
| --- | --- |
| | s.1 ............... A11–001 |
| | (1) ................ 6–017 |
| 1972 | Land Charges Act (c.61) |
| | s.2 ................ 2–005 |
| 1977 | Agricultural Holdings (Notices to Quit) Act |
| | (c.12) .............. 10–002 |
| | Rent Act (c.42) ........ 11–001, 11–002, 11–003, 11–004 |
| | Pt VII. .............. 11–006 |
| | s.1 ............... A12–001 |
| | s.2 ............... A12–002 |
| | (1) ............... 11–002 |
| | s.3 ............... A12–003 |
| | (1) ............... 11–004 |
| | ss.4–16 ............. 11–002 |
| | s.24(3) ............. 11–002 |
| | s.98 ........ 11–006, A12–004 |
| | Sch.15 |
| | Pt I .............. 11–006 |
| | Protection from Eviction Act (c.43) .............. 11–005 |
| | s.5 ......... 11–018, 11–020, A13–001 |
| | (1) ........ 11–019, 11–020 |
| | (a), (b) ......... 11–020 |
| 1981 | Senior Courts Act (c.54) |
| | s.35A ............. A5–003 |
| 1985 | Companies Act (c.6) |
| | s.654(1) .............. 6–012 |
| 1986 | Agricultural Holdings Act (c.5) ........ 10–001, 10–002, 10–015 |
| | s.1 ......... 10–001, A14–001 |
| | (1), (2) ............. 10–003 |
| | s.2 .......... 10–004, A14–002 |
| | s.3 .......... 10–004, A14–003 |
| | s.12 ............... 10–008 |
| | s.25 ........ 10–004, 10–006, A14–004 |
| | (1) ....... 10–005, 10–006, 10–008, 10–010 |
| | (2)(a) .............. 10–008 |
| | (b) ..... 10–008, 10–009 |
| | (c), (d) ......... 10–008 |
| | (3) ................ 10–008 |
| | (5) ................ 10–008 |
| | s.26 ......... 10–004, 10–011, 10–013, A14–005 |
| | (1) ........ 10–010, 10–011 |
| | (2) ............... 10–011 |
| | s.27 .............. A14–006 |
| | (1) ........ 10–011, 10–013 |
| | (2) ............... 10–013 |
| | (3) ........ 10–011, 10–012 |

| | (a)–(f). ......... 10–012 |
| --- | --- |
| | (4) .............. 10–013 |
| | s.31 ............... 10–005 |
| | s.60 ............... A14–007 |
| | s.96 ........ 10–014, A14–008 |
| | s.98(1) ............... 10–002 |
| | (2) ............... 10–008 |
| | Sch.3 |
| | Pt I .............. 10–010 |
| | para.9 .......... 10–008 |
| | Sch.12 |
| | para.4 ............ 10–008 |
| | Insolvency Act (c.45) |
| | s.144(1) .............. 5–028 |
| | s.145 .......... 5–028, 6–012 |
| | s.283(1) .............. 5–026 |
| | (5) ................ 6–010 |
| | s.306(1) ........ 5–026, 6–010 |
| | s.436 ................ 5–026 |
| | Sch.B1 ............... 5–027 |
| | para.43(6) .......... 6–011 |
| | para.52 ............ 5–027 |
| | para.67 ............ 5–027 |
| | para.68(1) .......... 5–027 |
| | Sch.4 |
| | para.7 ............. 5–028 |
| 1988 | Housing Act (c.50) ..... 11–008, 11–012 |
| | Pt I. ................ 11–007 |
| | s.1(1) .............. 11–007 |
| | s.5 ......... 11–013, A15–001 |
| | (1) ............... 11–008 |
| | (a), (b) ......... 11–009 |
| | (2) ........ 11–009, 11–010 |
| | (3) ............... 11–010 |
| | (4) ........ 11–009, 11–010 |
| | (5) ............... 11–010 |
| | s.7 .......... 11–008, 11–009 |
| | (4) ............... 11–011 |
| | s.19A ............... 11–013 |
| | s.21 ......... 11–008, 11–014, 11–015, A15–002 |
| | (1) ........ 11–014, 11–015, 11–016 |
| | (b) ............ 11–017 |
| | (5) ................ 11–014 |
| | s.45(1) .............. 11–008 |
| | Sch.1 ................ 11–007 |
| | Sch.2 ................ 11–011 |
| | Sch.2A ............... 11–013 |
| 1989 | Law of Property (Miscellaneous Provisions) Act (c.34) |
| | s.2 ................ 2–002 |
| 1990 | Agricultural Holdings (Amendment) Act (c.15) ............. 10–002 |

| | | | |
|---|---|---|---|
| 1995 | Agricultural Tenancies Act | | s.38 ............... A17–007 |
| | (c.8)............... 10–001 | | (1)............... 10–022 |
| | s.1 ............... A17–001 | | Landlord and Tenant |
| | (1)........ 10–015, 10–016 | | (Covenants) Act |
| | (2)–(4)........... 10–016 | | (c.30).........2–001, 5–004, |
| | s.2 ................. 10–016 | | A16–001 |
| | s.4(1)............... 10–002 | | s.3 ...... 3–010, 3–011, 3–015 |
| | s.5 .........10–023, A17–002 | | (1).......... 3–011, 3–013 |
| | (1)........ 10–018, 10–019 | | (a), (b) .......... 3–012 |
| | (4)............... 10–018 | | (2)................ 3–011 |
| | s.6 .........10–023, A17–003 | | (3)................ 3–011 |
| | (1)–(3)............ 10–019 | | (6).... 3–011, 3–012, 3–013 |
| | s.7 ..........10–020, 10–023, | | s.28 .............. A16–002 |
| | A17–004 | | (1)................ 3–013 |
| | (1)–(3)............ 10–020 | 2000 | Postal Services Act |
| | s.16 ............... A17–005 | | (c.26)............... 6–015 |
| | (1)............... 10–022 | 2002 | Land Registration Act (c.9) |
| | s.36 ...............A17–006 | | s.4(1)(c).............. 2–006 |
| | (1)–(3)............ 10–021 | 2006 | Companies Act (c.46) |
| | (5)............... 10–021 | | s.1012(1)............. 6–012 |

# Table of Statutory Instruments

1987 Agricultural Holdings
(Arbitration on Notices)
Order (SI 1987/710)
art.7 . . . . . . . . . . . . . . . 10–008
1988 Notices to Quit (Prescribed
Information) Regulations
(SI 1988/2201) . . . . . . 11–005
Schedule . . . . . . . . . . . 11–019

2005 Insolvent Partnerships
(Amendment) Order (SI
2005/1516) . . . . . . . . . . 5–027
Limited Liability Partnerships
(Amendment) Regulations
(SI 2005/1989) . . . . . . . 5–027

# Chapter 1

# The Nature of a Break Clause in a Lease

## 1 A definition

A break clause is a type of option entitling a landlord or a tenant unilaterally to determine a fixed-term lease before the fixed term expires by effluxion of time.  **1–001**

## 2 A break notice is not a notice to quit

A notice served pursuant to a break clause is sometimes referred to, in cases and elsewhere, as a notice to quit. However, it is not a notice to quit. A notice to quit, although it is one form of unilateral mechanism for bringing a tenancy to an end, only applies where there is a periodic tenancy. A periodic tenancy involves a succession of "periods" or "terms", and only continues for so long as all the parties to it agree that it shall continue. It only takes one person (e.g. one of the landlords or one of the tenants) to object to the continuance of a periodic tenancy, to enable that tenancy to be brought to an end. Thus a notice to quit is valid even if served by only one of two or more joint tenants (*Hammersmith and Fulham London Borough Council v Monk* [1992] A.C. 478).  **1–002**

In contrast to a notice to quit, a break notice seeks to end an existing fixed term of a lease. Therefore a break notice has to be served by, or on behalf of, all of the parties in whom the interest is vested. Thus if the interest of the tenant is vested in more than one party all those parties must join in serving a break notice.  **1–003**

In this book we intend to refer to a notice served pursuant to a break clause as a break notice, and not a notice to quit.  **1–004**

### 3 The right to terminate is unilateral

**1–005** Provided that a break clause satisfies all contractually agreed conditions, it will determine the fixed term of a lease. Thus, whether the break notice is served by a landlord or a tenant, the recipient's consent is not needed in order for the break to be effective. Indeed, the recipient is often unwilling for a lease to be broken, hence the plethora of case law dealing with disputes over the exercise of break clauses.

**1–006** Even if the recipient of a break notice is happy to see a lease ended, and cooperates in a break, this does not constitute the surrender of the lease. Surrenders are consensual and do not involve the operation of an existing provision within a lease. This distinction was emphasised by Lord Millett in *Barrett v Morgan* [2000] 2 A.C. 264.

**1–007** One consequence of there being a surrender of a lease is that any sublease granted out of that lease survives the surrender. This is because "it is a general and salutary principle of law that a person cannot be adversely affected by an agreement or arrangement to which he is not a party" (p.271D in *Barrett* above). However, the ending of the term of a lease by the operation of a break clause will automatically put an end to the term of any sublease created out of that lease. This position is deemed fair because the parties to the sublease could, by looking at the lease, make themselves aware of any break clause within it.

**1–008** Since a valid break notice automatically ends the term of the sublease carved out of it, any attempt to preserve the sublease, upon the execution of a break clause, will fail, whatever language is used (*PW & Co v Milton Gate Investments Ltd* [2004] Ch. 142, per Neuberger J.).

### 4 Forfeiture/Acceptance of repudiatory breach distinguished

**1–009** Where a landlord or tenant has committed a breach of a significant term of the lease amounting to a repudiation, the innocent party is faced with a choice between accepting that repudiation and thereby terminating the lease, or affirming the lease and thereby waiving the breach. So, a tenant was found to have accepted a repudiatory breach of the lease by the landlord in *Hussein v Mehlman* [1992] 2 E.G.L.R. 87. Similarly, in the case of a lease where the tenant commits a breach of covenant entitling the landlord to forfeit, the landlord must decide whether to forfeit the lease (whether by action or otherwise) or, for example, to accept rent and thereby waive the right to forfeit the lease for that breach.

**1–010** The acceptance of a repudiatory breach of contract and the act of forfeiture are two methods by which a lease may be terminated unilaterally. They are distinct from the exercise of a break clause because the right to accept a repudiatory breach of contract and the right to forfeit have the effect of putting the party with the right to terminate to an election of the sort described by Lord Diplock in *Kammins Ballrooms Co Ltd v Zenith Investments (Torquay) Ltd* [1971] A.C. 850, at p.882. The right to terminate a lease by the exercise of a break clause is different. This was emphasised by Patten L.J. in *BDW Trading Ltd (T/A Barratt North London) v JM Rowe (Investments) Ltd* [2011] EWCA Civ 548, at para.78, where he said:

"The lease with a break clause entitling the landlord or tenant to terminate the lease after the end of part of the term does not have to be exercised immediately unless the lease so provides. In most cases it will remain exercisable at any time after the right has arisen. The continued acceptance of rent by the landlord will not, without more, operate as a waiver of his rights under the break clause because there is nothing inconsistent between the continuation of the landlord and tenant relationship and the reservation of the right to break. If it is exercisable at any time during the remainder of the term the landlord is not put to an election and does not make an election by continuing to perform the contract until he chooses to exercise his right to break."

## 5 A break clause is a type of option

In *Spiro v Glencrown Properties Ltd* [1991] Ch. 537, at p.544, Hoffmann J. (as he then was) described an option as follows:    **1–011**

"An option is not strictly speaking either an offer or a conditional contract. It does not have *all* the incidents of the standard form of either of these concepts. To that extent it is a relationship sui generis. But there are ways in which it resembles each of them."

Many of the detailed points discussed in this book arise as a consequence of a break clause being a type of option. This key point was explained by Lord Salmon in *United Scientific Holdings Ltd v Burnley Borough Council* [1978] A.C. 904, where at p.951A he said as follows:    **1–012**

"Options to determine or to renew are not agreements to determine or renew. They are no more than irrevocable offers (kept open for good consideration) to do so providing the tenant complies with certain conditions usually before a certain date. If the tenant complies with the conditions in time, he thereby accepts the offer. The offer plus the acceptance constitutes a fresh agreement determining or renewing the lease as the case may be (see the *United Dominion Trust case* [1968] 1 W.L.R. 74, per Lord Denning M.R. at p.81). The same is true, mutatis mutandis, of an option to acquire the reversion. Neither equity nor the common law would ever intervene to make a contract for the parties. Anything which falls short of a complete acceptance of the offer is of no effect except sometimes as a counteroffer."

**1-013** There are two vital consequences of the above reasoning:

(i) The rule of strict compliance—All the requirements of any break clause must be completely complied with. The courts will give effect to this rule and not be deflected by submissions that to do so is unfair. As Lewison J. (as he then was) has explained in *Standard Life Investments Property Holdings Ltd v W & J Linney Ltd* [2010] EWHC 480 (Ch); (2011) L. & T.R. 9, at para.25:

"one part of fairness is that contractual stipulations are complied with. The exercise of a break clause has important consequences for both landlord and tenant and there are powerful policy considerations for certainty in this area of the law."

(ii) The rule of inflexibility—Just as the courts will not make a contract for the parties, they will not unmake it. Therefore if all the requirements of a break clause have been satisfied, the courts will determine that the lease is "broken". There is no scope for equity to intervene or grant "relief" against the loss of a lease (unlike the law of relief against forfeiture of a lease).

## 6 Break clauses can appear in all types of tenancies and in many different forms

**1-014** Since break clauses form part of the parties' contract, in principle they can take any form that the parties choose. Also break clauses can feature in all types of lease, commercial, residential, agricultural or anything else.

**1-015** Although the parties are the arbiters of the language used in any lease, in practice, standard clauses (appearing in practitioners' textbooks or in solicitors' standard precedents) mean that there are various concepts or phrases that repeatedly feature in practice or in the cases. This book seeks to consider various forms of break clause and how they should be approached.

Chapter 2

# Formalities and Registration

**1 Formalities**

Break clauses (if they exist at all) normally appear in leases. However they may appear in a separate document, either entered into at the same time as the lease (as a side letter or agreement) or subsequently (as a variation of the lease). Provided that the side letter/agreement or variation is supported by consideration then it should be valid. There was a break clause (expressed as a landlord's agreement to accept a surrender) in a side letter in *System Floors Ltd v Ruralpride Ltd* [1995] 1 E.G.L.R. 48. The letter was a not a deed; however there was no challenge to its validity. This case also establishes that a break clause in an "old lease" (pre-January 1, 1996, before the Landlord and Tenant (Covenants) Act 1995 had come into force) "touches and concerns" the land, and therefore binds a successor to the landlord. Break clauses in new leases also bind successors to the original parties, e.g. *Standard Life Investment Property Holdings Ltd v W & J Linney Ltd* [2011] L. & T.R. 9, at para.21.   2–001

However the courts approach alleged side or collateral agreements with circumspection. Thus in *Business Environment Bow Lane Ltd v Deanwater Estates Ltd* (2007) L. & T.R. 26 the Chancellor stated at para.43:   2–002

"In a normal conveyancing transaction in a commercial context with both parties represented by experienced solicitors the usual course of dealing is to ensure that all agreed terms are put into the contract and conveyance, transfer or lease. Accordingly those who assert a collateral contract in relation to a term not so contained must show that it was intended to have contractual effect separate from the normal conveyancing document. Otherwise it will be invalidated by s.2 Law of Property (Miscellaneous Provisions) Act 1989 even if evidence as to its existence is admitted."

**2–003** Therefore the more formally the break clause is documented, the better.

**2–004** If the term of the lease is more than three years then the existence of a clause permitting termination before three years will not obviate the obligation for the lease to be by deed; *Kushner v Law Society* (1952) 1 K.B. 264.

## 2 Registration

**2–005** A break clause is not a land charge and does not have to be protected by registration in order to bind successors in title (s.2 of the Land Charges Act 1972).

**2–006** The grant of a lease "for a term absolute of more than seven years from the date of the grant" must be registered at the Land Registry (s.4(1)(c) of the Land Registration Act 2002). The Land Registry will normally record the existence of a break clause that appears in a lease on the register. Transfers of unregistered leases, with more than seven years unexpired at the date of the disposition, must also be registered.

**2–007** Assuming that a registered lease has been successfully "broken" it will be appropriate to close the leasehold title. Any record of the "broken" lease should also be removed from a superior registered title.

Chapter 3

# Assignment

**1 The common law position relating to assignment**

In *City of London Corporation v Fell* [1994] 1 A.C. 458, at pp. 464–465, **3–001**
Lord Templeman said:

> "At common law, after an assignment, the benefit of a covenant by the original landlord which touches and concerns the land runs with the term granted by the lease. The burden of a covenant by the original tenant which touches and concerns the land also runs with the term: see Spencer's Case (1583) 5 Co Rep 16a.
>
> ...
>
> The principle that the benefit and burden of covenants in a lease which touch and concern the land run with the term and with the reversion is necessary for the effective operation of the law of landlord and tenant. Common law, and statute following the common law, recognise two forms of legal estate in land, a fee simple absolute in possession and a term of years absolute: see section 1 of the Act of 1925. Common law, and statute following the common law, were faced with the problem of rendering effective the obligations under a lease which might endure for a period of 999 years or more beyond the control of any covenantor. The solution was to annex to the term and the reversion the benefit and burden of covenants which touch and concern the land. The covenants having been annexed, every legal owner of the term granted by the lease and every legal owner of the reversion from time to time holds his estate with the benefit of and subject to the covenants which touch and concern the land. The system of leasehold tenure requires that the obligations in the lease shall be enforceable throughout the term, whether those obligations are affirmative or negative. The owner of a reversion must be able to enforce the positive covenants to pay rent and keep in repair against an assignee who in turn must be

able to enforce any positive covenants entered into by the original landlord. Common law retained the ancient rule that the burden of a covenant does not run with the land of the covenantor except in the case of a lease, but even that rule was radically modified by equity so far as negative covenants were concerned: see Tulk v Moxhay (1848) 2 Ph. 774."

3–002 Thus, the effect of common law on a lease is to create rights and obligations which are independent of the parallel rights and obligations of the original human covenantor who and whose heirs may fail, or the parallel rights and obligations of a corporate covenantor which may be dissolved. Common law achieves that effect by annexing those rights and obligations so far as they touch and concern the land to the term and to the reversion. Nourse L.J. summarised the position in *City of London Corporation v Fell* [1993] Q.B. 589 at p.604, when he said:

"The contractual obligations which touch and concern the land having become imprinted on the estate, the tenancy is capable of existence as a species of property independently of the contract."

3–003 The right of a landlord or a tenant to bring a tenancy to an end by notice is an incident of the relationship of landlord and tenant. This is the common law position in relation to notices to quit in respect of a periodic tenancy: *Wordsley Brewery v Halford* (1903) 90 L.T. 89 (notice to quit invalid when served by the original lessor who had, prior to the service of the notice, granted a concurrent lease). In the same way, the benefit and burden of a break clause in a lease will, on an assignment, ordinarily pass with the reversion or the term, as "touching and concerning" the respective estates of the landlord and the tenant and as conditions of the enjoyment of those estates. See *Linpac Mouldings Ltd v Aviva Life and Pensions UK Ltd* [2010] EWCA Civ 395, at para.44, per Etherton L.J.

3–004 Over time there has been criticism of the "touch and concern" test, the rules of which have long been said to be arbitrary. See, for example, *Grant v Edmondson* [1931] 1 Ch. 1, at p.28, per Romer L.J. and *Swift (P&A) Investments v Combined English Stores Group Plc* [1989] A.C. 632, at p.640, per Lord Oliver. Be that as it may, the common law position relating to the passing of the benefit and burden of landlord and tenant covenants on an assignment has now been supplanted by various statutory provisions, as shall be detailed in the following paragraphs.

## 2 Section 63 of the Law of Property Act 1925

3–005 Section 63 of the Law of Property Act 1925 ("the 1925 Act") provides as follows:

## ASSIGNMENT

"(1) Every conveyance is effectual to pass all the estate, right, title, interest, claim, and demand which the conveying parties respectively have in, to, or on the property conveyed, or expressed or intended so to be, or which they respectively have power to convey in, to, or on the same.

(2) This section applies only if and as far as a contrary intention is not expressed in the conveyance, and has effect subject to the terms of the conveyance and to the provisions therein contained.

(3) This section applies to conveyances made after the thirty-first day of December, eighteen hundred and eighty-one."

This provision is a statutory "all estate" clause, the effect of which is that, unless a contrary intention appears, a conveyance will automatically pass the whole estate, title and interest which the vendor has in, to, or on the property conveyed, without the need for express mention. Under s.205(1)(ii) of the 1925 Act, a "conveyance" includes a mortgage, charge, lease, assent, vesting declaration, vesting instrument, disclaimer, release and every other assurance of property or of an interest therein by any instrument, except a will. As was said by Lindsay J. in *Harbour Estates Ltd v HSBC Bank Plc* [2005] Ch. 194, at p.208D, the object of s.63 of the 1925 Act "was to avoid the litany of express mentions of ancillaries and sweepings up which, in order to ensure that everything passed that could pass with the conveyance, had become the standard language of conveyancers. That standard language was, by statute, instead to be read into every conveyance (including a written assignment of a lease) unless a contrary intention was expressed in the conveyance."  **3–006**

Thus, save where a contrary intention appears (for example, where the break clause is expressed to be purely personal to the tenant), upon an assignment, the effect of s.63 of the 1925 Act will be for the option to determine the lease to pass automatically upon assignment of the term or the reversion.  **3–007**

## 3 Section 142 of the Law of Property Act 1925

Section 142 of the 1925 Act provides as follows:  **3–008**

"(1) The obligation under a condition or of a covenant entered into by a lessor with reference to the subject-matter of the lease shall, if and as far as the lessor has power to bind the reversionary estate immediately expectant on the term granted by the lease, be annexed and incident to and shall go with that reversionary estate, or the several parts thereof, notwithstanding severance of that reversionary estate, and may be taken advantage of and enforced by the person in whom the term is from time to time vested by conveyance, devolution in law, or otherwise; and, if and as far as the lessor has power to bind the person from time to time entitled to that reversionary estate, the obligation aforesaid may be taken advantage of and enforced against any person so entitled.

(2) This section applies to leases made before or after the commencement of this Act, whether the severance of the reversionary estate was effected before or after such commencement: Provided that, where the lease was made before the first day of January eighteen hundred and eighty-two, nothing in this section shall affect the operation of any severance of the reversionary estate effected before such commencement."

**3–009** This provision only applies in respect of leases entered into prior to January 1, 1996. It is concerned with obligations under conditions or covenants entered into by a lessor with reference to the subject matter of a lease. A break clause will fall into this category. See *Weg Motors Ltd v Hales* [1962] Ch. 49 (concerning an option to renew a lease). The effect of s.142 of the 1925 Act is broadly similar to s.63 (see paras 3–005–3–007 above).

### 4 Section 3 of the Landlord and Tenant (Covenants) Act 1995

**3–010** The Landlord and Tenant (Covenants) Act 1995 ("the 1995 Act") came into force on January 1, 1996 and, with certain limited exceptions, applies in relation to leases granted on or after that date.

**3–011** Insofar as is relevant, s.3 of the 1995 Act provides as follows:

"(1) The benefit and burden of all landlord and tenant covenants of a tenancy—
  (a) shall be annexed and incident to the whole, and to each and every part, of the premises demised by the tenancy and of the reversion in them, and
  (b) shall in accordance with this section pass on an assignment of the whole or any part of those premises or of the reversion in them.
(2) Where the assignment is by the tenant under the tenancy, then as from the assignment the assignee—
  (a) becomes bound by the tenant covenants of the tenancy except to the extent that—
    (i) immediately before the assignment they did not bind the assignor, or
    (ii) they fall to be complied with in relation to any demised premises not comprised in the assignment; and
  (b) becomes entitled to the benefit of the landlord covenants of the tenancy except to the extent that they fall to be complied with in relation to any such premises.

(3) Where the assignment is by the landlord under the tenancy, then as from the assignment the assignee—
 (a) becomes bound by the landlord covenants of the tenancy except to the extent that—
  (i) immediately before the assignment they did not bind the assignor, or
  (ii) they fall to be complied with in relation to any demised premises not comprised in the assignment; and
 (b) becomes entitled to the benefit of the tenant covenants of the tenancy except to the extent that they fall to be complied with in relation to any such premises.

. . .

(6) Nothing in this section shall operate—
 (a) in the case of a covenant which (in whatever terms) is expressed to be personal to any person, to make the covenant enforceable by or (as the case may be) against any other person . . ."

**3–012** The effect of this provision is that the benefit of all "landlord covenants" and the burden of all "tenant covenants" are annexed and incident to the whole, and each and every part of the demised premises. Likewise, the benefit of all "tenant covenants" and the burden of all "landlord covenants" are annexed and incident to the reversion, and each and every part thereof (s.3(1)(a)). The benefit and burden of all landlord and tenant covenants pass on an assignment of the whole or any part of the demised premises or the reversion (s.3(1)(b)). The exception to this general rule is in the case of a covenant which is expressed to be personal to any person (s.3(6)).

**3–013** Section 28(1) of the 1995 Act defines "landlord covenant" as, in relation to a tenancy, a covenant falling to be complied with by the landlord of premises demised by the tenancy. A "tenant covenant" means, in relation to a tenancy, a covenant falling to be complied with by the tenant of premises demised by the tenancy. A "covenant" is itself defined as including a term, condition and obligation. A break clause does not obviously fall to be described as a "landlord covenant" or a "tenant covenant" (as defined) since such a clause confers merely a unilateral right to determine the lease, and not an obligation "falling to be complied with" by either the landlord or the tenant. If (which will be unlikely) on a true construction, any given break clause constitutes either a tenant or landlord covenant (as defined), then the benefit and burden of the same will be transmitted upon an assignment by operation of s.3(1) of the 1995 Act (unless s.3(6) applies).

## 5 The position where the tenant assigns the term

(a) *Leases entered into before January 1, 1996*
**3–014** By reason of the general common law rule mentioned in para.3–003 above, and/or by operation of ss.62 and/or 142 of the 1925 Act (see paras

3-005-3-009 above), the benefit and burden of a break clause will ordinarily pass automatically to an assignee of the term upon the assignment, and then without express mention. The position may be otherwise where the benefit of the break clause is expressed to be personal to the original tenant (on which, see para.3-017), or can only be assigned to a limited category of persons (on which, see para.3-018) or where the tenant assigns only part of the demise (on which, see para.3-019).

(b) *Leases entered into on or after January 1, 1996*

3-015 The observations made in the previous paragraph are equally valid here save that, if applicable in the case of a break clause (which is doubtful), s.3 of the 1995 Act operates in place of s.142 of the 1925 Act.

(c) *Restrictions on assignability*

3-016 On a true construction of the lease, it may be that the break clause is expressed to be purely personal to the original tenant or assignable only to a limited class of people. So, for example, the break clause may refer to "the tenant, here meaning X only" or it may only be assignable to "the tenant, or a permitted assignee, being a group company in the X group of companies."

3-017 The benefit of purely personal break clause (i.e. one in favour of a specific tenant only) will not pass on an assignment of the term, either at common law or under statute. In this scenario difficult questions arise as to what happens if the lease is then re-assigned back to the original tenant. These questions are considered in Ch.5 at paras 5-009-5-017. Generally, the courts will be slow to infer that the benefit of a break clause is purely personal in the absence of clear words. See, for example, *Re 120 Packington Street, Islington* (1960) 110 S.J. 672 (assignee of the reversion entitled to exercise break clause even though 'lessee' was defined to include persons claiming under him and there was no corresponding definition of "lessor").

3-018 In the case of a break clause which is assignable only to a limited class of people, it may be that the break clause is, nonetheless, sufficiently impersonal that it will pass under the statutory provisions referred to above (see paras 3-005-3-013). An interesting example of this is to be found in *Harbour Estates Ltd v HSBC Bank Plc* [2005] Ch. 194, which concerned an unusual 'hybrid' break clause, which was neither wholly personal, nor freely assignable. Nonetheless, Lindsay J. held that the benefit of the break clause passed on an assignment by operation of s.63 of the 1925 Act.

(d) *Assignment of part*

3-019 In *Kaiser Engineers & Constructors Inc v E R Squibb & Sons Ltd* (Unreported November 12, 1971), Russell L.J. (as he then was) said: "It is common ground that for [a break notice to be effective] it must on its true construction be a determination of the whole relationship of landlord and tenant under [the] lease." This reflects the common law position that a notice to quit referring to part only of the demise is invalid and ineffective: see *Re Bebington's Tenancy* [1921] 1 Ch. 559. Thus, where a break clause refers to the whole of the demised premises, and the tenant assigns part of those premises, neither the original tenant nor the assignee will be able to exercise the option to determine (unless, perhaps, they can jointly exercise the break).

## 6 The position where the landlord assigns the reversion

(a) *Leases entered into before 1 January 1996*
In relation to old tenancies, the benefit and burden of an option to deter-    **3–020**
mine will usually pass to an assignee of the reversion, whether at common law, or under ss.63 and/or 142 of the 1925 Act. The observations in para.3–014 apply here.

(b) *Leases entered into on or after January 1, 1996*
The observations made in para.3–015 are equally applicable here.    **3–021**

(c) *Restrictions on assignability*
The observations made in paras 3–016–3–018 apply in the case of a    **3–022**
landlord's break clause as with a tenant's break clause.

(d) *Severance of the reversion*
Insofar as is relevant, s.140 of the 1925 Act provides as follows:    **3–023**

"(1) Notwithstanding the severance by conveyance, surrender, or otherwise of the reversionary estate in any land comprised in a lease, and notwithstanding the avoidance or cesser in any other manner of the term granted by a lease as to part only of the land comprised therein, every condition or right of re-entry, and every other condition contained in the lease, shall be apportioned, and shall remain annexed to the severed parts of the reversionary estate as severed, and shall be in force with respect to the term whereon each severed part is reversionary, or the term in the part of the land as to which the term has not been surrendered, or has not been avoided or has not otherwise ceased, in like manner as if the land comprised in each severed part, or the land as to which the term remains subsisting, as the case may be, had alone originally been comprised in the lease.

(2) In this section "right of re-entry" includes a right to determine the lease by notice to quit or otherwise; but where the notice is served by a person entitled to a severed part of the reversion so that it extends to part only of the land demised, the lessee may within one month determine the lease in regard to the rest of the land by giving to the owner of the reversionary estate therein a counter notice expiring at the same time as the original notice."

**3–024** The effect of this provision is that, where a landlord grants part of his reversion to an assignee, all covenants, all conditions and rights of re-entry are apportioned on the severance of the reversion and are annexed to the severed parts thereof. This means that, so far as the benefit of a landlord's break clause is concerned, both reversioners will be able to determine the lease of the part of the reversion with which they are interested. See *Smith v Kinsey* [1936] 3 All E.R. 73. It should be noted that s.140(2) of the 1925 Act gives the tenant of a split reversion the statutory right, within one month of the service of the reversioner's notice, to elect to end the lease on the rest of the land by giving to the owner of that other part a counter-notice expiring at the same time as the first notice.

**3–025** In *Jelley v Buckman* [1975] Q.B. 488, it was emphasised by the Court of Appeal that severance of the reversion does not operate to replace the existing lease by two separate leases. Stamp L.J. said at pp.497–498:

> "Now it is no doubt correct that the effect of the legislation is that each reversioner has rights and remedies similar to those which he would have had if he had granted a separate tenancy of the land in respect of which he is owner. But it is one thing to say that each reversioner has rights and remedies similar to or even indistinguishable from the rights and remedies which he would have had if there had been two separate tenancies and quite another thing to say that this operates against the tenant and that he therefore has two tenancies; and we cannot read section 140 as producing the latter result. We can find nothing in the section to suggest for a moment that the legislature intended that following a severance to which the lessee was not a party he should find himself holding part of his land under one tenancy and part under another. In relation to a lease for years as opposed to a weekly tenancy the change in the law would be dramatic and had the legislature intended to create that result one would expect to find some clear expression of that intention. Not only is there an absence of such an expression of intention but we find in this section positive indications that what was assumed or contemplated was the continued existence of the pre-existing lease. We refer in this connection first to subsection (1) speaking as it does of 'the term' – not 'the respective terms' – 'whereon each severed part is reversionary' and subsection (2) speaking of the right to determine 'the lease', emphasising the definite article preceding 'lease'."

**3–026** Prudence would dictate that, where the landlord has severed the reversion, and the tenant has the benefit of a break clause, the break notice should be served on both reversioners. This is because the burden of the tenant's break clause will be apportioned, and shall remain annexed to the severed parts of the reversionary estate as severed.

## 7 Equitable assignees

Save where it is expressly provided otherwise, it is only the legal assignee **3–027**
of the term or the reversion who can exercise a break clause. So much
was held in *Seaward v Drew* (1898) 67 L.J.Q.B. 322, per Channell J.
(concerning the purported exercise of a break clause by an equitable
chargee of the term) and also in *Stait v Fenner* [1912] 2 Ch. 504, at
p.512, per Neville J.: "the legal estate in the term being outstanding, it
was not competent for the lessee or any assignee of the lessee who had
not the legal estate vested in him to give a notice [to quit]".

In *Brown & Root Technology Ltd v Sun Alliance and London Assurance* **3–028**
*Co Ltd* [2001] Ch. 733, on July 24, 1989, Sun Alliance and London
Assurance Co Ltd ("Sun Alliance") granted to Brown & Root Technology
Ltd ("Technology") a lease which entitled Technology to give notice to
terminate the same by serving not less than 12-months notice expiring at
the end of the seventh year of the term. In 1993, Technology became a
wholly-owned subsidiary of Brown & Root Ltd ("B&R") and, at the end
of May 1993, it was decided that B&R would take a transfer from
Technology of its business and assets, including the lease in question;
Sun Alliance granted a licence to assign. The necessary conveyancing
documents were duly executed, but the transfer of the lease, which was
registrable, was never registered at HM Land Registry in the name of
B&R. On September 10, 1994, Technology served a break notice on Sun
Alliance, but Sun Alliance refused to accept that the break notice was
valid. The question was whether there was an assignment of the lease by
Technology. If there had been, then Technology was not entitled to serve
the break notice; if there had not been, then it was. At trial, Sun Alliance
persuaded the judge that the break notice was invalid. Technology
appealed.

Allowing the appeal, Mummery L.J. said at pp.741–742: **3–029**

"It is common ground that there has been no transfer (and therefore no
assignment) of the legal title to the lease; that, as between Technology
and B&R, the equitable title to the lease was capable of passing by
virtue of a specifically enforceable contract to assign the lease; that, if
this were unregistered land, the assignment would occur on the execution of the deed of assignment and the conveyance of the legal estate
thereby, and not on the conclusion of the contract to assign; and that,
depending on the context, the passing of the equitable or beneficial
interest may amount to a transfer or assignment of the property in
question, even though there has been no registration of the transfer, as
required by statute, to perfect the legal title. The judge referred to the
cases of In re Rose [1949] Ch 78 and In re Rose [1952] Ch 499 as
instances of a bequest of shares and an inter vivos gift of shares which
took effect as between donor and donee and in accordance with donative intent before the registration of the transfers of the shares pursuant

to the provisions of the Companies Act. Until registration there was no transfer so far as the company was concerned, but that did not prevent the gift from being effective as between others.

. . .

This case is not a matter of beneficial ownership between parties to the transfer of the lease: the issue of assignment or no assignment affects the legal position of a third party, the lessors, who have given their licence to assign but are not a party to the transfer. As was observed by Jenkins L.J. in In re Rose [1952] Ch 499, 518 it is necessary to keep clear and distinct the position between the transferor and the transferee and the position of a third party. Transfer of the beneficial title is not, in this context, relevant to the legal relationship between the lessees and the lessors. The issue is not what rights Technology and B&R have against each other, but what rights Technology and Sun Alliance have against each other. That is a question of legal, not equitable, rights.

. . .

As between lessors and lessees, there is binding Court of Appeal authority in Gentle v Faulkner [1990] 2 QB 267 for the proposition that assignment means, in the absence of a context showing an extended meaning, an assignment of the legal estate, and not of the beneficial interest, e g by declaration of trust of the lease. It is not a matter of intention to assign, a point highly relevant to the passing of beneficial title, but of whether a defined event has occurred. That event is not completion, as [Counsel for Sun Alliance] contended; it is the transfer of the legal title to the lease, so as to create the legal relationship of lessor and lessee between B&R and Sun Alliance."

**3–030** Thus, the Court of Appeal had no hesitation in finding that the original lessee's notice to terminate was valid. There had been no transfer of legal title to the lease, and so the original tenant retained the right to exercise the break clause.

### 8 The position where the option is not contained in the lease

**3–031** An option to determine a lease may be conferred by an instrument other than a lease, for example, by a side letter. This does not present any particular conceptual problems so far as assignments are concerned. Thus, in *System Floors Ltd v Ruralpride Ltd* [1995] 1 E.G.L.R. 48, Midland Oak Properties Ltd ("Midland Oak") granted to System Floors Ltd ("System Floors"), under its then name, three leases for terms of 21 years from

June 24, 1977 of units 20, 22, 23 and 24, respectively, Marlissa Drive, Coventry. On the same day Midland Oak wrote on its headed paper to System Floors a letter headed "Re: Units 20, 22, 23 and 24 Marlissa Drive, Coventry", one copy of which was countersigned by System Floors by way of acknowledgment and agreement. The letter was in the following terms: "In consideration of your today taking from us Leases respectively of Units 20, 22 and 23 and 24 Marlissa Drive, Coventry WE HEREBY AGREE with you in relation to the Leases as follows . . . If within three months after any of the dates for review of rent contained in any of the Leases or (if later) the date upon which the rent payable from any such review date shall be agreed or determined in accordance with the Lease you shall desire to surrender any of the Leases (as a whole but not in part) and if you shall within three months after such review date or such alternative date as aforesaid (as to which period of time is of the essence) give to us notice in writing of your intention so to do, then . . . we will upon the date occurring three months after such notice accept a surrender of the demised premises from you." Although drafted in terms of a surrender, this side letter amounted to granting to System Floors an option to determine the leases. The question was whether this side letter bound Ruralpride Ltd ("Ruralpride"), Midland Oak's successor in title, to the reversion of the leases.

Morritt L.J. said at p.50: 3–032

"It is contended that the obligations undertaken in the letter . . . come within [s.142(1) of the 1925 Act] with the consequence that they may be enforced against Ruralpride, as the person now entitled to the reversionary estate. That is disputed by Ruralpride.

It was established by the decision of this court in Weg Motors Ltd v Hales [1962] Ch 49, that [s.142(1) of the 1925 Act] applies to promises contained in an independent document not under seal. In its written submissions Ruralpride sought to distinguish the case on the basis that in that case the independent document defined the parties as including their successors in title. But in the view I take of the construction of the letter in this case, that is not a distinction which can be drawn. Thus, the subsection may apply notwithstanding that the obligations are undertaken in a letter. The question is whether the obligations 'were entered into by a lessor with reference to the subject-matter of the lease'".

Thus, System Floors was entitled to rely on the side letter as against the assignee of the reversion. 3–033

## 9 General good practice

As a matter of best practice a practitioner acting for an assignee of the term or the reversion who wishes to take the benefit of a break clause 3–034 (assuming the benefit is assignable) should include appropriate express provision in the contract of assignment. In the absence of any express mention of the option to determine in the assignment of the lease, it may be necessary to decide whether the language of the documentation can be construed as extending to the option. See, for example, the decision of the Supreme Court of Queensland in *Denham Bros Ltd v W Freestone Leasing Pty Ltd* [2003] Q.C.A. 376 (whether the words "all the rights title and interest of the lessor under the said lease including the option" were sufficient to transfer the benefit of an option to renew).

3–035 It should be recalled that the assignor of the term or the reversion is not obliged to assign the benefit of a break clause upon the assignment. He may, if he so wishes, retain the benefit for himself (although quaere whether, and in what circumstances, it could then be exercised – see Ch.5, paras 5–009–5–017).

Chapter 4

# Contents of a Break Clause

**1 Introduction**

Consistent with the fact that a break clause is a type of option (see paras 1–011–1–012), the notice that exercises the option in the break clause needs strictly to satisfy the procedural requirements of that clause. Such requirements commonly refer to: **4–001**

  (i) The date or dates upon which the lease is to end, if the break clause is exercised.
  (ii) The length of notice to be given for the exercise of the break clause.
  (iii) The language of the break notice and/or its form (e.g. whether it is to be sent in accordance with a prescribed form, or to contain a set form of words or to be written on a particular colour of paper).
  (iv) The party who is to serve the notice, the party or parties to whom it is to be addressed and the mode of service.

The last of the above topics (service) is sufficiently extensive to justify two chapters of its own. See Chs 5 and 6. This chapter deals with the first three requirements. It also considers the question of mistakes in a notice, and several other miscellaneous issues. **4–002**

**2 The date of termination—general observations**

Since break clauses are a matter of contract, the parties to a lease can choose any date or dates of termination they wish. Probably the most typical tenant's break clauses include one or more pre-determined break dates, say every five years. This mechanism is to enable the landlord to organise cash flow. A lease that might end whenever the tenant chooses (i.e. a "rolling break") is unpopular with institutions. **4–003**

**4–004** Landlord's break clauses tend to be fixed less by reference to preordained dates than by reference to the triggering of particular events. An obvious example is a landlord's break clause which is operable when it has the necessary intention or desire to redevelop.

**4–005** Some mutual break clauses are also fixed by particular events. Quite a common example is where notice to break a lease can be given by either party after the expiry of, say, two years when damage to the demised premises has not been repaired.

**4–006** However, the foregoing are merely illustrations. Ultimately, it is up to the parties to choose a date or event upon which a lease might be broken. Whatever the date or event that is stipulated, the clearest method of achieving certainty for the service of a notice is to specify the actual date or dates in the lease. Modern leases often do this by inserting termination dates in a definition clause.

**4–007** Any mechanism that requires a calculation, on the part of the server, of the termination date, can prove problematic. Thus a break clause that refers to termination "upon the expiry of the seventh year of the term" or "within six months of a rent day", will require a calculation to be performed. Like all calculations, there is the possibility of a mistake occurring. Wherever possible, if a break clause contains a formula for the fixing of the break date, then the break notice should deploy that formula and resist the temptation to replace it with a date, or even to add a date after the formula. Thus, the lease might permit termination on the Michaelmas rent day. The server might muddle up his rent days, and stipulate termination on March 25 (Lady day) rather than September 29 (Michaelmas). Simply repeating the terminology in the break clause should avoid this problem.

**4–008** If the break clause is a "rolling break", then it follows that it will not be possible to tell from the clause itself the date when the break will take effect. It is considered that the date of the break must be specified in the break notice. Care should therefore be taken to ensure that any minimum period of notice will be satisfied. It is prudent to allow a margin for delayed receipt of the break notice. For example, if the clause requires six months' notice, then it would be wise to specify a date that is several days more than six months from the date that the notice is given.

**4–009** Assuming that it is necessary to know the termination date, or to identify it, then a number of well known words or phrases are considered below.

### 3 Notices—length and termination dates

**4–010** Some words or phrases that appear in break clauses might be uncertain, and it is therefore useful to know how the courts might approach them. Some such words or phrases are considered below.

**4–011** "Quarter"—If a break clause requires a quarters' notice to be given, then it will be a question of construction as to whether the particular lease means a quarter of a year (viz. three months) or a quarter between rent days. Brightman L.J. recognised that the former was possible in *East v Pantiles (Plant Hire) Ltd* [1982] 2 E.G.L.R. 111. Traditional quarter days are March 25 (Lady day), June 24 (mid summer), September 29 (Michaelmas) and December 25 (Christmas). In modern leases, one often finds other dates specified as rent dates (e.g. January 1, April 1, etc.) and break clauses might mirror such dates. The whole lease will need to be examined to see how the break clause is intended to "work".

"Month"—By s.161 of the Law of Property Act 1925, "in all deeds, contracts, . . . and other instruments executed, made or coming into operation after [January 1, 1926], unless the context otherwise requires— **4–012**

(a) "Month" means calendar month . . ."

Where a break clause requires several months notice to be given, the corresponding date rule is applied. This rule was discussed by the judges in the *Dodds v Walker* litigation. *Dodds v Walker* was concerned with the four-month time limit that used to operate for a tenant to apply to the court for a new lease, after receiving a landlord's notice pursuant to s.25 of the Landlord and Tenant Act 1954. The Court of Appeal was divided on the point. When the case reached the House of Lords (per [1981] 1 W.L.R. 1027), Lord Diplock stated in his speech at p.1029B: **4–013**

"That when the relevant period is a month or specified number of months after the giving of a notice, the general rule is that the month ends upon the corresponding date in the appropriate subsequent month, i.e. the date of that month that bears the same number as the day of the earlier month on which the notice was given".

Lord Russell illustrated the application of the rule in the case of months of different lengths by saying, at p.1030E:

"The application of the corresponding date principle inevitably produces variation in the number of days involved, depending upon the date upon which a four month notice is served and the irregular allotment of days in different months. Sometimes it is not possible to apply directly the principle, for instance if a four month notice is served on October 30 (the time beginning to run at midnight October 30/31), there being in February but 28 (or 29) days, it is not possible to find a corresponding date in February and plainly a corresponding date cannot be sought in March: The application of the corresponding date principle in such a case can only lead to termination of the four month period at midnight February 28/March 1 (or midnight February 29/ March 1 in a leap year), that is an inevitable outcome."

"From"—The tendency since 1808 (viz. *Lester v Garland* (1808) 15 Ves. Jr. 248) has been to construe "from" as excluding the specified date (see Salmon L.J. in *Trow v Ind Coope (West Midlands) Ltd* [1967] 2 Q.B. 899, at p.925). **4–014**

**4–015** "Commencing on or with"—"Any period of time to be calculated as commencing or beginning with a certain day must include that day", per Salmon L.J. in *Trow v Ind Coope* (above) at p.925.

## 4 The language of the break notice and mistakes—the general approach

**4–016** The question as to the form of words to be used in a break clause was discussed by the House of Lords in *Mannai Investment Co Ltd v Eagle Star Life Assurance Co Ltd* [1997] A.C. 749 when reviewing the circumstances when a mistake in that language would not deprive the notice of legal effect. In view of the crucial importance of the *Mannai* case to the validity of break notices, it is worth briefly considering its facts and then considering the reasoning adopted by the majority of their Lordships when explaining their conclusions.

**4–017** *Mannai* concerned two leases of office premises containing break clauses (at Clause 7(13)) exercisable "on the third anniversary of the term commencement date". The tenant gave notice to the landlord to determine both leases on January 12, 1995. On a proper calculation the third anniversary was January 13, 1995, so the tenant understated the date by one day. The Court of Appeal found that the notices were invalid. The House of Lords, by three to two, overturned this decision.

**4–018** All three Judges, who were in the majority in *Mannai*, and who decided that the break notices were valid, made speeches. It is important to note the test that each formulated, to decide whether a break notice is valid.

**4–019** The first speech was from Lord Steyn. Beginning at p.767D he stated as follows:

"On reflection I have come to the conclusion that the question of the construction of the notices should be answered by holding that the notices were effective to determine the leases . . .

The reasons for my conclusion can be stated in the form of numbered propositions.
(1) This is not a case of a contractual right to determine which prescribes as an indispensable condition for its effective exercise that the notice must contain specific information . . .
(2) The question is not how the landlord understood the notices. The construction of the notices must be approached objectively. The issue is how a reasonable recipient would have understood the notices . . . Given that the reasonable recipient must be credited with knowledge of the critical date and the terms of clause 7(1) the question is simply how the reasonable recipient would have understood such a notice . . .

(3) It is important not to lose sight of the purpose of a notice under the break clause. It serves one purpose only: to inform the landlord that the tenant has decided to determine the lease in accordance with the right reserved. That purpose must be relevant to the construction and validity of the notice. Prima facie one would expect that if a notice unambiguously conveys a decision to determine a court may nowadays ignore immaterial errors which would not have misled a reasonable recipient.

(4) There is no justification for placing notices under a break clause in leases in a unique category. Making due allowance for contextual differences, such notices belong to the general class of unilateral notices served under contractual rights reserved, e.g. notices to quit, notices to determine licences and notices to complete: Delta Vale Properties Ltd v. Mills [1990] 1 W.L.R. 445, 454E–G. To those examples may be added notices under charter parties, contracts of affreightment, and so forth. Even if such notices under contractual rights reserved contain errors they may be valid if they are 'sufficiently clear and unambiguous to leave a reasonable recipient in no reasonable doubt as to how and when they are intended to operate': the Delta case, at p.454E–G, per Slade L.J. and adopted by Stocker and Bingham L.JJ.; see also Carradine Properties Ltd v. Aslam [1976] 1 W.L.R. 442, 444. That test postulates that the reasonable recipient is left in no doubt that the right reserved is being exercised. It acknowledges the importance of such notices. The application of that test is principled and cannot cause any injustice to a recipient of the notice. I would gratefully adopt it."

Lord Hoffman delivered the second speech in the majority. At p.773G he began by noting that: "It is remembered that such notices, operating as they do, unilaterally to alter the rights of the parties, must comply strictly with the terms of the lease". He then went on to address the question as to the appropriate test to be applied when considering the validity of a notice. He contrasted the test in *Carradine Properties Ltd v Aslam* [1976] 1 W.L.R. 442 with the test in *Hankey v Clavering* [1942] 2 K.B. 326. In examining the judgment of Lord Greene M.R. in *Hankey v Clavering* he said (at p.776A) as follows:

**4–020**

"I pass on to a second explanation which also seems to me inadequate. Lord Greene M.R. said, at pp.329–330, that because such notice is of unilateral operation, the conditions under which they may be served must be strictly complied with. I have already said that this principle is accepted on both sides. But, as an explanation of the method of construction used in Hankey v. Clavering, it begs the question: If the clause had said that the notice had to be on blue paper, it would have been no good serving a notice on pink paper, however clear it might have been that the tenant wanted to terminate the lease."

**4–021**  He then went on to explain that clause 7(13) of the leases before him had no special requirement.

**4–022**  After a further review of the authorities, at p.780D Lord Hoffmann approved the test used by Goulding J. in *Carradine Properties* (above), namely: "Is the notice quite clear to a reasonable tenant reading it? Is it plain that he cannot be misled by it?" We shall call this the *Carradine* Test.

**4–023**  The third judge in the majority was Lord Clyde. At p.782A he approved the *Carradine* Test. At p.782B he added as follows:

> "Delta Vale Properties Ltd v Mills [1990] 1 W.L.R. 445 concerned a vendor's notice to complete which was in condition 23 of the conditions of sale, but I see no reason why any different principle of construction should apply. Slade L.J. observed at p.454:
> 
> 'In my judgment, notices served under condition 23, if they are to be valid, must be sufficiently clear and unambiguous to leave a reasonable recipient in no reasonable doubt as to how and when they are intended to operate.'
> 
> The standard of reference is that of the reasonable man exercising his commonsense in the context and in the circumstances of the particular case . . . the test is an objective one. In circumstances where an estoppel might arise the act of understanding the recipient may be relevant, but in general the actual understanding of the parties is beside the point."

**4–024**  Thus all three judges in the majority in *Mannai* expressly approved the *Carradine* Test. Two Judges expressly approve the test formulated by Slade L.J. in the *Delta* case, which we will call the *Delta* Test.

**4–025**  As we shall see from the discussion of later cases below, the scope of *Mannai* is comparatively narrow. It is not an escape clause for inaccuracy or sloppy drafting. It is worth emphasising that Mannai involved an obvious error by one day in the termination date.

**4–026**  Before considering the question of mistakes in a notice, it is necessary to record that, if the break clause prescribes specific information "as an indispensable condition for its effective exercise" (per Lord Steyn) then the court has no power to correct a mistake. Lord Hoffman's example is using pink paper when blue paper was prescribed. All of the discussion that follows hereafter, regarding mistakes in the content of a notice, therefore assumes that the mistake does not relate to an "indispensable condition".

### 5 Mistakes as to the date of termination

**4–027**  The insertion of the wrong date in a break notice is, probably, the most basic type of mistake. If everything about a break notice is correct, other than the date of termination, then it should be relatively easy to satisfy the

*Carradine* Test. After all, if it is plain that the document received is a notice pursuant to a break clause, then it should be obvious that the server does not intend to serve an invalid notice. *Mannai* itself illustrates this proposition, as does *Garston v Scottish Widows Fund and Life Assurance Society* [1998] 1 W.L.R. 1583. In *Garston*, the tenant had a single opportunity to break a lease, on the expiration of the 10th year of the term. The tenant wrongly specified a date that was 10 years from the date of the lease. The Court of Appeal held the notice to be valid. However, this observation only works if there is only one possible termination date, or only one termination date that makes any sense. If there are two or more real possibilities, then the court cannot validate the notice by choosing one date in preference to another, simply in order to make the notice valid.

### 6 Mistakes in the identity of the landlord or the tenant

Since *Mannai* there have been various cases where the name of one of the parties is wrong. The courts' treatment of these cases has varied. A key ingredient has been whether the party name, that is alleged to be a mistake, was the name of a real person, or whether that name did not correspond to a real person. 4–028

An example of the latter situation is *Baker Tilly Management Ltd v Computer Associates UK Ltd* (Unreported December 11, 2009). In this case a lease was granted to a tenant, which then had the name Baker Tilly Services Ltd. When the time arrived to serve a break notice the tenant had changed its name to Baker Tilly Management Ltd, however, the break notice was served in its old name, viz. Baker Tilly Services Ltd. There was no company with that name, and the judge concluded that this was an obvious error, which could not have caused any reasonable landlord any confusion. 4–029

In contrast to the above, there have been three reported cases which involved doubts as to which company was the tenant, for the purposes of the service of a break clause. In these cases the allegedly mistaken name corresponded to a real person. The cases in question are *Lemmerbell Ltd v Britannia LAS Direct Ltd* (1999) L. & T.R. 102, *Procter & Gamble Technical Centres Ltd v Brixton Plc* [2003] 2 E.G.L.R. 24 and *Havant International Holdings Ltd v Lionsgate (H) Investment Ltd* (2000) L. & T.R. 297. 4–030

In *Lemmerbell* there were two leases, in each of which the defendant tenant was known as LAS Direct Limited ("Direct"). Each lease contained a break clause exercisable on six months' written notice. In 1992 solicitors acting for Direct informed the landlord's solicitors that they acted for the Life Association of Scotland ("Life"). It was explained that Life and Direct were wholly owned subsidiaries of LAS Holdings Limited. No request for consent to any assignment was made and no 4–031 assignment actually took place. However, in 1994 break notices were sent on behalf of "The Life Association of Scotland Limited successors in title to ... Direct". The Trial Judge decided the notices were valid, but the Court of Appeal unanimously reversed this decision.

**4–032** Peter Gibson L.J. delivered the principal judgment. At p.71G he explained that *Mannai* was concerned with a wrong date but that:

> "the present case seems to me to bear little resemblance to the type of error addressed in Mannai. There, words containing a mere slip, obvious to the reader of the notice when read in context, were construed as meaning what they were plainly intended to mean. In the present case there is no equivalent error: the break notice is not merely given on behalf of Life rather than Direct but it contains the explanation as to why it was so given, viz. Life was successor in title to Direct. I find it impossible to see how, in these circumstances, it is permissible to construe the break notices given on behalf of Direct."

**4–033** At p.71L the same judge added:

> "On the face of each notice, Life was said to be the tenant to the successor in title to Direct, and that, if true, could only have come about as a result of an assignment without consent. But such an assignment would be effective to make the assignee the lessee for the purposes of clause 7(x). The reasonable recipient could not know, in the absence of proof of the assignment, whether Life was the lessee: it might have been. If life was not in fact the lessee but Direct was, the reasonable recipient could not know whether Amery-Parkes [the solicitors serving the notice] were authorised by Direct to act for it and to serve the break notice, contrary to the express terms of the notice. To my mind, because it is not obvious from each notice that there was an error in the name of the lessee, nor is it obvious who the actual current lessee was, nor whether Amery-Parkes were duly authorised by anyone other than Life, it is impossible as a matter of construction to cure what we now know to be the defect by substituting Direct for Life as the person on whose behalf Amery-Parkes was giving each notice."

**4–034** *Procter & Gamble* was a decision of Neuberger J., as he then was. The premises were demised by a company, abbreviated by the judge, with the letters H&B, and the lease contained a break clause. There were assignments, so that the term of the lease became vested in a company, abbreviated by the judge, with the initials TC. A break notice was served on behalf of H&B as tenant. It was argued that it should have been obvious that it was the current tenant who wished to serve the notice. The judge, however, stated that a reasonable recipient of the notice would have been entitled to assume that the notice had been intentionally served on behalf of H&B. Neuberger J. reviewed the judgments in *Mannai* and added, at p.27C:

"It is important to read those observations as a whole because, like Lord Hoffman, Lord Steyn did not give a green light to inaccurate and sloppily drafted notices. The test, even in relation to the construction of notices, is relatively strict. In *Mannai*, what had gone wrong was that the tenant (or the tenant's agent that had served the notice) had got the break date one day wrong. He had therefore put forward in the notice an impossible date upon which to determine the lease, because the right to determine the lease could be effective only upon one specific date. By a bare majority, the House of Lords held that that did not invalidate the notice, because it would have been plain and obvious to a reasonable recipient of the notice what the notice intended to do, namely to determine the lease on the permitted date."

At p.27E the judge noted that "There is, of course, a potential difference between the wrong date and the wrong person identified in the notice." The judge then reviewed the case of *Lemmerbell* and decided, following that decision, that the notice in the case before him was invalid. **4–035**

*Havant* was factually different from *Lemmerbell* and *Procter & Gamble*. In *Havant*, a tenant (HIHL) had a personal right to break two leases. The leases remained vested in HIHL at the date of service of the break notices. However, the notices, wrongly, stated that they were served on behalf of HIL. HIL was a wholly owned subsidiary of HIHL. Hart J. decided the notices were valid, observing that, "The personal nature of HIHL's right ... makes the only explanation of the notice which carries conviction". **4–036**

## 7 Mistakes in the description of the premises

The simplest type of mistake, in the description of premises, is where the address stated in the notice does not exist. Lord Hoffman referred to such a case, decided as long ago as 1803, in his speech in *Mannai*. He said: **4–037**

"In *Doe d. Cox v. Roe* 4 Esp. 185, the landlord of a public house in Limehouse gave notice to quit 'the premises which you hold of me ... commonly called ... the Watermans Arms'. The evidence showed that the tenant held no premises called the Watermans Arms; indeed, there were no such premises in the parish of Limehouse. But the tenant did hold premises of the landlord called the Bricklayers Arms. By reference to the background, the notice was construed as referring to the Bricklayers Arms. The meaning was objectively clear to a reasonable recipient, even though the landlord had used the wrong name."

Thus a reference in a break notice to premises that do not exist should not invalidate a break notice, provided that it is clear what premises are intended to be referred to. **4–038**

**4–039**  However, if the break notice referred to premises of which the server and the served were landlord and tenant, but the premises referred to were not those the subject of the lease that was sought to be broken, then the notice would only be valid if the *Carradine* Test could be satisfied.

## 8 The relevance of the reaction of the party receiving the break notice

**4–040**  When disputes arise as to the validity of a break notice, one party or the other often seeks to refer to the reaction of the recipient, either to bolster a submission or to undermine it. There are cases, pre *Mannai*, that contain dicta that would appear to justify a reference to the reaction of the recipient to a break notice. However, the better view, post *Mannai*, is that the reaction of the recipient is legally irrelevant.

**4–041**  The above point was discussed by the Court of Appeal in *Lancecrest Ltd v Asiwaju* (2005) L. & T.R. 22. *Lancecrest* was a case that involved a disputed rent review, in which the validity of the counter notice was in issue. However the reasoning therein directly adopted a *Mannai* approach. Neuberger L.J. delivered the first judgment, the contents of which made it clear that he had seen a draft of the judgment of Clarke L.J. At para.36 of the report, Neuberger L.J. explained that he agreed with this judgment, with one exception. At paras 38–43 he then explained that the exception related to the reaction of the recipient of the notice. The judge's reasoning appears in the said paragraphs as follows:

> "[38] The one point that he makes with which I am inclined to disagree, is that, when deciding whether a particular notice is valid, it is permissible to place some weight on the reaction of the actual recipient. As Lord Steyn emphasised in Mannai, the question is not how the actual recipient landlord understood the letter, but how a reasonable person in his position would have understood it. I see the attraction of the argument that the reaction of the actual landlord might, in some circumstances, have evidential value as to how a reasonable recipient would react, and that that can be said to be consistent with what was said in Patel [*Patel v Earlspring Properties Ltd* [1991] 2 E.G.L.R. 131] and not inconsistent with the analysis of Lord Steyn.
>
> [39] However, it appears to me, when deciding on the validity of a notice, to rely in any way upon the reaction of the actual recipient is unsound in principle, and could well lead to inconsistency and unfairness. It is well established that, when interpreting contract, it is not permissible to rely upon the subsequent conduct of the parties as an aid to construction. The proper approach to the interpretation of notices is the same as that of contracts: see per Lord Hoffmann in Mannai, at p.779H. Accordingly, it appears to me that the same principle must apply to interpretation of notices.

[40] The question of whether a particular document is a valid notice must, of course, depend upon the contractual provisions under which it is said to have been served, and the precise terms of the document and the matrix of facts in which it is received. However, it is obviously desirable that the courts adopt a consistent approach to the construction of alleged notices as a matter of principle. If the reaction of the recipient of an alleged notice is to impinge upon its validity, this would almost inevitably lead to additional uncertainty in an area that (judging by the number of cases on the topic) is already bedevilled by uncertainty, and where certainty is highly desirable.

[41] Further, if the fact that the recipient treats the document as a valid notice is a factor in favour of it being a valid notice, the corollary must be that the recipient who treats the document as ineffective is entitled to rely upon that fact in order to support his contention that it is not a valid notice. In my view, that would be unfair on the sender of the document. Furthermore, it appears to me that to take into account the reaction of the recipient would actually benefit an ill-advised recipient as opposed to one who is well advised. A well-advised recipient of a document that is almost certainly not a valid counter-notice might protect himself by treating the document as a valid counter-notice, in case he turns out to be mistaken, would thereby be improving the chances of the document being held to be a valid counter-notice.

[42] It is true that Woolf LJ in Patel could be said to have relied upon the fact that the landlord appears to have treated the letter in question as a valid counter-notice, but it was little more than a throwaway line. In any event, the decision in Patel predated by some years the more detailed and principled analysis of the House of Lords in Mannai."

The view of Clarke L.J. is at para.67. He said, "I can see no reason why the Court should not have regard to the actual reaction of the landlord in deciding what the reaction of the reasonable landlord, in the position of this landlord, would be". The third judge in *Lancecrest* was Brooke L.J. He obviously felt that he had to express his own view on the point. He did so at para.88, by saying, "I agree with Neuberger LJ, for the reasons he gives, that the landlord's actual reaction plays no part in the legal test that has to be applied." **4–042**

## 9 Break notices that incorporate the phrases "without prejudice" and "subject to contract"

The phrase "without prejudice" may appear in break notices, or in covering letters, in two contexts. Firstly, a break notice might be served "without prejudice to the service of the earlier notice . . ." (or with similar wording). **4–043**

The quoted language was used by a landlord in serving a break notice, in *Keith Bayley Rogers & Co v Cubes Ltd* (1976) 31 P. & C.R. 412. Templeman J. stated at p.416, "In my judgment the landlord may contend that the first notice is good, but if it is not, he may rely on the second notice".

**4–044** A similar situation arose in *Royal Bank of Canada v Secretary of State and Defence* (2004) 1 P. & C.R. 20. In that Lewison J. was concerned to assess the validity of break notices served on June 21, 2002 and July 29, 2002. The second notice included the statement, "This is without prejudice to our previous notice of 21$^{st}$ June 2002". Lewison J. remarked, at the foot of p.459, "It is common ground that the test is where the notice was clear to a reasonable recipient of its statement. In my judgment it was. The notice followed clause 8 exactly. The meaning of the quoted sentence was that the giver of the notice was not to be taken to withdraw the earlier notice and was to remain free to argue that it had validly terminated the lease . . ."

**4–045** The second situation in which "without prejudice" might occur is where the words appear, without any further qualification, in a break notice or in a covering letter. Such a situation occurs quite often in practice, particularly where the server is not a lawyer, and is therefore not aware of the normal significance attached to these words (viz. they are included when negotiations are initiated or continued, in order to signify that the text of the document is privileged and is never to be used in court).

**4–046** There have been a number of cases where "without prejudice" has occurred in documents, alone or in combination with the phrase "subject to contract", in the context of rent review notices. Depending upon the circumstances, the notice has sometimes been held to be valid and sometimes invalid. A useful and interesting review of the relevant authorities was carried out by Nolan J. in *Royal Live Insurance v Phillips* [1990] 2 E.G.L.R. 135 (a case notable for the representation of the landlord and the tenant by, respectively, Lord Neuberger and Lewison L.J. when they were practising at the Bar). The facts of the individual cases tend to dictate the result, and reference can be made to specialist rent review textbooks for a discussion of all the cases. It is suggested that the tests to be employed are those found in the majority judgments in *Mannai*.

**4–047** Just as "without prejudice" might appear alone in a break notice, so can the phrase "subject to contract". Such a case did arise, involving an option to purchase, in *Westway Homes Ltd v Moores* [1991] 2 E.G.L.R. 193. In that case the Court of Appeal rejected the argument that the addition of the phrase "subject to contract", appearing on a notice that was otherwise quite clear, rendered the notice invalid. Dillon L.J. distinguished one of the rent review cases (*Shirlcar Properties Ltd v Heinitz* [1983] 2 E.G.L.R. 120) and a case involving an option in a charterparty (*The Trado* [1982] 1 Lloyds Rep. 157) and said at p.195B, "It seems to me that any solicitor reading the letter of February 18 would necessarily and reasonably have inferred that the words 'subject to contract' in the heading were in the context meaningless". Russell L.J. agreed, saying at p.197C, "I recognise that the approach must be an objective one in respect of the intent of the writer, but, that said, I agree that the words were mere surplusage in the context of this case and have no legal significance".

Although *Westway* preceded *Mannai*, it is suggested that it remains 4–048
good law today.

## 10 Sequential break notices

If the server of a break notice has any doubts as to its validity (either self- 4–049
induced or because of something said by the recipient) then the server
might choose to serve a second notice. If nothing is said about the first
notice, when serving the second notice (e.g. the second notice is not
served without prejudice to the validity of the first notice) then there is a
risk that the server might be estopped from relying upon the first notice.
A comparable situation occurred, with two rent review notices, in the
case of *Cordon Bleu Freezer Food Centres Ltd v Marbleace Ltd* [1987]
2 E.G.L.R. 143. At the end of the judgment, H.H.J. Paul Baker QC
(sitting as a Deputy High Court Judge) said, at p.146M:

> "Mr Neuberger, who, as always, put his points attractively, put it this
> way in regard to these two notices: it does not matter which of the two
> notices was valid. If the party serving the notice, the tenant in this
> case, serves two notices, having served the second one you cannot go
> back to them with the first one unless the second one is served without
> prejudice to the others, and the second counter-notice refers to the
> two, and so one cannot then withdraw it.
>
> In the ordinary way I would accede to that. That perhaps would raise
> an estoppel. The notice itself is some sort of representation that the
> landlord is entitled to act on it. But ... the notices of April 15 and
> April 28 are alternative notices, not cumulative notices, in the partic-
> ular circumstances of this case."

## 11 Invalid notices and estoppels

Barring an estoppel, or similar, an invalid break notice will have no legal 4–050
effect. So, in *Bebington v Wildman* [1921] 1 Ch. 559, at p.565, Peterson
J. said:

> "Assuming that regard can be had to the second notice, the question
> arises whether the tenant could when he received the first notice have
> acted upon it. It has been argued that the defendant after giving a bad
> notice could not have said that it was invalid at any time thereafter and
> accordingly that the tenant when he received the second notice was
> able to act with security on the two notices. If the opinion expressed
> by the Court on various occasions is correct — namely, that in order
> to be valid a notice to quit must be good when received, it follows that

the notice by the defendant was bad when received by the plaintiff; and it seems to me to be established further by the authorities to which I have been referred — Doe v Johnston, Johnstone v Hudleston, and Doe v Milward — that a man who gives a bad notice, that is, a notice which does not operate as a defeasance of the estate of the tenant, is not afterwards precluded or estopped from saying it is void."

4–051   Since the server of an invalid notice has not properly exercised the option contained within the break clause (see Ch.1), the lease will continue. However, depending upon the particular circumstances of the case, the server of an invalid notice, or its recipient, might be estopped from the alleging that the notice is invalid.

4–052   There are various variants of the doctrine of estoppel. Those that are likely to be pertinent for break notices are promissory estoppel and estoppel by convention. These doctrines are the subject of extensive learning, and indeed are the subject of textbooks of their own. It is suggested that reference be made to such books for a detailed account of the law. We will confine our discussion to two cases that are concerned directly with estoppel in the context of break notices.

4–053   In *Dun & Bradstreet Software Services (England) Ltd v Provident Mutual Life Assurance Association* [1998] 2 E.G.L.R. 175 one of the issues before the Court of Appeal was whether the landlord was estopped from disputing the validity of break notices, that had been served upon the landlord, because of a conversation between representatives of the landlord and the tenant. Peter Gibson L.J. said, at p.179E:

> "Mr Wilkes was asked whether the notices were acceptable, that is to say whether the landlord did in fact have any objections to them as break notices, and he gave the unequivocal assurance that they were acceptable. That is a factual representation. The fact that Mr Wilkes is a surveyor did not detract from that assurance: he was the person responsible on the landlord's side and he told Miss Moret that the notices had been passed to the landlord's solicitors. If Mr Wilkes had wanted to leave it to the solicitors, or otherwise qualify his assurance he could have done so, but he did not . . ."

4–054   In reliance upon the landlord's forgoing assurance no further break notices were served by the tenant. The Court of Appeal upheld the Trial Judge's finding that the landlord was estopped from contending that the break notices were invalid.

4–055   In *Prudential Assurance Co Ltd v Exel UK Ltd* (2010) 1 P. & C.R. 7 a lease was vested in the joint names of E and its wholly owned subsidiary C, a dormant company. A break notice was served in the name of E only and therefore (subject to estoppel) it was invalid. The tenants argued that the landlord was estopped from denying the validity of the notice, relying upon both promissory estoppel and estoppel by convention. Jeremy Cousins QC (sitting as a Deputy High Court Judge) rejected both contentions for the various reasons that he set out in his judgment.

Chapter 5

# Who May Exercise the Break Clause

## 1 General observations

There is now a long line of authorities in which the courts have had to consider service of a break notice by the 'wrong' party. In every case, an objective approach is to be taken when construing the break notice. This accords with the approach set out by the House of Lords in *Mannai Investment Company Ltd v Eagle Star Life Assurance Co Ltd* [1997] A.C. 449, at p.767G, where Lord Steyn said: "the question is not how the [recipient] understood the notices. The construction of the notices must be approached objectively. The question is how a reasonable recipient would have understood the notices." See, further, *Havant International Holdings Ltd v Lionsgate (H) Investment Ltd* (2000) L. & T.R. 297, at p.306 which clarifies that ambiguity in a notice as to who is purporting to give is not a category of mistake outside the scope of *Mannai*. What has to be considered is how a reasonable person, in light of the information which could reasonably have been expected to be available to the parties, would have understood the break notice. This proposition is illustrated by the following cases.  **5–001**

In *Lemmerbell Ltd v Britannia LAS Direct Ltd* (1999) L. & T.R. 102, two commercial units had been let to the tenant under two different (but similarly-worded) leases. In August 1992, solicitors acting for the tenant and an associated group company called The Life Association of Scotland Ltd ("Life") gave notice to the landlords of the commercial units that the demised premises would be used by employees of Life, as well as by employees of the tenant. In October 1994, the same solicitors sent purported break notices in respect of both commercial units, saying: "We act on behalf of [Life], successors in title to . . . [the tenant] . . . We therefore give notice of our Client's intention . . . to determine this lease." Life was not, as it so happened, the successor in title to the tenant at all. The Court of Appeal allowed the landlords' appeal and found that the  **5–002** break notices were invalid. Giving the lead judgment, Peter Gibson L.J. said at p.114:

"... I cannot see how the [landlords] could act upon the notices safely as being notices which were in fact, or which they had reason to believe were, binding on [the tenant]. They would have been aware that no consent had been given to any assignment by [the tenant], but that was not inconsistent with there having been an effective assignment. Without the production to them of an assignment, they could not know if Life was the right person to be giving the notices."

5–003  In *Havant International Holdings Ltd v Lionsgate (H) Investment Ltd* (2000) L. & T.R. 297, break notices were given in the name of a company called Havant International Ltd ("HIL"), a wholly-owned subsidiary of Havant International Holdings Ltd ("HIHL") (the tenant), and the main operating company in the group of which HIHL was the ultimate holding company. The break notices were signed by a director of HIL, who was not a director of HIHL. On the evidence before him, Hart J. found that the break notices were valid. He said at p.306:

"The question therefore resolves to this. Would the reasonable recipient assume that there had been a mistake in the description of the company giving the notice? Or would he entertain, as a matter giving rise at least to a reasonable doubt, the possibility that HIL had taken an unlawful assignment and had done so in the mistaken belief that it had thereby become entitled to the benefit of HIHL's personal right? Without claiming to find the answer altogether easy, I have concluded that the latter construction of the notice is not one which would have been seriously entertained by a reasonable recipient. The reasonable recipient would, rather, conclude that a mistake had been made in not naming HIHL as the giver of the notice."

5–004  In *Procter & Gamble Technical Centres Ltd v Brixton Plc* [2003] 2 E.G.L.R. 24, a lease granted in 1995 to Procter & Gamble Health & Beauty Care Ltd ("H&B") contained a break clause in favour of the tenant. Following a series of permitting assignments, in 1998 the lease was vested in another Procter & Gamble company, namely, Procter & Gamble Technical Centres Ltd ("TC"). In 2000, a rent review memorandum was said to be executed by the landlord and the tenant, but the identity of each was wrongly stated; H&B was identified as the tenant. In 2002, a solicitor for Procter & Gamble, relying on the memorandum, purported to serve a break notice, but did so in the name of H&B. Neuberger J. (as he then was) held that the notice was invalid. He said:

"[42] There had been a rather complex series of transactions in 1998–1999 ... It is by no means inconceivable that, after those transactions, there had been one or more other transactions relating to the property which had accidentally not been communicated to the landlord.

. . .

[44] Additionally, in this case, unlike in Lemmerbell, the person on whose behalf the notice was stated to be served, was the original tenant. There is therefore . . . the additional possibility that a reasonable person in the [landlord's] position could not have ruled out, that the Notice was being served on behalf of someone who had good reason for wishing to put an end to the lease, but in fact had no right to do so. That is not a fanciful idea, because . . . the lease was not subject to the Landlord and Tenant (Covenants) Act 1995 and therefore H&B, as the original tenant, remained liable on the tenant's contracts, despite the subsequent assignments . . ."

Neuberger J. emphasised, at para.46, that break notices "particularly if served near the last minute . . . have to be clear and unambiguous because the recipient is entitled, and may need, to make dispositions in the faith of such notices, i.e. on the basis that such notices can be confidently relied on." A mistake which could reasonably mislead a reasonable recipient cannot be overridden.

**5–005**

In *Baker Tilly Management Ltd v Computer Associates UK Ltd* (Unreported December 11, 2009), the landlord had underlet premises to a firm of accountants who, at that time, went by the name Baker Tilly Services Ltd ("BTS"), but subsequently changed its name to Baker Tilly Management Ltd ("BTM"). The underlease included a break clause allowing the tenant to determine the underlease by service on the landlord, within a certain timeframe, of a notice of its intention to do so. The break notice was served on the landlord by BTM, using its old name of BTS. Mr Peter Prescott QC (sitting as a Judge of the High Court) held that when BTM served the notice, it was still the same legal person as BTS. The landlord had to be taken as knowing that and, accordingly, the notice to quit, despite the disparity in the names used by BTM, was valid.

**5–006**

In *Prudential Assurance Co Ltd v Exel UK Ltd* (2010) 1 P. & C.R. 7, Prudential Assurance Co Ltd ("Prudential") had granted a lease to Tibbett & Britten Ltd ("T&B") and Tibbett & Britten Consumer Group Ltd ("Consumer"). At all material times, Consumer was a wholly-owned subsidiary of T&B, and a dormant company. The lease contained a break clause entitling "the Tenant" to determine the lease on March 24, 2007 by giving to the landlord not less than nine months' prior written notice. In August 2004, the Exel Group of companies acquired the Tibbett & Britten group of companies, including T&B and Consumer. On December 29, 2004, T&B's name was changed to Exel UK Ltd ("Exel"). Consumer's name was not changed. On June 13, 2006, solicitors purporting to act solely for Exel (and not for Consumer) served a break notice on Prudential. The court found that, although the solicitors were authorised to serve the

**5–007**

break notice on behalf of Exel and Consumer, the break notice would not unambiguously have been understood to be an effective notice by a reasonable recipient. At p.139, Mr Jeremy Cousins QC (sitting as a Judge of the High Court) said of the notice: "Its own terms would generate real doubt as to whether it was served on behalf of Consumer, because they suggested that although Consumer was known to have been a lessee, the Notice was not being served on its behalf."

5–008  From the above authorities, it appears that, to be effective, a break notice served by or on behalf of a landlord/tenant must clearly and unambiguously communicate to the tenant/landlord that the person entitled to exercise the break provision is determining the lease on the permitted date. A mistake in the notice, even as to the identity of the person giving it, will not necessarily invalidate it, provided that, in all the circumstances its meaning is clear, the mistake is obvious, and the recipient can safely rely upon it. See *Prudential v Exel*, at p.136.

## 2 Where the break clause is personal to the original tenant

5–009  The right of a landlord or a tenant to bring a tenancy to an end by notice is an incident of the relationship of landlord and tenant. This is the common law position in relation to notices to quit in respect of a periodic tenancy. See *Wordsley Brewery v Halford* (1903) 90 L.T. 89 (notice to quit invalid when served by the original lessor who had, prior to the service of the notice, granted a concurrent lease). In the same way, the benefit and burden of a break clause in a lease will, on an assignment, ordinarily pass with the reversion or the term, as "touching and concerning" the respective estates of the landlord and the tenant and as conditions of the enjoyment of those estates. See *Harbour Estates Ltd v HSBC Bank Plc* [2005] Ch. 194, *City of London Corporation v Fell* [1993] Q.B. 590, at pp.603–604 (per Nourse L.J.) and, generally, Ch.3.

5–010  It is not uncommon, however, for a break clause to be expressed to be personal to the original tenant (e.g. "the tenant, here meaning X only"). In this scenario, interesting questions arise as to what happens to the option upon assignment, and re-assignment, of the lease.

5–011  It has been held that, where a break clause is personal to the original tenant, then, once the lease is assigned, an option to determine ceases to have any contractual life. So, in *Max Factor Ltd v Wesleyan Assurance Society* (1997) 74 P. & C.R. 8, at p.13, Auld L.J. said, in relation to a personal break clause: "Once [the tenant] assigned the [lease] to [the assignee] I do not see what continuing contractual life there was in the break clause. It did not pass to [the assignee] with the term, and [the tenant] retained nothing to which it could relate. It was dead. [The assignee] could not, by re-assignment of the [lease], bring it to life again." In a similar vein, Aldous L.J. said at p.18: "There can be no commercial sense in the tenant bargaining for, or the landlord conceding, that once the tenant had chosen to assign the lease and realised any value it had, the right to determine the lease should revive if the tenancy should be reassigned to the original tenant."[1]

An illustration of this principle can be found in *Equinox Industrial (GP2) Ltd v Sketchley Ltd* [2003] EWHC 2 (Ch). In that case, a lease was granted to a company called Sketchley Plc. Clause 8 of the lease contained a break clause exercisable by "the Tenant". However, the clause also included the following wording: "For the purposes of this clause 8 . . . the Tenant shall mean Sketchley Plc only and not its successors in title or its assigns." On September 8, 1999, Sketchley Plc assigned the lease to a third party. On January 15, 2002, the lease was then reassigned into the name of the original tenant (save that, by this time, Sketchley Plc had changed its name to Sketchley Ltd). On June 19, 2002, Sketchley Ltd served a notice under clause 8 of the lease purporting to determine the lease at the end of the 10th year of the term. The landlord sought a declaration that the notice was invalid. So, the issue before the court was whether Sketchley Ltd was entitled to serve a notice to determine the lease having regard to the fact that the break clause was made personal to Sketchley Plc and did not pass to its successors in title or assigns. Granting judgment in favour of the landlord, Lawrence Collins J. held, at para.33, that the wording of the break clause had the effect of "making it clear . . . that it is only the original lessee, as original lessee, which can exercise the break clause. For the purposes of the break clause, Sketchley Ltd falls within the category of those who are excluded from the benefit of the clause."

So, where a break clause is expressed to be personal to the original tenant, it is only the original tenant, in that capacity, who can exercise the break clause. Furthermore, only the party in whom the interest of the tenant is vested can exercise a tenant's break clause. This is reflected in *Linpac Mouldings Ltd v Aviva Life and Pensions UK Ltd* [2010] EWCA Civ 395, where Etherton L.J. said, at para.45:

5–012

5–013

". . . provision for a former tenant to bring a lease to an end at a time when the lease is not vested in them would be extraordinary, even if technically possible. It would be extraordinary . . . because of the difficulties of obtaining vacant possession from the business tenant entitled to the benefit of the security of tenure conferred by the 1954 Act, the improbability of the landlord or any assignee from the tenant being content to accept such a provision, and the availability of a more

---

[1] In a dissenting judgment, Staughton L.J. said at pp.12–13: "In this court it was argued (without a respondent's notice), and I understand that my colleagues accept, that the right conferred by clause 5.09 on the Lessee [i.e. the right to determine the lease] 'disappeared' when there was an assignment to [the assignee] because it was a personal right; and it could not be created once more on a reassignment. I do not agree that the right disappeared. In my view it was assigned like all the other rights of the original Lessee; it was merely of no value while it belonged to [the assignee]; but it became once more a right of some value when there had been a reassignment."

obvious and straightforward route to achieve the same practical end by the tenant subletting rather than assigning. It is not surprising, in the light of such considerations as these, that Lightman J and the Court of Appeal in Max Factor gave very short shrift to the argument of [the tenant] that it could exercise the right to determine even at a time when the lease was not vested in them."

5–014 Similar comments were made by Lewison J. at first instance ([2009] EWHC 1602 (Ch)), where he said, at para.49: "Although it would, I accept, be theoretically possible to create a fixed-term lease capable of termination by someone who was neither the landlord nor the tenant, it would be an extraordinary, if not a unique creation." Lewison J. also decided that the right to break could not be re-acquired by the original tenant on a re-assignment. This decision was not challenged on appeal.

5–015 So far as the ability for the original tenant to re-acquire a right to break is concerned, this is possible if the language of the lease so provides. This is evident from *BP Oil UK v Lloyds Bank Plc* [2004] EWHC 496 (Ch), at para.14, where Mr Michael Brindle QC (sitting as a Deputy Judge of the High Court) accepted the submission on behalf of the claimants that no clear principle arises from the *Max Factor* and *Equinox* cases which is not dependent on the particular wording of the document in question. His decision was upheld on appeal ([2004] EWCA Civ 1710) where Arden L.J., at para.15, reiterated the point that those cases turned on "the construction of the leases in question". In *BP Oil* itself, it was held that a "put" option requiring Lloyds to take a lease, was capable of being revived on, and exercisable following, re-assignment of that lease to the tenants.

5–016 The foregoing accords with the decision of the Court of Appeal in *Olympia & York Canary Wharf Ltd v Oil Property Investment Ltd* (1995) 69 P. & C.R. 43. In *Olympia*, E granted a lease to N for a term of 25 years from March 8, 1985. The lease contained a common form provision prohibiting assignment without the lessor's previous consent, such consent not to be unreasonably withheld. The lease also contained a tenant's break clause which enabled the lease to be determined at the end of the 10th year of the term. The right conferred by the break clause was exercisable only by N, the original lessee. In October 1987, N assigned the lease to O. However, N remained liable on its covenant to pay rent for the whole of the term of the lease. In March 1991, the freehold reversion of the property was acquired by L. Subsequently, in May 1992, O became insolvent and an administration order was made. O did not wish to retain the lease and desired to re-assign it to N. N was willing to accept a re-assignment because this would enable it to exercise the break clause and thereby put an end to its continuing rental liability as original lessee. So it came about that the administrators of O sought L's consent for assignment of the lease to N. L refused. O then sought various declarations, including a declaration that L was unreasonably withholding its consent to the assignment. The case was argued on the assumption that, if N re-acquired the lease, it would be able to exercise the break clause. As Lewison J. noted in *Linpac*, at para.30:

> "The case was argued on the basis that (1) unless the lease was vested in it, [the tenant] could not operate the break clause, and (2) if it re-acquired the lease, it would be able to exercise that right. Although Sir Donald Nicholls V-C, questioned the latter assumption, he did not question the former. Leggatt and Henry L.JJ. appeared to accept both assumptions as correct."

Also of note is the decision of the Supreme Court of New Zealand in *Taita Hotel Ltd v Spelman* [1963] N.Z.L.R. 206. In that case, the lease provided that the lessee could renew the lease on notice "if the lessee shall still be the lessee." The original lessee assigned the lease and, when the landlord challenged the right of the assignee to give notice of renewal, the assignee sought the landlord's consent to re-assign the lease to the original lessee. It was held by McGregor J. that the original tenant would be entitled to the benefit of the right to renew if the lease was re-assigned to him. It was held that the fact that there had been an assignment would not prevent the original lessee from "still" being the lessee. **5–017**

### 3 Where the lease is silent/ambiguous

Where the lease is silent or unclear as to who is entitled to exercise a break clause, the option will usually be interpreted as being confined to the benefit of the tenant alone. Thus, in *L R Wingfield Ltd v Clapton Construction and Investment Co Ltd* (1967) 201 E.G. 769, in which a lease contained a clause in these terms: **5–018**

> "In case either the lessor or the lessee shall desire to determine the term hereby granted at the end of the seventh ... year ... and shall give to the lessor not less than six months' previous notice in writing ... the present demise ... shall cease and be void."

The lessor served a notice purporting to terminate the lease. Stamp J. held that the words "either the lessor or" were inconsistent with the rest of the clause and, having regard to the general principle that a lease was to be construed against a landlord, and the fact that the burden was on the landlord to satisfy the court that the clause conferred on him a right to determine, the notice to quit would be declared invalid.

## 4 Assignees

5–019  Barring quite an exceptional case (see para.5–014 above), a break clause will only be exercisable by the party in whom the legal estate is vested. Thus, on an assignment, the benefit and burden of a break clause in a lease will usually pass, with the reversion or the term, as "touching and concerning" the respective estates of the landlord and the tenant. See, generally, Ch.3.

## 5 Joint lessees

5–020  *In Re Viola's Indenture of Lease* [1909] 1 Ch. 244 concerned an indenture of a lease dated February 2, 1906, made between O F Viola (the lessor) of the first part and Mr and Mrs Humphrey (the lessees) of the second part. The lease contained a proviso that if "the lessees" should be desirous of terminating the lease at the end of the first three years of the term, and of such desire should give to the lessor six months' previous notice in writing, then at the end of such three years the term would come to an end. On October 3, 1907, Mr Humphrey, the husband, alone gave notice in writing to the lessor to determine the lease at the end of the first three years of the term. The lessor did not accept the notice. The lessees sought a declaration that a valid notice to determine the lease had been given.

5–021  At trial, Warrington J. declared that, upon a true construction of the lease, no effective notice to determine the term had been given. He said, at p.247 of the report: "The terms of the proviso are express; both lessees must be desirous and express their desire to determine the term. A notice therefore by one of them cannot be a notice by both to determine the lease." Absent any express term to the contrary, a break notice given by one of two joint lessees on behalf of both could only be good if the court was able to infer an agency, or facts which expressly prove an agency.

5–022  In *Hounslow London Borough Council v Pilling* [1993] 1 W.L.R. 1242, at p.1247A, Nourse L.J. approved of *Re Viola's Indenture of Lease* and held that a break notice cannot be given by one only of two (or more) joint tenants. In *Pilling*, the Council had granted, and Mr Pilling and Miss Doubtfire had taken, a joint weekly tenancy of a dwelling-house. In the agreement, Mr Pilling and Miss Doubtfire were together defined as "the Tenant." By Clause 14, "the Tenant" was obliged "to give the council four weeks' written notice or such lesser period as the council may accept when the tenant wishes to end the tenancy and give possession of the premises." On December 6, 1991, having left the demised premises following incidents of domestic violence, Miss Doubtfire wrote to the Council giving notice that she wished to terminate the tenancy, however Mr Pilling refused to give up possession. The Council commenced possession proceedings and obtained a possession order.

Mr Pilling successfully appealed on the basis that Miss Doubtfire's December 6, 1991 letter was an invalid break notice.

The position in relation to the service of a break notice by one of two (or more) joint lessees may be contrasted with the service of a notice to quit terminating a periodic tenancy. In *Hammersmith and Fulham London Borough Council v Monk* [1992] 1 A.C. 478, the House of Lords held that a contractual periodic tenancy held by two or more joint tenants continued only so long as they all agreed to its continuation, so that, in the absence of any contrary term in the agreement, the tenancy was determinable by a notice to quit given by one joint tenant without the concurrence of the other or others. In *Pilling*, Nourse L.J. distinguished *Monk* on the basis that all that *Monk* decided was that the continuation of a periodic joint tenancy beyond the end of each period of it depends on the joint will of the tenants, so that if one of them gives notice determining it at the end of a period, it does not continue. In *Pilling*, the notice purported to determine the tenancy not at the end of a period but in the middle of one.

5–023

## 6 Joint lessors

The above principle applies equally to break notices given by joint lessors. All of the joint lessors must join in the giving of a notice to exercise a landlord's break clause.

5–024

## 7 The survivor of joint lessees/joint lessors

There is no authority concerning the question whether an option to determine a lease in favour of A and B is exercisable by A only after the death of B. However, it is thought that (absent an express provision to the contrary) a break clause exercisable by "the lessee" or the "the lessor" can be exercised by the survivor of joint lessees/joint lessors.

5–025

## 8 Trustees in bankruptcy

Once a bankruptcy order is made, the bankrupt's estate vests in the Official Receiver, until a trustee in bankruptcy is appointed, at which point the property vests in the trustee: see s.306(1) of the Insolvency Act 1986. The bankrupt's estate comprises, inter alia, all property belonging to or vested in the bankrupt at the commencement of the bankruptcy. See s.283(1) of the Insolvency Act 1986. Given the wide definition of the word "property" in s.436 of the Insolvency Act 1986, this is apt

5–026

to include leases and options in gross. The trustee is thus entitled to exercise a break clause (subject to its terms).

## 9 Administrators

5–027 The administration of companies is governed by Sch.B1 to the Insolvency Act 1986, with effect from September 15, 2003. The administration regime was applied to partnerships from July 1, 2005 (by the Insolvent Partnerships (Amendment) Order 2005) and from October 1, 2005 to limited liability partnerships (by the Limited Liability Partnerships (Amendment) Regulations 2005). After the appointment of an administrator, he takes "custody or control of all property to which he thinks the company is entitled" (para.67 of Sch.B1) and is under a duty to manage the company's affairs, business and property in accordance with any creditors' proposals approved under para.52 and any revisions to those proposals (para.68(1) of Sch.B1). So, although, during the period of administration, the company's property remains vested in the company, the decision whether or not to exercise an option must be taken by the administrators, acting as agents of the company. A break notice should be given by the administrators in this capacity.

## 10 Liquidators

5–028 Liquidation is the corporate equivalent to bankruptcy. Under s.144(1) of the Insolvency Act 1986, when a winding-up order has been made, or where a provisional liquidator has been appointed, the liquidator or the provisional liquidator (as the case may be) is required to take into his custody or under his control all the property and things in action to which the company is or appears to be entitled. So, in contrast to the position of a trustee in bankruptcy, the company's property does not vest automatically in the liquidator (although an application for a vesting order may be made under s.145). By para.7 of Sch.4 to the Insolvency Act 1986, a liquidator has the power "to do all acts and execute, in the name of and on behalf of the company, all deeds, receipts and other documents." This means that, unless the company's property is vested in the liquidator, if the company wishes to exercise a break clause, notice should be given by the liquidator on behalf of the company.

## 11 The use of agents

5–029 Since a break notice must be given by the lessee/lessor (save for an exceptional case), a notice given by someone who is not the lessee/lessor is invalid. However, unless the wording of the lease expressly or impliedly forbids it, a notice may be validly given by an agent acting on behalf of the lessee/lessor if: (i) the notice states that it is given by the agent on behalf of the lessee/lessor, and (ii) the agent is duly authorised so to give it. So, for example, in *Lemon v Lardeur* [1946] 1 K.B. 613, a notice to quit, purportedly given by the husband of the tenant, was held to be ineffective. Similarly, in *Divall v Harrison* [1992] 2 E.G.L.R. 64, the Court of Appeal held that a notice to quit, served by a firm of solicitors, but not expressed to be given in the name of the landlord, was invalid.

In an appropriate case, a break notice may be given effectively in the name of a person other than the lessee/lessor if that person has general authority from the lessee/lessor in relation to dealings in respect of the lease. It should be noted, however, that a general agency is an "unusual commercial relationship" since the agent will have authority to do anything in relation to the subject matter of the agency, "even to the extent of destroying that subject matter without reference to the principal". Thus, the inference of a general agency, in the absence of express authority creating the agency, "requires clear evidence to support it". See *Lemmerbell Ltd v Britannia LAS Direct Ltd (formerly LAS Direct Ltd)* (1999) L. & T.R. 102 at p.110, per Peter Gibson L.J. **5–030**

There are a number of 'general agency' cases concerning notices to quit/break notices, starting with *Jones v Phipps* (1868) L.R. 3 Q.B. 567. In that case, the issue was whether Sir Maxwell Graves had authority from the trustees of a marriage settlement, in whom the legal estate of a farm vested, to give notice to quit, so as to determine the defendant's tenancy. Lush J. said, at pp.571–572: **5–031**

"The decision in this case must depend on the answers to be given to two questions, one of fact, the other of law. The question of fact is, whether Sir Maxwell Graves had authority from the trustees . . . to give notice to quit . . . The question of law is whether, assuming that he had such authority, a notice to quit given, in his own name, not purporting to be given as agent of the trustees is valid.

On the first point, we are of the opinion that the facts stated lead to the conclusion that Sir Maxwell Graves had the authority of the trustees to give a notice to quit. He had assumed the entire control over the farm from the time it was purchased in 1863 . . .We therefore infer that it was with the sanction of the trustees that he . . . dealt with it as his own . . . It was incidental to such an authority that he should determine the tenancy by notice to quit at such time as he should think proper. As regards the defendant, he could have been under no doubt whether the notice was binding, inasmuch as he was not aware that the estate was vested in trustees, but always treated with and considered Sir Maxwell as the legal, as he was in fact the equitable, owner of the farm.

On the second point, we are of the opinion that it is not essential to the validity of a notice to quit by such an agent, that his agency should appear on the face of the document itself."

5–032 In *Re Knight and Hubbard's Underlease* [1923] 1 Ch. 130, it was argued that a notice seeking to terminate an underlease, given by the solicitors acting on behalf of a friendly society, was invalid because the friendly society was the beneficial or equitable owner only of the leasehold interest which it sought to determine. The tenant contended that the notice ought to have been given by or on behalf of the legal owners of the leasehold interest, that is, the trustees of the friendly society. Rejecting this argument, at p.141, Sargant J. held that not only were the trustees the mere nominees of the friendly society, and bound to act under the direction of the committee of management, but also, the trustees did, in fact, leave the management of the various interests in the subject property in the hands of the friendly society and the friendly society's agent. On the evidence, it was clear that the trustees, as the legal owners of the property, allowed the friendly society, as the absolute beneficial owners, to have the full management of it, and to deal directly with the tenant.

5–033 In *Harmond Properties Ltd v Gajdzis* [1968] 1 W.L.R. 1858, a notice to quit was served on a tenant by a firm of solicitors stating that they were acting "[on] behalf of your landlord Mr R P Harvey". In fact, the landlord was Harmond Properties Ltd, and Mr Harvey was its director. At trial, the evidence was that Mr Harvey had acted as if he was the landlord in every way and it was clear that the tenant had always thought of him as the landlord. Thus, the County Court Judge decided that he was acting as a general agent and could give a valid notice to quit. This decision was upheld on appeal, although it may be observed that Willmer L.J. said, at pp.1864–1865, that the case was "rather peculiar" and turned "on [its] particular facts".

5–034 In *Townsends Carriers Ltd v Pfizer Ltd* (1977) 33 P. & C.R. 361, a break notice had been served, not by the tenant company, but by an associated company, not on the landlord company, but on an associated company. The tenant and the landlord had consigned the whole conduct and management of the tenancy and of the tenancy itself to agents on their behalf, allowing their respective associated companies to deal with the property as if they were landlord and tenant respectively in respect of matters such as an increase in rent and variations of the lease. In the circumstances, Sir Robert Megarry V.C. held that the break notice had been validly served saying, at p.365:

"It has long been settled that if a landlord leaves the general control of the property in the hands of an agent, a notice to quit may be perfectly valid even if it is given by the agent in his own name, as if he were the landlord, and does not disclose any agency or purport to be given as agent for the landlord."

In *Peel Developments (South) Ltd v Siemens Plc* [1992] 2 E.G.L.R. 85, a  **5–035**
break notice was served by the tenants on a subsidiary of the landlord
company. That subsidiary was found to have acted as managing agent of
the property. Judge Paul Baker QC (sitting as a Deputy Judge of the High
Court), on the evidence that the management of the property was carried
out by the subsidiary, held that the subsidiary was the general agent of
the landlord and the notice was validly served on the subsidiary.

In *Dun & Bradstreet Software Services (England) Ltd v Provident*  **5–036**
*Mutual Life Assurance Association* [1998] 2 E.G.L.R. 175, the Court of
Appeal reversed a decision that the subsidiary of the tenant was the
general agent of the tenant, in circumstances where the tenant held the
lease on bare trust for the subsidiary, and the subsidiary was in occupation and paid the rent on the tenant company's behalf. Peter Gibson L.J.
said, at p.178, that:

"... both sides were fully alert to the fact that [the subsidiary] was not
the tenant ... The payment of the rent and other sums due under the
leases by [the subsidiary] was an act associated with occupation of the
demised premises ... The payment and the occupation were not to my
mind indicative of agency, still less of general agency ... What [the
subsidiary] did in relation to the demised premises seems to me to fall
some way short of demonstrating that it was the general agent of [the
tenant]. All that it did ... was consistent with the beneficial occupation of the premises. The termination of the leases was an act of a
different nature, aimed at destroying the assets in question."

In *Hexstone Holdings Ltd v AHC Westlink Ltd* [2010] EWHC 1280  **5–037**
(Ch), the primary issue was whether the term created by an underlease
entered into between Hexstone Holdings Limited ("Hexstone") and
AHC Westlink Limited ("AHC") on January 7, 2008 was determined on
October 31, 2009 through the exercise by the tenant of a break provision.
Importantly, AHC was part of the Stobart Group of companies, one of
which was Eddie Stobart Limited ("ESL"). On or about August 19, 2008,
Hexstone received a letter on ESL's notepaper informing it that, with
effect from July 1, 2008, AHC would change its name and be known as
ESL. In reliance on this letter, Hexstone directed all future rent invoices
to the accounts department of ESL. In fact, the change of name never
occurred, and the true name of the original tenant under the underlease
remained AHC (with AHC and ESL remaining entirely separate companies). In April 2009, it was desired to exercise the break provision
contained in the underlease. To that end, ESL served a break notice on
Hexstone. Hexstone subsequently challenged the validity of this notice,
claiming that it had not been served by the tenant under the underlease.
Edward Bartley Jones QC (sitting as a Deputy Judge of the High Court)
rejected the contention that ESL was acting as AHC's general agent
because he did not have any material before him to enable him to find
that a general agency was created.

**5–038**  It should be emphasised that, if a break notice is given by a general agent without stating that that person is acting as an agent, it is not sufficient for the person relying upon the notice to show merely that the giver was in fact duly authorised to give it. In addition, it must be shown that the circumstances of the case are such that the recipient can act upon the notice safely in the knowledge that it will be binding on the principal of the giver. See *Jones v Phipps* at p.572, and *Lemmerbell* at p.111. Such circumstances will include where: (i) the recipient knows that the giver was authorised to give the notice; (ii) the principal has held out the giver of the notice as authorised to give the notice; or (iii) the recipient has been led to believe that the giver of the notice is the principal.

**5–039**  An illustration of this is to be found in *Hexstone*, where Edward Bartley Jones QC said, at pp.42–43:

> "... even if [ESL] ... had been duly authorised by AHC to give the Notice still, because of the absence of reference to agency on the face of the Notice, the same could not possibly have been valid ... unless the circumstances were such that Hexstone, as recipient, could act on the Notice safely in the knowledge that it would be binding on the principal (AHC).
>
> ...
>
> I find it impossible to see how Hexstone could safely have acted on the Notice in the knowledge that it would be binding on AHC. There is no question of Hexstone knowing that [ESL] had been authorised to give the Notice ... Nor is there any question of AHC having held out [ESL] as authorised to give the Notice ... What in fact had happened [by the August 19, 2008 announcement] is not a case of 'holding out' but, rather, an assertion that AHC would, henceforth, be known as [ESL]."

Chapter 6

# Service (and Withdrawal) of the Break Notice

**1 Who may serve the break notice**

This topic is considered in Ch.5.                                                    6–001

**2 On whom a break notice must be served**

As a general rule, the terms of the lease must be observed. However, the   6–002
following specific scenarios merit comment.

(a) *Joint lessors/joint lessees*
Where there are joint lessors or joint lessees, in the absence of any   6–003
express term to the contrary, break notice should be given to each of
them. The observations made in Ch.5 at paras 5–020–5–024 are equally
applicable here.

(b) *Concurrent lessees*
A concurrent or overriding lease is one granted subject to and with the   6–004
benefit of a lease which is already in existence. It entitles the concurrent
lessee to the rent reserved in the previous lease, and to the benefit of
the covenants contained in it during the then residue of the term granted
by the first lease, and the continuance of the concurrent lease. See,
generally, Woodfall, *Landlord and Tenant*, Vol.1, para.6.018.

In *Standard Life Investments Property Holdings Ltd v W&J Linney*   6–005
*Ltd* [2010] EWHC 480 (Ch), the court had to consider whether the original landlord, or the concurrent lessee, was the appropriate person on
whom a break notice should be served. The facts were as follows. On
April 4, 1996, M demised commercial premises to S for a term beginning
on April 4, 1997 and expiring on September 29, 2116. On June 6, 1997,

the lease was assigned to C. On February 4, 2004, C granted a sub-lease of part of the commercial premises to L. The sub-lease contained a definition of "Landlord" as follows: "... the party so described at the head of this Lease and where the context so admits the person for the time being entitled to the reversion immediately expectant on the determination of the term." Clause 9 of the sub-lease stated: "If the Tenant wishes to determine this Lease on the 5th anniversary of the date of this Lease and shall give to the Landlord not less than six months' prior notice in writing to such effect ... then this Lease shall come to an end ..." On November 26, 2004, C demised the commercial premises to S for a term beginning on April 4, 1997 and expiring September 26, 2116. Thus, C's interest in the premises was limited to three days in 2116. In 2008, L wished to exercise the break clause and so, on July 23, 2008, its solicitors wrote to C at its registered office enclosing a break notice addressed to C. C took the view that the notice ought to have been served upon S. The court had to decide the issue.

**6–006** At trial, L argued first that C was defined in the sub-lease as "the Landlord" and that that definition continued to apply even after C ceased to be the holder of the immediate reversion. Thus, the break notice was properly served on C. Lewison J. held, at para.21, that such a construction of the sub-lease did not make commercial common sense. For:

> "It would mean that the current reversioner could have his income stream removed from him without his knowledge. Someone who was once the landlord but no longer is would have no interest in checking whether the conditions applicable to the exercise of the break clause, whether as to timing or compliance with covenants, had been complied with and would have no interest in communicating with the current landlord. One of the conditions applicable to the exercise of the break clause is the giving of vacant possession. Vacant possession can only be given to the current landlord. It cannot, in my judgment, have been contemplated that the tenant could simply move out of the premises and return the keys to the landlord without having given him any notice of his intention to do so ... In my judgment ... the only person on whom a valid notice could be served was [S]."

**6–007** Thus, absent express wording to the contrary, a break notice must be served by the tenant on the holder of the current reversion.

(c) *Multiple parties*

**6–008** Occasionally, the lease will specify that the break notice has to be served on more than one party (e.g. a landlord and it's managing agent). This may well be the case where, for example, the landlord holds the lease on trust for a beneficiary, and the beneficiary has, in turn, entrusted responsibility of the management of the demised premises to a third party. Thus, in *The Hotgroup Plc v The Royal Bank of Scotland Plc (as Trustee of Schroder Exempt Property Unit Trust)* [2010] EWHC 1241 (Ch),

Clause 14.2 of the lease in question provided: "... no notice will be deemed to be validly served on the Landlord unless a copy of the notice is also served on Schroder Property Investment Management Limited." The latest date for exercise of the break clause in that case was October 3, 2009, and the landlord was served with the necessary break notice on September 14, 2009. However, Schroder Property Investment Management Limited was not served with a break notice until November 19, 2009. Mr Charles Hollander QC (sitting as a Deputy Judge of the High Court) held that the break clause had not been validly exercised; with the consequence that The Royal Bank of Scotland was entitled to a declaration that the break clause option had not been complied with.

(d) *Agents*
In *Galinski v McHugh* (1989) 21 H.L.R. 47 at p.55, Slade L.J. said: **6–009** "under the general law of landlord and tenant, it is possible for good service of a landlord's notice to be effected by serving it on the duly authorised agent of the tenant (and vice versa)." So, for example, in *Hawtrey v Beaufort Ltd* [1946] K.B. 280, a notice addressed to the directors of a company and received by them was held to be effectual to determine a tenancy vested in the company.

(e) *Bankrupts/Trustees in bankruptcy*
Where the grantor of an option to determine is made bankrupt, the break **6–010** clause can still be exercised because, by operation of s.283(5) of the Insolvency Act 1986, the property comprised in a bankrupt's estate is so comprised subject to the rights of any person other than the bankrupt. Invariably, once the lease/option to determine has vested in the trustee by operation of s.306(1) of the Insolvency Act 1986, a break notice will need to be served on the trustee, as the party in whom the property which is subject to the option is vested. This is analogous with the position of a concurrent lessee.

(f) *Companies in administration*
As for the exercise of a break clause against a company in administra- **6–011** tion, the break notice can be given to the company (subject to the terms of the lease). As mentioned in Ch.5 at para.5–027, during the period of administration, the company's property remains vested in the company. Where proceedings are commenced, or continued, for the purpose of enforcing an option against a company in administration, either the consent of the administrator or the leave of the court will be required under para.43(6) of Sch.B1 to the Insolvency Act 1986.

(g) *Companies in liquidation*
In a similar manner to a company in administration, where a company is **6–012** in liquidation, unless its property has vested in the liquidator under s.145 of the Insolvency Act 1986, a break notice can continue to be served on the company itself (of course, subject to the terms of the lease). Once a

company in liquidation has been dissolved after the winding up of its affairs, any property of whatever nature or any right then vested in the company is deemed to be bona vacantia and will vest in the Crown, the Duchy of Lancaster, or the Duke of Cornwall, as appropriate. See s.1012(1) of the Companies Act 2006 (replacing s.654(1) of the Companies Act 1985 with effect from October 1, 2009). This means that, once the company has been dissolved, and assuming that the liquidator has not disclaimed the lease prior to the date of dissolution, a party desirous of exercising a break clause will need to serve the break notice on the Crown (i.e. to the Treasury Solicitor or the Duchy offices).

## 3 Method of service

**6–013** The method of service of a break notice will often be governed by express provisions in the lease. Frequently, the lease will expressly apply s.196 of the Law of Property Act 1925 ("the 1925 Act") to the service of any notices thereunder.

**6–014** Section 196 of the 1925 Act extends to "notices required to be served by any instrument affecting property executed or coming into operation after the commencement of this Act unless a contrary intention appears" (s.196(5)). In *Wandsworth London Borough Council v Attwell* (1995) 27 H.L.R. 536 at p.541, Glidewell L.J. said, in relation to a notice to quit: "... a tenancy agreement which makes no express provision for the service of a notice to quit to determine the tenancy does not 'require' such notice to be served. Thus in that situation section 196(5) does not apply." See, further, *Enfield London Borough Council v Devonish* (1997) 29 H.L.R. 691 at p.697, per Kennedy L.J. It follows from these authorities that a break notice served pursuant to a break clause will be "required" to be served within the meaning of s.196(5) since, unlike in the case of a notice to quit, the lease will make express provision for the service of a break notice. Accordingly, even where it is not expressly incorporated into a lease, s.196 will apply to the service of break notices (unless a contrary intention appears).

**6–015** In a case where s.196 of the 1925 Act does apply, any notice required or authorised by the 1925 Act to be served shall be sufficiently served if:

(i) It is left at the last-known place of abode or business in the United Kingdom of the lessee, lessor, or other person to be served, or, in case of a notice required or authorised to be served on a lessee, is affixed or left for him on the land or any house or building comprised in the lease (s.196(3)); and/or

(ii) If it is sent by post in a registered letter addressed to the lessee, lessor, or other person to be served, by name, at the aforesaid place of abode or business, and if that letter is not returned by the postal operator (within the meaning of the Postal Services Act 2000) concerned undelivered (s.196(4)).

In *Cannon Brewery Co v Signal Press Ltd* (1929) 139 L.T. 384, Humphreys J. said that the expression "left for him" in s.196(3) of the 1925 Act "includes the case of a notice which is left in the hands of some person who is in fact on the premises, and in regard to whom there is reasonable ground for supposing that she will hand it to the [intended recipient], if the [intended recipient] should be available for that purpose." A notice will be "left for" the recipient if it is left in a proper way, that is to say, in a manner which a reasonable person, minded to bring the document to the attention of the person to whom the notice is addressed, would adopt. See *Newborough (Lord) v Jones* [1975] Ch. 90 (a case concerning s.92 of the Agricultural Holdings Act 1948), where a landlord's notice to quit ended up being slipped under the linoleum behind the tenant's door and did not come to the tenant's attention. **6–016**

Where service under s.196(4) is effected, then service is deemed to be made at the time at which the registered letter would in the ordinary course be delivered. By operation of s.1(1) of the Recorded Delivery Service Act 1962, any enactment (including s.196 of the 1925 Act) which requires or authorises a document or other things to be sent by registered post (whether or not it makes any other provision in relation thereto) shall have effect as if it required or, as the case may be, authorised that thing to be sent by registered post or the recorded delivery service; and any enactment which makes any other provision in relation to the sending of a document or other thing by registered post or to a thing so sent shall have effect as if it made the like provision in relation to the sending of that thing by the recorded delivery service or, as the case may be, to a thing sent by that service. **6–017**

Where s.196 of the 1925 Act does not apply, and there are no other express deeming provisions in the lease (see e.g. *Hogg v Brooks* (1885) 15 Q.B.D. 256), then the person serving the notice will have to rely upon the common law rules relating to service. At common law, a notice is regarded as having been served only if it has been received by, or if it has come to the attention of, the recipient (or his duly authorised agent). See *Holwell Securities Ltd v Hughes* [1974] 1 W.L.R. 155, at pp.157–158, per Russell L.J. (concerning the exercise of an option to purchase a property); and, also, *Blunden v Frogmore Investments Ltd* [2002] 2 E.G.L.R. 29, at p.32, per Robert Walker L.J. So, for example, in *Beanby Estates Ltd v Egg Stores (Stamford Hill) Ltd* [2003] 1 W.L.R. 2064, at p.2075, Neuberger J. (as he then was) said: "a common law notice is not served merely by putting it in the post unless, of course, the terms of the contract under which the notice is served indicate otherwise . . . [The] point I wish to emphasise is that the notion of a person being bound by a document which was put in the post but which he did not actually receive is by no means unknown or foreign to English law." **6–018**

**6–019** A break clause may provide for a notice to be transmitted in a particular way, for example, by registered post. However, failure to comply with the prescribed method of service will not necessarily be fatal if, on a true construction of the break clause, it is not mandatory. Thus, in *Yates Building Co Ltd v R J Pulleyn & Sons (York) Ltd* [1976] 1 E.G.L.R. 157 (CA), an option to purchase a certain plot of land was expressed to be exercisable by notice in writing "such notice to be sent by registered or recorded delivery post." In the event, the option was sent from the intending purchaser's solicitors to the intending vendor's solicitors by ordinary post. The Court of Appeal held that the prescribed form of posting was directory and not mandatory and, accordingly, the option had been validly exercised. Lord Denning said, at p.157K:

"... the question is whether the words 'such notice to be sent by registered or recorded delivery post' are mandatory or directory ... The distinction is this: a mandatory provision must be fulfilled exactly according to the letter, whereas a directory provision is satisfied if it is in substance according to the general intent ... In applying the rule of construction, you must look to the subject-matter, consider the object to be fulfilled, and then see whether the provision must be fulfilled strictly to the letter or whether the substance of it is enough ... Looking at the object of this provision, it seems to be this. It is inserted for the benefit of the buyer so that he can be sure of his position. So long as he sends the letter by registered or recorded delivery post, he has clear proof of postage and the time of posting. But if the buyer sends it by ordinary post, he will have no sufficient proof of posting, or of the time of posting."

**6–020** In *Orchard (Developments) Holdings Plc v Reuters Ltd* [2009] EWCA Civ 6, at para.34, Rix L.J. said that, in *Yates*, the reference to "such notice to be sent by registered or recorded delivery post" was evidential only, and not as a requirement of the validity or effectiveness of the notice. In other words, those words could be read: "and for the purpose of evidencing the timely receipt of the notice, it will be of assistance to the buyer to use registered or recorded delivery post but he may use other methods of delivery." *Orchard* itself concerned the service of a break notice under the terms of a lease which provided: "Unless the receiving party or its authorised agent acknowledges receipt a notice is valid only if it is given by hand or sent by registered post or recorded delivery." Rix L.J. said, at para.35, that: "What is remarkable about the present case ... is the introduction of the words 'is valid only' ... That, in my judgment, is a provision which goes to essential validity, not evidence." Thus, service by hand, by registered post or recorded delivery was mandatory.

**6–021** Where a particular method of service of a break notice is prescribed in a lease, but not in terms insisting that only service in that method shall be binding, service on the recipient by any other mode which is no less advantageous to him will be effective. See *Manchester Diocesan Council* *for Education v Commercial & General Investments Ltd* [1970] 1 W.L.R. 241, at p.246C, per Buckley J. (a case concerning acceptance of an offer to purchase a property).

## 4 When a break notice should be served

(a) *Occasion for exercise*
In the case of a landlord's break clause, the power to determine a lease is often expressed to be exercisable only when the landlord requires the demised premises for building or redevelopment. Here, the lessor's right to terminate the lease requires a bone fide intention to use the land for the stipulated purpose. This is illustrated by the decision of the House of Lords in *Commissioners of Inland Revenue v Southend-on-Sea Estates Co Ltd* [1915] A.C. 428. In that case, undeveloped land duty was claimed by the Attorney General. This duty was not payable on land which was under a lease prior to the coming into force of the Finance (1909–1910) Act 1910, save where the landlord had the power to determine the tenancy. The question was whether the landlord had such power. As to this, Earl Loreburn said, at p.431: 6–022

"Now here the lease enables the landlord to resume possession for building or other purposes, which means in my opinion purposes of the same kind. It is admitted that the landlord had no such purpose. Under these circumstances, had the landlord in this case the power to determine the tenancy? I think he had not. This power only arose when there was a purpose. If in an action between him and the tenant the landlord had said, 'I wish very much to determine but I have no purpose within the covenant,' he had not power to determine the lease."

(i) See also *Gregson v Cyril Lord Ltd* [1963] 1 W.L.R. 41, at p.45, per Upjohn L.J.

When construing such a landlord's break clause, useful reference may be made to authorities concerning the meaning of "intention" in s.30(1)(f) of the Landlord and Tenant Act 1954 ("the 1954 Act") (i.e. opposition to a tenant's application for a new tenancy based on an intention to demolish or reconstruct the premises) or s.30(1)(g) (i.e. opposition to a tenant's application for a new tenancy based on an intention to occupy the premises for the purposes of a business or as a residence). In *Patel v Keles* [2010] Ch. 332, at p.338H, Arden L.J. observed that, insofar as s.30(1)(g) of the 1954 Act was concerned, the courts have "set a high hurdle for establishing the necessary subjective intention" because, if the landlord succeeds in making out his ground of opposition to the tenant's application for a new tenancy, the tenant 6–023 will have no right to renew his lease and will have to vacate the premises (thereby losing any goodwill attached to the business at those premises). In *Cunliffe v Goodman* [1950] 2 K.B. 237 (which concerned the statutory predecessor of s.30(1)(f) of the 1954 Act), Asquith L.J. explored the requirement for an intention to be shown and held, at p.253:

> "An 'intention' to my mind connotes a state of affairs which the party 'intending' – I will call him X – does more than merely contemplate it: it connotes a state of affairs which, on the contrary, so far as in him lies, to bring about, and which, in point of possibility, he has a reasonable prospect of being able to bring about, by his own act of volition."

(ii) In *Zarvos v Pradhan* [2003] EWCA Civ 208, at para.46, Ward L.J. observed that the motive behind a landlord's intention is irrelevant, save to the extent that an ulterior motive leads to the conclusion that the expression of intent is not genuine.

**6–024** Ultimately, however, each case will turn on the language of the lease in question. So, for example, in *Aberdeen Steak Houses Group Plc v The Crown Estate Commissioners* [1997] 2 E.G.L.R. 107, the lease contained a break clause worded as follows:

> "If the [landlord] shall desire to demolish or reconstruct the Building or a substantial part thereof or to carry out substantial work of construction on part thereof . . . and of such desire shall give to [the tenant] at least six months' previous notice in writing . . . then on the expiration of the said notice the term hereby granted shall cease."

Mr Anthony Grabiner QC (sitting as a Judge of the High Court) held that the word "desire" is quite different from the word "intention" and, for the purposes of the break clause, it was sufficient if the landlord contemplated, in general terms, demolition or reconstruction of the building or a substantial part of it. See, further, 7–057–7–060.

**6–025** In any case, it is important to consider whether a development break clause extends to the lessor's actual intended purpose. So, in *Coates v Diment* [1951] 1 All E.R. 890, the landlord had reserved the right to re-enter at any time without notice upon such of the demised premises (an agricultural holding) as he required "for building sites or planting or other purposes". The landlord had obtained permission from the local planning authority to construct a sports stadium on part of the agricultural holding; and, as a consequence, he sent to the tenant a notice to quit in the following terms:

> "I . . . hereby give you one months' notice from the date hereof . . . to quit [the land which was the subject of the planning permission] as I wish . . . to enter upon the said lands for the purpose of effecting preparatory works for which permission has been granted."

Streatfield J. held, at pp.898–899, that the words "or other purposes" in the break clause ought to be construed ejusdem generis with the preceding words. He said:

"In so far as a genus is to be found in the words, I think it is the normal user of land of the character concerned, and I cannot think that it was ever the intention for the parties to this contract that part of the land within a quarter of a mile of the farm-house should be used for building a sports stadium . . . I do not think that this was the kind of 'building site' contemplated, nor that the words 'or other purposes' construed ejusdem generis with the earlier words, cover such buildings as a sports stadium and other buildings purely ancillary to the main purpose of providing a sports ground."

(b) *Time for exercise—where time is expressed*
Well-drafted leases will almost certainly contain: (i) a time limit for the exercise of the break clause; and (ii) a minimum break notice period. In all cases, time limits should be strictly complied with; see paras 6–028–6–031 below. Because a failure to serve the break notice within the applicable time limit will almost certainly result in the loss of the ability to terminate the lease, care must be taken to ensure that the lease terms are followed. In practice, this may be difficult, as is demonstrated by *Biondi v Kirklington & Piccadilly Estates Ltd* [1947] 2 All E.R. 59. In that case (which concerned an option to renew a lease), the lease, granted for a period of 35 years from February 8, 1911, contained the following covenant:

**6–026**

"The lessor hereby covenants with the lessees that the lessor will on the written request of the lessees made 6 calendar months before the expiration of the terms hereby granted . . . grant to them a lease of the demised premises for the further term of 14 years from the expiration of the said term at the same rent and containing the like covenants and provisos as are herein contained with the exception of the present covenant for renewal, the lessees on the execution of such renewal lease to execute a counterpart thereof."

Roxburgh J. noted, at p.60, that the phrase "On the written request of the lessees made 6 calendar months before the expiration of the term hereby granted" was capable of at least four different meanings: (i) made on August 8, 1945; (ii) made at any time before August 8, 1945; (iii) made on or a reasonable time before August 8, 1945; and (iv) given so as to take effect on August 8, 1945. The judge did not say which construction was correct, only that the second construction was incorrect.

As a general rule, where a break clause is to be exercised "from" a certain date, it is presumed that the period is calculated from the day after the stipulated date. See *Trow v Ind Coope (West Midlands) Ltd* [1967] 2 Q.B. 899. Similarly, where the break clause must be exercised "within" a certain period of time, the initial day of the period is generally not

**6–027**

included, and the break notice may be given up to midnight on the last day of the period. See *Manorlike Ltd v Le Vitas Travel Agency and Consultancy Services Ltd* [1986] 1 All E.R. 574. See, generally, Ch.4, paras 4–009–4–014.

(c) *Time for exercise—where time is not expressed*
6–028 Where no time is specified for the exercise of a break clause, notice of a reasonable period should be given. This is a question of fact dependent upon the circumstances of each individual case. In *Goodright on the demise of Hall v Richardson* (1789) 3 Term Reports 462, a lease granted in 1785 was expressed to be determinable in the years 1788, 1791 and 1794. Lord Kenyon C.J. said, at p.463: "It was intended . . . that it should be in the election of either of the parties to put an end to [the lease] . . . at the end of six years, giving reasonable notice to the other."

(d) *Equitable relief for late service*
6–029 Formal leases invariably provide a time limit for the exercise of a break clause. Time is of the essence of stipulations in break clauses. Accordingly, unlike the normal time limits for rent review clauses, when dealing with options to determine, a time stipulation must be strictly complied with. In *United Scientific Holdings Ltd v Burnley BC* [1978] A.C. 904, at p.962, Lord Fraser explained the rationale behind this as follows:

"There is a good reason why time limits should be strictly enforced in relation to an option to purchase or renew a lease, because so long as it remains open the grantor is not free to dispose of his property elsewhere, although the grantee is under no obligation to him. Similarly where a tenant has an option to break his lease, he can break it or not as he chooses, but the landlord is not free to let his property to anyone else until the time for exercising the tenant's option has expired. It is fair and reasonable, and in accordance with what I would take to be the intention of the parties,that the time limit of the restriction on the grantor should be strictly enforced. That however does not apply in relation to a rent review clause in a continuing lease."

6–030 Equitable relief is not normally available to a party who gives notice late in circumstances where time is of the essence. An extraordinary and extreme example of this principle is to be found in the decision of the Privy Council in *Union Eagle Ltd v Golden Achievements Ltd* [1997] A.C. 514. In that case, time for the completion of the sale of a flat was of the essence and was to take place at 17.00 on a specified date. The purchase price was tendered at 17.10. The vendor refused to accept the money tendered and successfully forfeited the purchaser's deposit.

6–031 However, it may be that relief would be granted if late service of the notice came about as a result of some event which the serving party could not reasonably have avoided/prevented. See *Reid v Blagrave* (1831) 9 L.J. (OS) (Ch) 245. Relief might also be granted in circumstances where unconscionable conduct has been made on the part of the recipient of the notice. Thus, in *Samuel Properties (Developments) Ltd v Hayek* [1972] 1 W.L.R. 1296, at pp.1307–08, Edmund Davies L.J. said:

"The circumstances in which relief against forfeiture is granted are widely different from those under present consideration. In the former, a right of forfeiture is expressly reserved or implied by law in order to ensure the performance by the lessee of his obligations, and the court will grant relief if terms can be imposed which will ensure due protection to the lessor. But the power of a lessor on due notice to increase rent involves, in effect, the making of a new contract between the parties, subject in the present case to compliance by the lessor with a condition precedent. It resembles options and these are undoubtedly required to be exercised in strict conformity with the terms by which they were created: see Hinds v Randall (1961) 177 E.G. 733 and Peeling v Guidice, 186 E.G. 113. If this is not done, relief will in general be granted only where, by unconscionable conduct by the proposed recipient of the notice to exercise the option, the other party has been led to believe that strict adherence to its terms will not be insisted upon."

*Peeling v Guidice* (referred to by Edmund Davies L.J. in *Samuel Properties*) emphasises the general rule. In that case, Mr Guidice was the tenant of premises under a lease which conferred an option to renew which was to be exercised three months before the expiration of the term. On the date for exercise of the option Mr Guidice was in prison; and he gave no notice pursuant to the terms of the option. Judge Lane gave judgment for possession for the plaintiff landlord. The Court of Appeal, dismissing Mr Guidice's appeal, held that there was no ground in equity for giving Mr Guidice relief against his failure to give notice to renew.

6–032

(e) *Acceptance of short service of a break notice*
Where one party has given short notice which does not comply with the requirements of the break clause, it is open for the recipient to accept the notice, thereby waiving the requirement in relation to the appropriate length of notice or the time for service. So, for example, in *Elsden v Pick* [1980] 1 W.L.R. 898, the defendant was the tenant of a farm under an agreement which was determinable on one year's notice in writing expiring on April 6 in any year. On April 4, 1977, the tenant discussed with the landlords' agent the possibility of his having to give up the farm, and on April 7 he delivered to the agent a notice of his intention to quit the farm in April 1978, together with a letter requesting the agent to accept the notice. The agent agreed to treat the notice as valid notwithstanding that the length of the notice was short. When, later, the tenant contended that the notice was ineffective to determine his tenancy, the landlords brought an action for a declaration that they were entitled to possession of the farm in April 1978. The judge held that the tenant's

6–033

notice was invalid as it contravened s.23(1) of the Agricultural Holdings Act 1948, and he dismissed the landlords' action. On appeal by the landlords, the Court of Appeal held that the landlord was entitled to waive the requirement for 12 months' notice and, having done so, was not entitled to insist upon compliance with the statute. See, further, para.6–035.

## 5 Estoppel and waiver

6–034   It may be possible for the recipient of a break notice to waive any defects contained in the notice or the method by which the notice was served. Equally, an estoppel may arise which prevents the recipient from asserting that a break notice is invalid or was served incorrectly. Estoppel and waiver are considered more fully in Ch.4.

## 6 Withdrawal of a break notice

6–035   In *May v Borup* [1915] 1 K.B. 830, at p.832, Lawrence J. said:

> "A tenant who has given a good notice to quit cannot subsequently cancel it without the consent of the landlord. If the tenant desires to continue his tenancy after giving notice it is a matter for negotiation with the landlord, who can accept or reject the tenant's proposals as he pleases."

Similarly, in *Tayleur v Wildin* (1868) L.R. 3 Ex. 303, at p.305, Kelly C.B. said: "whether [a] notice to quit is given by the landlord or the tenant, the party to whom it is given is entitled to insist upon it, and it cannot be withdrawn without the consent of both." This was followed by the Court of Appeal in *Freeman v Evans* [1922] 1 Ch. 36, notwithstanding the fact that, as was acknowledged by Lord Sterndale M.R. at p.45, *Tayleur* had previously been very strongly criticised and, indeed, disapproved of entirely by the Court of Appeal in Ireland in *Lord Inchiquin v Lyons* (1887) 20 L.R. Ir. 474. It is thought that the observations here made in connection with notices to quit are equally applicable to the case of a break notice (unless the express terms of the lease provide otherwise). See also *Lower v Sorrell* [1963] 1 Q.B. 959.

6–036   Where a notice to quit is treated by the parties as withdrawn, then a new tenancy may be created to take effect at the expiry of the old one. So much was said by Bramwell B. in *Tayleur v Wildin,* at pp.305–306: "If the notice is given, the tenancy is at an end; the parties may by a parol contract create a new tenancy, which is what is meant by the phrase withdrawing the notice, but the old tenancy no longer exists" and by Lord Sterndale M.R. in *Freeman v Evans,* at p.45. This does not present any real practical difficulties in the case of a periodic tenancy, but gives rise to a number of problematic implications in the case of a break notice withdrawn during the course of a fixed term tenancy. In the latter scenario, it is thought that the parties would be left with a new tenancy for a fixed term equal to the residue of the old tenancy. However, if this happens, then presumably:

(i) The landlord would lose the ability to claim against former tenants liable under privity of contract (for pre-1996 'old' leases) or under an authorised guarantee agreement (under post-1996 'new' leases).

(ii) As regards liability to keep the demised premises in repair, any repairing obligation on the part of the tenant would be construed by reference to the condition of the premises at the time when the deemed new lease takes effect. See *Walker v Hatton* (1842) 10 M. & W. 249.

(iii) If the rent under the previous lease was payable, say, quarterly in advance on the usual quarter days, and the break notice is withdrawn half way through a quarter, the tenant would find himself liable to pay twice over for the remaining part of that quarter.

(iv) The new lease (if for a term of longer than seven years) would have to be registered at HM Land Registry. Failure to register the new lease will mean that the tenant has no legal title, and thus, only an equitable tenancy (which interest is vulnerable upon a transfer of the landlord's reversion).

In *Lower v Sorrell* [1963] 1 Q.B. 959, at pp.973–974, Donovan L.J. **6–037** felt compelled to follow *Freeman v Evans*, but advanced a more simple solution to these difficulties, as follows:

"I take the ratio of the decision in Freeman v Evans to be this: that a notice to quit converts a tenancy from year to year into one which is to end on a fixed date, and that if thereafter the notice to quit is by agreement withdrawn, then another tenancy from year to year—which is a new tenancy altogether—replaces the tenancy ending on a fixed date.

A different view, however, is, I think, open. Any tenancy from year to year possesses the inherent characteristic that by a valid notice to quit it may be determined at the end of some year of the tenancy; so that its full description is really a tenancy from year to year and until the date when it is validly determined. When the notice is given, the inherent characteristic becomes an actual feature of the tenancy. But no new tenancy comes into being. It is simply the old one with its ending fixed. If by agreement this date is cancelled, again no new tenancy is created. The life of the old one is simply prolonged, and it continues once more with its inherent quality of determination by a valid notice.

I respectfully think that this more nearly represents the reality of the matter, and where it is what the parties intend shall happen, I can see no reason for imposing upon the parties the notion that they have agreed to a completely new tenancy."

**6–038** Interestingly, for SDLT purposes, HMRC takes the approach advocated by Donovan L.J. in *Sorrell*. Thus, under HMRC's SDLT Manual 17030 ('Miscellaneous Provisions: Withdrawal of a Notice to Quit or Break Notice'), it is expressly stated that:

> "In circumstances where a break notice or notice to quit is withdrawn, by agreement between the parties, before it takes effect the lease will be treated as continuing for SDLT purposes, notwithstanding any rule of law to the effect that a break notice or notice to quit may not be withdrawn and that any purported withdrawal creates a new lease."

Accordingly, a tenant will not have to file a land transaction return for the new tenancy.

**6–039** It should be noted, however, that in any case, the server of a break notice may be able to countermand it (as opposed to withdrawing it), at least before the notice has been served. In *Kinch v Bullard* [1999] 1 W.L.R. 423, at p.429, Neuberger J. said:

> "I am inclined to think that the position would be different if, before the notice was 'given', the sender had informed the addressee that he wished to revoke it. In such a case, it appears to me that the notice would have been withdrawn before it had been 'given'. After all, as is clear from the reasoning at first instance and in the Court of Appeal in Holwell Securities Ltd v Hughes [1973] 1 W.L.R. 757, 761–762; [1974] 1 W.L.R. 155, 158–159, 160–162, a notice sent by post is not 'served' in accordance with section 196(3) until it arrives at the premises to which it has been addressed. Accordingly, it seems to me that, while the notice is still in the post, it has not been given, and, until it is given, the sender has in effect a locus poenitentiae whereby he can withdraw the notice, but only provided his withdrawal is communicated to the addressee before the notice is given to, or served on, the addressee. I should emphasise, however, that this is no more than a tentative view."

## 7 Professional liability in connection with invalid break notices

**6–040** Absent express instructions to carry out the steps required to bring about the termination of a lease by the exercise of a break clause, it is doubtful whether a solicitor would be under a duty to remind the person wishing to exercise the break clause that the time for service of the break notice was approaching. This is illustrated by the decision of the Court of Appeal in *Yager v Fishman & Co* [1944] 1 All E.R. 552. In that case, Mr Yager, an experienced businessman, was the guarantor under a lease which contained a break clause entitling the lessee (a company which he owned and controlled) to determine the lease by six months' previous notice at the end of the third, seventh and fourteenth years of the term. Mr Yager had, from time to time, retained the services of a firm of solicitors to advise him about certain legal difficulties he had in connection with the lease. On the facts, the solicitors were justified in assuming that Mr Yager was alive to the terms of the break clause in the lease. Further, Mr Yager was found never to have expressly raised the question of how the break clause should be exercised. In the circumstances, the solicitors could not be criticised for failing to advise Mr Yager as to when the break clause should have been exercised, and how. As with almost every case, however, the facts will be determinative of the issue. In *Yager* itself, Goddard L.J. said, at p.556:

> "The nature and amount of advice which, in a matter of this sort, a solicitor would be expected to give to a person wholly unacquainted with business may differ very materially from what he would offer to an experienced business man, who would naturally decide for himself the course he thought it in his interest to take [viz. to exercise the break clause or not]."

Professional liability in connection with a failure to exercise a break notice was established against a managing agent and a firm of solicitors in *The Secretary of State for the Environment, Transport and Regions v Unicorn Consultancy Services Ltd* (Unreported October 19, 2000). In that case, the Secretary of State for the Environment, Transport and Regions ("SoS") was the lessee of premises in Bristol. The lease contained a break clause in the following terms: **6–041**

> "If the Tenant . . . shall be desirous of determining this Lease on the 25$^{th}$ day of December 1995 and of such his desire shall serve on the Landlord not less than six months' notice in writing . . . and shall also pay to the Landlord a sum equal to one half of the annual rent payable as at the date of such notice such sum to be payable not later than the 18$^{th}$ day of December 1995 . . . then and in such case this Lease shall cease and be void at midnight on the 24$^{th}$ December 1995."

In 1993, Unicorn Consultancy Services Ltd ("Unicorn") was appointed as managing agent in respect of a large portfolio of properties held by the SoS, including the premises in Bristol. In March 1994, the SoS appointed Veale Wasbrough ("VW") to provide various legal services. By March 1995, the SoS had decided to exercise the break option in the lease and, to that end, instructed Unicorn and VW to serve the break notice. The break notice was properly served, but both Unicorn and VW forgot about the requirement to pay to the landlord a sum equal to one half of the annual rent payable as at the date of the notice (being £100,000.00). Because this sum had not been paid in full and on time, the break clause was not properly exercised and the SoS had to negotiate an expensive surrender of the lease. On the facts, Rimer J. found that Unicorn owed a contractual duty to advise the SoS of the impending need to make the one-off payment of £100,000.00 due no later than December 18, 1995 (notwithstanding the fact that there was no specific provision in Unicorn's contract of engagement showing that it clearly had a duty to advise about the need to make such a payment). Similarly, VW was found to have owed to the SoS a duty to arrange for the making of the payment of £100,000.00 in the correct manner and in time to comply with the conditions of the break option. Unicorn and VW failed to discharge these obligations and were liable in damages to the SoS. Notably, the SoS was found to be guilty of contributory negligence in that it did not take care of its interests in the way in which it reasonably ought to have done. Given the importance of the payment of £100,000.00, Rimer J. found it astonishing that the SoS was so passive about the matter. Rimer J. said, at para.128: "I can see no reason at all why [the SoS] could not and should not at least have put in hand its own internal reminder of the need to make the payment on time."

Chapter 7

# Conditions in a Break Clause

## 1 The principle of strict compliance

As a consequence of break clauses being a type of option (see paras 1–011–1–012), in order that the "offer to break" contained in a break clause can be accepted, all the conditions of that offer must be strictly complied with.   **7–001**

The principle of strict compliance with the terms of an option was settled in 1876, by the Court of Appeal, in *Finch v Underwood* (1876) 2 Ch.D. 310. In *Finch* the landlord had covenanted with the tenant, on receipt of notice from the latter, to renew the lease "in case the covenants and agreements on the tenant's part shall have been duly observed and performed". Notice was duly given by the tenant but the landlord refused to renew the lease because the interior of the property needed repairs at a cost of £13. Malins V.C. decided that the landlord was obliged to renew the lease because the want of repair was "trifling". The Court of Appeal disagreed.   **7–002**

James L.J. considered that the case was one of compliance with a condition precedent. He held that the tenant had lost his right to a renewal of the lease by a breach of the covenant to repair. He added, at p.315:   **7–003**

> "No doubt every property must at times be somewhat out of repair, and a tenant must have a reasonable time allowed to do what is necessary: but where it is required as a condition precedent to the granting of a new lease that the lessee's covenant shall have been performed, the lessee who comes to claim the new lease must show that at that time the property is in such a state as the covenants require it to be. He can easily send in his builder, get a report of what repairs are necessary, and do them before he applies for the lease. There is no hardship in requiring this of him, and I think he is not entitled to excuse himself by saying that the want of repair is trifling. The answer to that is, 'No matter; your bargain was to leave the property in thorough repair'. If he has not fulfilled his legal bargain, which is also his bargain in equity, he cannot sustain his claim for a lease."

**7-004**  Although *Finch's* case concerned an option to renew a lease, rather than to break a lease, the principle of strict compliance established in that case has been consistently applied to break clauses, (see, for example, the comments made by the Judges in the Court of Appeal in *Bass Holdings Ltd v Morton Music Ltd* [1988] 1 Ch. 493).

**7-005**  The principle of strict compliance means that if a precondition to the exercise of a break clause has not been satisfied then it will not avail the party in breach of covenant to contend that only minimal damages would be recoverable. Thus in *Bairstow Eves (Securities) Ltd v Ripley* [1992] 2 E.G.L.R. 47, the option (to renew a lease) was exercisable "if the tenant shall perform and observe all the covenants and obligations herein on the tenant's part contained". The tenant's covenants included a provision to paint and decorate in the last year of the term (which was from March 25, 1988 to March 24, 1989). The premises were not painted and decorated in the last year of the term but 17 to 20 months before the end of the term. This made no practical difference to the premises, but it meant there was a technical breach of the tenant's covenants. The tenant's counsel submitted that the only breaches that mattered were those for which substantial damages would be recoverable. The Court of Appeal disagreed. Scott L.J. said, at p.49: "There is no authority that permits the Court to re-write the condition precedent so as to exclude from account a subsisting breach on the ground that only nominal damages are recoverable". At p.50 he added: "The Court is not entitled to re-write that covenant or to presume to inform [the landlord] that breach of the covenant was only trivial and should be ignored for the purposes of the condition precedent".

**2 Subjectivity and motive**

**7-006**  The principle of strict compliance can appear to create unfairness. In efforts to correct this perceived unfairness, judges have sometimes distorted the law (e.g. the judge at first instance in *Bairstow Eves,* despite the breach of covenant, found in favour of the tenant). One distortion, that has now been corrected, involved introducing fairness or subjectivity when it came to the exercise of a break clause. Thus in *Commercial Union Life Insurance Co Ltd v Label Ink Ltd* (2001) L. & T.R. 380, Judge Rich QC considered the concept of "material breach". In dealing with this phrase he said that a breach:

> "was only material if, but only if, having regard to all the circumstances, and to the proper efforts of the tenant to comply with his covenants as well as the adverse effect on the landlord of any failure to do so, it will be fair and reasonable to refuse the tenant the privilege which the lease otherwise grants".

In *Fitzroy House (No.1) Ltd v Financial Times Ltd* [2006] 1 W.L.R. **7–007**
2207 the judge at first instance adopted the *Label Ink* approach. The Court
of Appeal disagreed. The Chancellor, when delivering judgment in *Fitzroy*,
at para.16, said: "The word 'material' is susceptible to a number of nuances
but what is fair and reasonable between landlord and tenant is not one of
them". At para.24 he added: "It cannot, I think, be seriously disputed that
the issue of 'material compliance' whatever it involves must be determined
on an objective basis". The chancellor also cited with approval the
comments of Pearson L.J. in *Chapman v Honig* [1963] 2 Q.B. 502 that "a
person who has a right under a contract or other instrument is entitled to
exercise it and can effectively exercise it for good reason or a bad reason
or no reason at all". The same sentiment was expressed in a recent Court
of Appeal decision containing a right to rescind, dependent upon conditions being satisfied, namely, *BDW Trading Ltd v JM Rowe (Investments)
Ltd* [2011] EWCA Civ 548. Patten L.J. stated, in para.12, "Reasons do not
matter. The right to rescind by Clause 6.2 does not depend upon Barratt
having any particular intention or justification beyond the non-fulfilment
of one or more of the clause 6.2 conditions".

Thus, unless the language of a break clause expressly introduces **7–008**
concepts of motive or subjectivity then these concepts are irrelevant.

One situation where it will be necessary to inquire into a party's inten- **7–009**
tions is in a landlord's development break clause, of a type that makes
express reference to "the landlord's intention to develop". If the landlord
asserts that it has such an intention then it will be open to the tenant to
deny this. See, further, paras 6–022–6–026 and 7–057–7–060.

## 3 Spent breaches

In *Bass Holdings* (para.7–004 above) a lease included a covenant stating **7–010**
that:

"If the tenant shall be desirous of taking a further lease of the demised
premises . . . and shall not later than 29 September 1985 give to the
lessors notice in writing of such a desire and if it shall have paid
the rent hereby reserved and shall have performed and observed the
several stipulations on its part herein contained and on its part to be
performed and observed up to the date thereof then the lessors will . . .
let the demised premises to the tenant for a further term of 125
years . . ."

The tenant served such a notice, but the landlord contended that the
tenant had not observed all its covenants. The tenant admitted that it had,
in the past, breached its covenant, but contended that these were spent
and that there were no current breaches. A preliminary issue was argued

as to whether any past or spent breaches could be relied upon by the landlord in order to oppose the tenant's renewal notice. The Court of Appeal decided that spent breaches could not be relied upon, whatever their nature. It is important to note that its decision was not based upon the language of the clause but upon the long history of break and renewal clauses, coupled with commerciality and commonsense. As Nicholls L.J. (as he then was) explained, at p.528F: "A 'never any breach' construction would mean that in practice the condition would be impossible of fulfilment in almost all cases of leases of buildings containing a full range of repairing and other covenants by a tenant".

7–011 In his judgment Kerr L.J., at p.518H, noted that: "While it would of course be possible to formulate a proviso which is sufficiently explicit to cause spent breaches to preclude the exercise of the option, there appears to be no reported case in which this was so".

7–012 Thus it would take wholly unambiguous wording in a break clause before a court would conclude that spent breaches prevented a tenant exercising its break.

**4 The time for compliance with any conditions**

7–013 A break clause, being an option, requires a notice of some kind in order for it to be exercised. The notice will be served on day 1 and expire on some later date, day X. Issues often arise as to whether any conditions have to be satisfied:

(i) on day 1;

(ii) on day X; or

(iii) on both day 1 and day X.

7–014 The language of the break clause should make the position explicit, however this is often not so. It is therefore appropriate to examine certain earlier decisions, and the language used therein, to see how judges have approached the matter.

7–015 In *Finch's* case (para.7–002) the landlord covenanted that he:

"shall and will, at the expiration of the term hereby granted (in case the covenants and agreements on the said tenant's part shall have been duly observed and performed), grant unto the said tenant . . . a fresh lease of the hereby demised premises . . . provided the said tenants . . . shall 21 days before the expiration of the term hereby granted give unto the said landlord . . . a notice in writing . . . of the intention and desire to take such fresh lease . . ."

Mellish and Baggallay L.JJ. appear to have been of the opinion that compliance with the covenant at the date of service was required. James

L.J. seems to have been of the opposite view. However, since it was agreed that at all material times there was disrepair, and since the notice only had to be 21 days long, the "time" issue was not significant in that case.

In *Bastin v Bidwell* (1881) 18 Ch.D. 238 the judge declined to offer **7–016** any answer to the "timing" question. In that case there was a covenant to renew, on six months' notice, "upon the lessees paying the rent and performing and observing the covenants". Kay J., at p.253, said:

> "I have considerable difficulty in determining which of these two constructions should be preferred, that is, whether this clause means that there should be no breach at the time the notice was given, or that there should be no breach at the time that the notice expired, but I purposely avoid determining it because in this case it is quite immaterial."

In *Robinson v Thames Mead Park Estate Ltd* [1947] 1 Ch. 334 the **7–017** tenant had a tenancy of a piece of land, from July 22, 1941 until April 22, 1944. The tenant covenanted to erect a dwelling on the land in the first 12 months. By clause 19 of the lease the landlord covenanted that "subject to the tenant having faithfully performed and observed all her agreements herein contained the tenant shall have the option of continuing the tenancy under the grant of a building lease . . ." Evershed J. referred to *Bastin*'s case (para.7–016 above) saying:

> "This is a case where the tenant was entering into obligations as to the erection of new premises, both during the first 3 years term and later; and, I think in those circumstances, the problem which Kay J found it unnecessary to decide in the case before him, I decide in the plaintiff's favour here, namely, that it is sufficient for the purposes of this clause 19 that the tenant, when she comes to give her notice calling on the landlord to grant the lease, has then ended any previous breaches of covenants or failure to perform covenants."

In *West Country Cleaners (Falmouth) Ltd v Saly* [1966] 1 W.L.R. 148 **7–018** a lease contained a covenant to renew which stipulated that:

> "If the lessee shall be desirous of renewing this lease (except this present sub-clause thereof) for a further term of 7 years and shall give to the lessor 12 months notice in writing before the expiry of this demise then the lessor will providing all covenants herein contained have been duly observed and performed grant to the lessees a further term of the demised premises for 7 years from the expiration of this lease . . ."

The lease included a covenant to repaint in the last year of the term. It **7–019** was agreed that this covenant had been broken. An issue arose as to whether the renewal covenant required performance at the date of service of the notice or at the date of its expiry. Danckwerts L.J. said, at p.1490E:

> "On the wording of the clause in the present case it is quite plain that the date of the expiration of the lease is the material time because after the period of 12 months has been fixed for giving the notice the clause proceeds: 'then the lessor will' – and then, and not before, comes the proviso requiring the covenant to paint in the last year to be duly observed and performed."

**7–020** Winn and Sellers L.JJ. agreed.

**7–021** In *Bass Holdings* (where the wording of the covenant is as set out at para.7–010 above) the parties agreed that the covenant required compliance with the tenant's covenants at the date of service of the notice.

**7–022** On the basis of the above authorities no presumptions as to the date for compliance with covenants emerge. In order to resolve the "timing" question, the language of the break clause must be closely examined, together with the remaining terms of the lease, plus the commercial context.

### 5 Words qualifying the principle of strict compliance

**7–023** In view of the principle of strict compliance, if a tenant's break clause requires performance of repairing and painting covenants, then achieving full compliance will be extremely difficult. Faced with such difficulty it is suggested that the tenant should consider two steps:

(i) Engaging a building surveyor, and then following all of his recommendations as to the work needed to comply with repairing and painting covenants. If this is done then some words in *Finch* (para.7–002), might provide a 'lifeline'. At p.316 in that case, Mellish L.J. said: "The Court would be inclined to give credit to a survey thus honestly made and would lead towards holding the condition precedent to have been complied with."

(ii) Liaise with the landlord, and invite the landlord to agree a schedule of works that are needed to achieve compliance with the tenant's covenants. If all the work that is stipulated by the landlord is duly carried out, to the landlord's satisfaction, then it would probably be too late for the landlord to allege further breaches after the tenant has departed from the premises (see the discussion as to waiver/estoppel at paras 7–048–7–049).The drawback with this approach is that there is no obligation upon a landlord to cooperate with its tenant, and a landlord should not be criticised in law for declining to inform its tenants as to the steps to be taken to comply with its covenants. (See *Fitzroy House*, para.7–007.)

To avoid the foregoing problem, occasioned by a break clause that  7–024
requires strict compliance with the covenants in a lease, the best advice
to a tenant, when the lease is being drafted, is to avoid including any
condition that requires compliance with the tenant's covenants. Failing
this being achieved, the tenant should seek to insert words that qualify
the principle of strict compliance. Qualifying words that are often
deployed are "reasonable", "material" and "substantial". The meaning of
each of these words is considered in the following sections.

### 6 "Reasonable" or "reasonably"?

The above words have been considered in a series of cases, addressed  7–025
below.

In *Gardner v Blaxill* [1960] 1 W.L.R. 75 Paull J. considered a provi-  7–026
sion for renewal contained in a home-drawn lease. The paragraph in the
lease read: "Provided that the tenant has reasonably fulfilled the covenants hereinbefore mentioned he has the option of continuing . . ." The
judge accepted the tenant's Counsel's submission "that by inserting the
word 'reasonably' the parties not only intended to mean, but must be
deemed to have meant, that the tenant can exercise his option provided
that he behaves during his tenancy in a way in which a reasonably
minded tenant might well behave."

*Bassett v Whiteley* (1983) 45 P. & C.R. 80 involved a provision for  7–027
renewal. The provision required the tenants to serve 6 to 12 months'
notice, and continued:

> "If they shall have paid the rent hereby reserved and shall have reason-
> ably performed and observed the several stipulations herein contained
> and on their part to be performed and observed up to the termination
> of the tenancy hereby created then the landlord will let the demised
> premises to the tenants . . ."

The tenants normally complied with their covenants, but, having become
upset about water leaking into their restaurant premises through the roof,
delayed payment of rent in protest. Waller L.J., at p.91, said:

> "In my judgment here are tenants who have regularly paid their rent on
> that which was regarded as the due date for the whole of their lease until,
> for the early part of the year, they (being concerned about the dampness
> in the wall) were minded to withhold the rent to try and put some pres-
> sure upon the landlord but, after 2 or 3 months, had paid the whole of the
> rent, one asks oneself: Can it be said that the tenants had not reasonably
> performed and observed the several stipulations therein contained? The
> Judge, who approached this matter not in precisely the same way, came
> to the conclusion that the tenants had complied with that covenant.

I have no hesitation in saying that, when one has a tenant who has performed throughout the currency of the lease all his obligations but who on one occasion, or perhaps I should say two because there are five days in issue on the second occasion, withholds the rent because he wishes to put some pressure upon his landlord to do some repairs that he has reasonably performed and observed 'the several stipulations herein contained'."

**7–028** Griffiths L.J. agreed, and, at p.92, added that:

"In my view, it is permissible to look at the conduct of the tenants throughout the term to determine whether or not they have reasonably performed and observed the several stipulations contained in their covenants."

**7–029** The above two cases were ones where the merits favoured the tenant. The final case is the reverse, namely *Reed Personnel Services Plc v American Express Ltd* [1997] 1 E.G.L.R. 229. In that case the tenant, Amex, had a lease with a "one off" break clause, that required six months' notice and stipulated that the tenant "shall up to the time of such determination pay the rent reserved by and reasonably perform and observe the covenants contained in this lease . . ."

**7–030** About £21,000 worth of work was needed to remedy breaches of covenant. The tenant knew about this work but did nothing. Jacob J. said:

"Of course, the word 'reasonably' does qualify the word 'perform' and there are plenty of examples one can think of here where AMEX might reasonably have performed the obligation without actually doing it to the letter. For example, there is a requirement that there should be two coats of paint: one coat might have been quite good enough. There is a requirement of re-carpeting at the very end of the lease and it may be that if the carpet was in perfectly good condition that it would not have been necessary to comply with that obligation. I am not concerned with that kind of case at all. I am concerned with a case of total non-compliance."

**7–031** From the above cases one can conclude that if it is a pre-condition to the exercise of a break clause that a tenant has reasonably performed its covenants then the whole history of the tenancy will be material. If a tenant, in advance of exercising a break, seeks advice regarding his compliance and then follows that advice, it is likely that a judge will find that the tenant has satisfied the precondition.

### 7 "Material"

**7–032** The leading case, where the qualifying word is "material" or "materially", is *Fitzroy House (No.1) Ltd v Financial Times Ltd* [2006] 1 W.L.R.

2207. In that case the tenant had a "one-off" break clause, exercisable on not less than 13 months' notice, and subject to preconditions. One of these preconditions was "The tenant has materially complied with all its obligations under this lease down to the date for which notice of termination has been given . . ." Having rejected the judge's subjective approach, as being wrong (see para.7-007 above) the Court of Appeal was required to find its own meaning for the word "materially". The Chancellor (at para.35) said:

> "In my view the commercial context in which the provision is to be interpreted and applied is that described by Bingham L.J. in Bass Holdings Limited v Morton Music Limited [1988] Ch. 493, 538, . . . Materiality must be assessed by reference to the ability of the landlord to relet or sell the property without delay or additional expenditure."

That Judge then refrained from giving any judicial "gloss" to the phrase "materially complied". He said, "the application of an ordinary English word to a set of primary facts is itself a question of fact".

*Fitzroy* was considered and applied by B Livesey QC (sitting as a Deputy High Court Judge) in *Mourant Property Trust Ltd v Fusion Electronic (UK) Ltd* [2009] EWHC 3659 (Ch). In that case it was decided that there were material breaches of the two leases, and therefore the leases had not been broken. 7–033

## 8 "Substantial"

"Substantial" or "substantially" are ordinary English words, like "material". Therefore, applying *Fitzroy House* (para.7–033 above), the courts will treat compliance as a question of fact. There are no known reported cases dealing with the word "substantial". In *Fitzroy House* the Chancellor said, "The words 'substantial' and 'material', depending on the context, are interchangeable". However it is important to appreciate that in construing words judges often point out that "the context is everything". This point was underscored in a recent Supreme Court case, where Lord Collins, delivering the judgment of the court, cited the words of Deane J. in an Australian case, noting that "the word 'substantial' is not only susceptible of ambiguity: it is a word calculated to conceal a lack of precision"; see *Agbaje v Agbaje* [2010] 1 A.C. 628, at para.32. 7–034

Therefore it is suggested that the dicta in *Fitzroy* may not assist in knowing whether in a given situation "substantial" will be construed in the same way as "material". Indeed it is tentatively suggested that, in the context of disrepair, establishing a material breach might be easier to prove than establishing a substantial breach. 7–035

### 9 Vacant possession

**7–036** Whether or not a tenant's break clause includes any other preconditions, it will almost certainly expressly require the tenant to give vacant possession by the break date. Indeed, since the term of the lease is to end on that date, it would be strange if vacant possession was not given.

**7–037** The concept of vacant possession is well known in property law. It not only occurs in leases but also in contracts for the sale of freehold and leasehold property. The leading case is *Cumberland Consolidated Holdings Ltd v Ireland* [1946] 1 K.B. 264. This authority was concerned with a contract for the sale of land, however it (and subsequent authorities) was considered in detail by Lewison J. in *Legal & General Assurance Society Ltd v Expeditors International (UK) Ltd* (2006) L. & T.R. 368.

**7–038** *Expeditors* was a tenant's break clause case. Lewison J. pointed out, that in the judgment of Lord Greene M.R. in *Cumberland*, two possible tests for deciding whether or not vacant possession had been given were set out. The first test was posed, at p.270 of Lord Greene's judgment, in the following terms:

> "Subject to the rule de minimis a vendor who leaves property of his own on the premises on completion cannot, in our opinion, be said to give vacant possession, since by doing so he is claiming a right to use the premises for his own purposes, namely as a place of deposit for his own goods inconsistent with the right which the purchaser has on completion to undisturbed enjoyment."

**7–039** The second test treated vacant possession as the right to actual unimpeded physical enjoyment of the premises. Thus Lord Greene M.R. stated, at p.271 of the report:

> "We cannot see why the existence of a physical impediment to such enjoyment to which a purchaser does not expressly or impliedly consent to submit should stand in a different position to an impediment caused by the presence of a trespasser. It is true that in each case the purchaser obtains the right to possession in law notwithstanding the presence of the impediment but it appears to us that what he bargains for is not merely the right in law but the power in fact to exercise the right. When we speak of a physical impediment we do not mean that any physical impediment will do. It must be an impediment which substantially prevents or interferes with the enjoyment of the right of possession of a substantial part of the property. Such cases will be rare and can only arise in exceptional circumstances and there would normally be (what there is not here) waiver or acceptance of the position by the purchaser."

**7–040** In *Expeditors*, on the break date, the tenant retained all the keys, kept one of its employees on the premises, and continued to use the warehouse for the storage of materials and for the arrival of vehicles to collect the same. Lewison J. decided that vacant possession had not been delivered up. However he found that this did not invalidate the tenant's break notice, because of a settlement agreement made by landlord and tenant. In the Court of Appeal the Judge's decision upon vacant possession was not challenged. Moreover, although his decision upon the construction of the settlement agreement was challenged, by a majority the Court of Appeal dismissed the appeal. See *Legal & General Assurance Society Ltd v Expeditors International (UK) Ltd* (2007) L. & T.R. 229.

Both *Cumberland* and *Expeditors* were examined by the Court of Appeal in *NYK Logistics (UK) Ltd v Ibrend Estates BV* [2011] EWCA Civ 683. That case concerned a lease of a large warehouse, with a break clause that, to be effectively operated, required the tenant to deliver up "vacant possession of the premises" on April 3, 2009, most probably by midnight on that day. The Trial Judge decided that the tenant did not do this, because from April 6 to 9 the premises were occupied by the tenant's contractors, who were carrying out works to remedy dilapidations. The Court of Appeal agreed with this decision. Rimer L.J. approved Lewison J.'s comment that there were two tests in *Cumberland*, but did not consider that case of particular significance to the appeal. At para.44 he stated as follows: **7–041**

"The concept of 'vacant possession' in the present context is not, I consider, complicated. It means what it does in every domestic and commercial sale in which there is an obligation to give 'vacant possession' on completion. It means that at the moment that 'vacant possession' is required to be given, the property is empty of people and that the purchaser is able to assume and enjoy immediate and exclusive possession, occupation and control of it. It must also be empty of chattels, although the obligation in this respect is likely only to be breached if any chattels left in the property substantially prevent or interfere with the enjoyment of the right of possession of a substantial part of the property."

There are a number of other cases that concern vacant possession. Whilst recognising that "the meaning of the words 'vacant possession' can ... vary from context to context" (per Templeman J. in *Topfell Ltd v Galley Properties Ltd* [1979] 1 E.G.L.R. 161) it is worth recording them briefly: **7–042**

(i) *Topfell's* case (above) — This was a claim for specific performance of the contract for the sale of a two-storey house, in which the first floor was let, but the ground floor was sold with vacant possession. Templeman J. decided that the contract had been breached, because, although physically vacant, the ground floor could not be occupied due to a Housing Act restriction.

(ii) *Hynes v Vaughan* (1985) 50 P. & C.R. 444 — A purchaser challenged the validity of a notice to complete. She said that the property was not vacant when she was called upon to complete. Scott J. noted that the property was a rural smallholding. He distinguished cases with rubbish indoors, from situations where debris had piled up outside over the years, and was "a part of the property sold".

(iii) *Royal Bank of Canada v Secretary of State for Defence* (2004) 1 P. & C.R. 448—Involved argument over the validity of several break notices of commercial premises. Lewison J. stated that various office equipment, none of which was unwieldy or difficult to move, did not prevent the premises being vacant.

7–043 In addition to all of the above vacant possession cases there is *John Laing Construction Ltd v Amber Pass Ltd* [2004] 2 E.G.L.R. 128. In this case Robert Hildyard QC (sitting as a Deputy Judge) had to consider the validity of a notice, served pursuant to a break clause that ended a lease, upon the tenant "yielding up the entirety of the demised premises". The landlord contended that the tenant did not yield up the premises on the appointed day because there was no formal event of yielding up. The tenant had not handed back the keys, nor offered to do so, the tenant continued to instruct a security firm to secure the premises without giving the landlord the option to take over the security, and the tenant left in place concrete barriers that impeded vehicular access to the premises. Despite these matters the Deputy Judge found in favour of the tenant, and concluded that the lease had been successfully broken. Although in *Merton LBC v Jones* [2009] 1 W.L.R. 1269 the Court of Appeal agreed with the Deputy Judge that the retention of keys was ambiguous, it is suggested that his overall decision may have to be approached with some caution. This is because, in *Expeditors* (paras 7–036–7–040), Lewison J. deliberately left open its correctness, noting (at para.46) that "none of the cases cited to me on the question of vacant possession appear to have been cited to Mr Hildyard".

## 10 Reinstatement obligations

7–044 One often finds, in a lease or in a subsequent deed permitting alterations, an obligation of some kind to reinstate at the end of the term. The nature of the reinstatement obligation can vary. Sometimes it is absolute (e.g. "the tenant upon the expiry or sooner determination of the term, will restore the premises to their condition prior to the alterations hereby permitted"). Sometimes it is at the landlords option (e.g. "the tenant will restore the premises to their condition prior to the said alterations, if the landlord serves notice upon the tenant requiring it to do so"). Issues quite often arise as to the interplay between such provisions and the operation of a break clause.

There are various possibilities. The simplest is where the break clause  7–045
itself requires reinstatement as a condition of a successful break. Plainly
reinstatement is required. However, more frequently, the break clause
only refers to the tenant complying with its obligations or covenants. If
the obligation to reinstate is of the absolute kind indicated above, then
reinstatement is probably needed, although there might be a distinction
between a condition in a break clause to comply with the tenants covenants (viz. the covenants just in the lease) and a condition to comply with
the tenants obligations (which may well extend to the obligations
contained in subsequent deeds). The bigger problems lie where the reinstatement obligation is conditional upon notice to reinstate given by the
landlord. If the landlord gives plenty of notice to allow reinstatement pre
the termination date in the break clause, there should not be a practical
problem. However the notice might be given just before the termination
date. The leading textbook on dilapidations (Dowding and Reynolds,
*Dilapidations: The Modern Law and Practice*, 4th Editon, 16.04)
suggests that such a reinstatement notice is valid, but the tenant has an
implied notice to remain on the premises to complete the reinstatement
work. But how can the concept of an implied licence "work" where the
break is to end the tenants occupation, and where (expressly or impliedly)
the tenant must give vacant possession? This is an unresolved question.

## 11 Paying the rent

Payment of the rent is the most commonplace of the preconditions in a  7–046
tenant's break clause, after the condition as to the giving of vacant
possession. Payment of rent might be mentioned explicitly in a break
clause, or be relevant simply as one of the tenant's covenants that has to
be complied with. As with all preconditions, save where qualifying
words appear, strict compliance is required. This means payment on or
before the due rent day. If the termination date is the day before a rent
payment day then there should be no problem in calculating the amount
to be paid. However in all other cases problems may arise. The break
date might be on the rent payment day or in between two rent payment
days.

If, as is normally the case, rent is payable in advance what should the  7–047
tenant do? Should it pay an amount apportioned to the break date or pay
rent for the whole of the period? The Apportionment Act 1870 does not
assist (see *Ellis v Rowbotham* [1900] 1 Q.B. 740). If one takes forfeiture
as an analogy, then rent for the whole period would have to be paid (see
*Capital and City Holdings v Dean Warburg Ltd* [1989] 1 E.G.L.R. 90).
In *Re A Company* [2006] EWHC 3436 (Ch); [2007] B.P.I.R. 1, Pumfrey
J. was impressed with the analogy. He had to decide whether to grant an
injunction to restrain the presentation or advertisement of a winding up
petition. One point that arose was whether (assuming that leases ended

in the middle of a quarter) this absolved the tenant from paying the full quarter's rent. The Judge decided not. After setting out a passage from *Capital and City* he said:

> "I am constrained for the reasons given by Ralph Gibson LJ to hold that it is not possible to apportion the rent to a lesser period than a quarter on expiry of the term whenever that term expires in any quarter following a quarter day on which payment of the rent has been made."

It is fair to point out however that Pumfrey J. does not appear to have heard any sustained argument on the point, nor was any other authority cited to him. Break clauses are inserted in a lease consensually, whereas a forfeiture involves a non consensual event, viz. forfeitable breach of covenant. It is understandable that a tenant who has broken his lease in so serious a way as to have it forfeit should not be able to escape payment of his full contractual obligation to pay for the quarter. However the bargain embodied in a break clause means that the parties had contracted for the term to end at a date between quarter days. Why should the tenant have to pay for a period after the contractual lease term has ended? Is not then the landlord unjustly enriched? Suffice it to say, that this vexed point remains to be fully considered by the courts.

**7–048** In practice any prudent tenant, being aware of the legal uncertainty, will avoid litigation and pay rent for the whole rent period. However, when doing so, the tenant should do so under protest and reserve the right to claim back any excess rent, once the break takes effect. This course of action was expressly sanctioned by Peter Gibson L.J. in *Dun & Bradstreet Software Services (England) Ltd v Provident Mutual Life Assurance Association* [1998] 2 E.G.L.R. 175 at p.180F.

**7–049** Some break clauses make it a condition of a successful break that the tenant pay a "penalty" rent, or equivalent lump sum, by a certain date. A failure to pay such money on time will defeat the operation of the break clause, as happened in *Dun & Bradstreet* (above).

## 12 Waiver of or estoppel of conditions in a tenant's break clause—the tenant's position

**7–050** Since the strict compliance principle can potentially defeat many tenant's break notices it is not unusual to find tenants resorting to the doctrines of waiver or estoppel, to try to save what would otherwise be a defective break notice. In such circumstances, the tenant's argument would need to be that the landlord has waived compliance with a condition or conditions, or is estopped from contending that a break notice is invalid. Experience shows that although waiver or estoppel are frequently raised they rarely succeed. So, for example, in *Bastin v Bidwell* (1880-1881) L.R. 18 Ch.D. 238, at p.249, Kay J. observed the following in relation to the acceptance of rent by the lessor after the time for compliance with a condition precedent has passed:

> "That brings me down to the case of Finch v Underwood. The marginal note is, 'A lease was granted to two, with a proviso for re-entry in case the rent should be in arrear for thirty days, or the tenants or either of them should become bankrupt, or let, assign, or part with the premises, or any part thereof, without license; or if the tenants should not keep the covenants (which were joint and several covenants), one of which was to keep the interior of the property in repair. The landlord covenanted that he would at the expiration of the term (in case the covenants on the tenants' part should have been duly performed), grant to "the tenants, their executors and administrators," a fresh lease.' It appears that the covenants had not been duly performed, but that the landlord had gone on receiving rent with full notice of the circumstances, and it was argued that this amounted to a waiver. Lord Justice Mellish answered that argument in this way: "Receipt of rent waives a forfeiture" (that is, of course, the right of re-entry under a power to re-enter), "because it admits the lease to be subsisting, but does it follow from that that a condition precedent to granting a new lease is waived?" I confess upon consideration that satisfies my mind completely. Supposing there was a waiver of the right of re-entry, it does not seem to me at all to follow that the precedent condition would be waived or affected in the least degree. The condition precedent is this: If you have performed your covenants altogether, then, that being the precedent condition, you shall be entitled to have the renewed lease; if you have not performed your covenants it does not matter that the lessor may have waived his right of forfeiting the lease; the condition precedent has not been performed, and if the precedent condition has not been performed, the right which depends upon it does not arise at all."

Waiver of a condition would require a clear and unequivocal representation by the landlord that the condition in the tenant's break clause will not be relied upon by the landlord, plus reliance upon that representation by the tenant. The ingredients of estoppel are broadly comparable. In *James v Heim Gallery (London) Ltd* [1980] 2 E.G.L.R. 119 (a case involving a rent review notice) Oliver L.J. said, at p.122K: 7–051

> "In order to found a promissory estoppel there has first to be found some clear and unequivocal representation either by words or conduct that the party claimed to be estopped will not rely upon his strict contractual rights. Secondly, the representation must be made with the intention, or at least the knowledge, that it is to be acted upon by the other party by altering his legal position; and thirdly, he must so alter his legal position in reliance upon the representation in such a way that it would be inequitable, or unfair, to permit the party claiming to be estopped from departing from the representation."

7–052 Citing cases where waiver or estoppel arguments have failed might not be very valuable, however one important Court of Appeal ruling justifies mention, namely *West Country Cleaners* (para.7–018). In that case the tenant was in breach of a decorating covenant. The County Court Judge found that the landlord had waived reliance upon the breach, or was estopped from relying upon it. The Court of Appeal disagreed. At its highest the evidence was that the landlord, who lived next door to the premises, knew about the breach and said nothing. Danckwerts L.J. explained, at p.1489C, that the "silence of the landlord here cannot amount to conduct which induced the tenants to change their position in any way".

7–053 Even if a landlord and tenant work closely together and agree a settlement agreement that deals with all the possible dilapidations, there may still be scope for argument that the settlement did not result in a waiver of other conditions. This is what happened in *Expeditors* (paras 7–036–7–040), which travelled to the Court of Appeal, and resulted in a "split" decision.

7–054 Thus, if a tenant wishes to avoid any particular precondition in a break clause then the tenant should obtain an unambiguous written waiver of that condition from the landlord.

7–055 A very recent decision, in which it was found that a defect had been waived, was *MW Trustees Ltd v Telular Corp* [2011] EWHC 104 (Ch). In that case the tenant's break clause stated that the notice "shall be valid only if . . . it is sent by special delivery post or delivered by hand". The tenant served a notice by special delivery that was correct in form, but sent to the old landlord. The notice thus would be ineffective unless the defect was waived. The notice was passed to the current landlord, whose representative emailed, saying "We accept the attached letter and can confirm we are happy for you to break the Lease . . ." Peter Smith J. stated that this went beyond an acknowledgement (which would have enabled the landlord to maintain its opposition to the break) and constituted a waiver of the defect.

## 13 Waiver of conditions in a tenant's break clause—the landlord's position

7–056 The foregoing discussion assumes that the tenant has failed to perform one or more conditions in a break clause, and the landlord wishes to utilise this fact to challenge the validity of the break. However situations sometimes arise where a tenant serves a break notice and then changes its mind, and wishes to remain in its demised premises. What is the position then? Of course, if the landlord agrees to the tenant remaining, there is no problem, they can consensually agree to treat the break as ineffective (although see discussion at paras 6–036–6–040). However the landlord might wish the lease to end, for example because it has negotiated better terms with another tenant, or proposes to include the premises within a development. What if the tenant deliberately fails to perform one or more of the conditions to which the break clause is subject? In those circumstances, the answer will probably lie in the well settled doctrine of waiver of conditions.

The doctrine of waiver of conditions has its roots in the law of specific performance. In *Bennett v Fowler* (1840) 2 Beav. 302, a purchaser obtained a decree of specific performance "if a good title can be made". The master reported that good title could not be made. The vendor sought to use this as justification for not completing. Lord Langdale M.R. disagreed. He said "I am of opinion that the obligation to which a vendor is subject to make out a title is intended for the benefit of the purchaser only, and that if he thinks fit to waive it, he has a right to do so". Brightman J. cited the above passage in *Heron Garage Properties Ltd v Moss* [1974] 1 W.L.R. 148, but declined to hold that the purchaser could waive a condition relating to planning permission, on the basis that this was not solely for the benefit of a purchaser. Planning can affect the seller. However waiver did succeed in *Ganton House Investments v Corbin* [1988] 1 E.G.L.R. 69. In that case Judge Finlay QC decided that a condition as to obtaining satisfactory local searches could be waived by the buyer, being solely for its benefit. The Judge also remarked (at p.72F) that conditions about change of use and alterations would also be capable of waiver by a prospective assignee. 7–057

Utilising the above law, one can say with reasonable confidence, that if a tenant left premises in disrepair after a break date, or failed to pay all the rent, then such breaches of condition would be capable of unilateral waiver by a landlord, and thus not prevent a valid break occurring. 7–058

## 14 Conditions in a landlord's break clause

Hitherto, the focus of much of the discussion has been upon tenants' break clauses. However leases can, and quite often do, contain clauses entitling a landlord to break the lease. The content of these clauses is plainly a matter for negotiation between the parties. Tenants may be loathe to agree an unconditional break. Hence a landlord's break clause often contains language that is referrable to some kind of development. 7–059

As with any break clause, the principle of strict compliance applies to the language used in a landlord's development break clause. Thus the landlord must satisfy whatever test the language of that break clause creates. This can be a trap for the unwary landlord. If a break clause makes it a condition that the landlord "intends" to develop premises then the courts will construe "intends" in the same way as it is construed pursuant to s.30(1)(f) of the Landlord and Tenant Act 1954 (as to which see the approach to "intends" in *Cunliffe v Goodman* [1950] 2 K.B. 237 7–060 at p.253). Moreover, whereas in order to prove ground (f) of s.30(1), a landlord need only show that it has the necessary intention at the date of the hearing (*Betty's Cafes Ltd v Phillips Furnishing Stores Ltd* [1959] A.C. 20) if a break clause requires the landlord to intend development at the date of service of the notice, then the notice will not be valid if the necessary elements of intention cannot be shown as at the time of service. See, further, paras 6–022–6–024 above.

7–061 In order to avoid the problems inherent in the word "intention", a landlord should opt for some word that creates a lesser hurdle. The word "desire" has been shown to create such a lower hurdle. The word occurred in *Aberdeen Steak Houses Group Ltd v Crown Estate Commissioners* [1997] 2 E.G.L.R. 107. In that case Anthony Grabiner QC (sitting as a Deputy Judge) said that " 'desire' is an ordinary English word meaning simply to wish for something".

7–062 Potentially all the words in a development's break clause can be litigated upon. Some examples are identified below:

(i) In *Parkinson v Barclays Bank Ltd* [1951] 1 K.B. 368 the bank let premises to a dental surgeon for 21 years, but with "liberty to determine the said term . . . at the expiration of the first 14 years thereof, if they shall require the premises hereby demised for the purposes of the business carried on by them". The Court of Appeal agreed with Sellers J. that the bank only needed to show they required the premises at some time during the last seven years. Moreover the bank did not have to show they required all of the premises.

(ii) In *Coates v Diment* [1951] 1 All E.R. 890 Streatfield J. decided that a landlords entitlement to determine a lease where the land was required "for building sites or planting or other purposes" did not extend to a requirement to build a sports stadium.

(iii) In *City Offices (Regents Street) Ltd v Europa Acceptance Group Plc* [1990] 1 E.G.L.R. 63 the lease excluded Pt II of the Landlord and Tenant Act 1954. Thus the tenant was very keen to show that the landlord's break clause was invalid, in order to continue its occupation. The tenant pursued its argument, unsuccessfully, to the Court of Appeal by challenging a notice that relied upon "redevelopment or reconstruction".

## 15 The server of a notice cannot rely upon its own wrong

7–063 Sometimes an agreement will permit a termination notice to be served if a condition or conditions have not been satisfied by a particular date. If the condition has not been satisfied because of the server's own breach, then the court will normally find that the server cannot serve a valid termination notice. This is because the court will find that the parties would not have contemplated a party being able to rely upon its own wrong. This proposition was considered by the House of Lords in *Cheall v Association of Professional, Executive Clerical and Computer Staff* [1983] 2 A.C. 180, in particular, at p.188, by Lord Diplock, and was applied by Vos J. in *Extra MSA Services Cobham v Accor UK* (Unreported March 17, 2011), where it was determined that the termination notice was invalid. See, also, *Richco International Ltd v Alfred C Toepfer International GmbH (The Bonde)* [1991] 1 Lloyd's Rep. 136, at p.144, per Potter J. and *Petroplus Marketing AG v Shell Trading International Ltd* [2009] EWHC 1024, at para.17, per Andrew Smith J.

Chapter 8

# The Effect of Exercising a Break Clause

## 1 As between landlord and tenant

(a) *The extent to which the parties are relieved of the further need to perform their covenants*
As was said in *Hankey v Clavering* [1942] 2 K.B. 326 at p.329, per Lord  **8–001**
Greene M.R., break notices served in the proper manner and in the proper form "have of their own force without any assent by the recipient the effect of bringing the demise to an end".

However, on the expiration of a valid break notice difficulties can  **8–002**
often arise in relation to the extent to which the parties are relieved of their need to perform the covenants which they would have been bound to perform if the length of the term had not been cut short. In relation to this difficulty, the answer will always depend upon the construction of the lease in each case. For example, a covenant to yield up the premises in a certain condition at the expiration or some sooner determination of the term will refer to the end of the demise, howsoever it terminates. By contrast, for example, in *Dickinson v St. Aubyn* [1944] K.B. 454, a tenant covenants to paint "in the last quarter of the term" was held to mean the last quarter of the original term of seven years; and, thus, the tenant was not obliged to paint the demised premises in the last quarter of the term shortened by the exercise of the break clause.

(b) *Liability for existing breaches of covenant*
It is sometimes argued that, where a break clause provides that, on the  **8–003**
expiration of the term "this demise and everything herein contained shall cease and be void," then, on termination of the lease, all rights of action for anything contained in the lease are brought to an end. As to this contention, in *Blore v Giuliani* [1903] 1 K.B. 356, at pp.357–358, Wright J. said:

"As a matter of common sense, it is impossible to suppose that it was ever intended by the parties that the liability of the lessees to pay damages for the breaches of covenant already committed by them should be put an end to by mere determination of the lease. I think the point is sufficiently decided against such a contention by the decision in Hartshorne v Watson. There Tindal CJ said: 'The argument [that the covenant to pay rent was gone] would equally apply to a covenant for repairs, or other services to be rendered by the lessee, and is so unreasonable that it cannot be upheld.'"

(c) *Effect on rent review provisions*

**8–004** In *United Scientific Holdings Ltd v Burnley Borough Council* [1978] A.C. 904, the majority of the Law Lords held that there was a general presumption that, in the case of rent review provisions, time is not to be treated as being of the essence. This is because the detriment to the landlord of losing his review altogether by failure to adhere strictly to the stipulated time limit will be wholly disproportionate to the disadvantage of the tenant of a delay in the assessment of the rent.

**8–005** However, Lord Simon said, in *Samuel Properties (Developments) Ltd v Hayek* [1972] 1 W.L.R. 1296, at pp.946C–D:

"Where a rent review clause is associated with a true option (a 'break' clause, for example), it is a strong indication that time is intended to be of the essence of the rent review clause – if not absolutely, at least to the extent that the tenant will reasonably expect to know what new rent he will have to pay before the time comes for him to elect whether to terminate or renew the tenancy."

Similarly, Lord Fraser said, at pp.962F–G:

"The rule [viz. that time is not be treated as being of the essence] would of course be excluded if the review clause expressly stated that time was to be of the essence. It would also be excluded if the context clearly indicated that that was the intention of the parties as for instance where the tenant had a right to break the lease by notice given by a specified date which was later than the last date for serving the landlord's trigger notice. The tenant's notice to terminate the contract will be one where the time limit was mandatory, and the necessary implication is that the time limit for giving the landlord's notice of review must also be mandatory."

**8–006** There are numerous examples of this principle in practice. So, for example, in *Legal & General Assurance (Pension Management) v Cheshire County Council* [1984] 269 E.G. 40 (CA), a 21-year lease contained provisions for the landlord to review the rent at 7 and 14 years and for the tenant to determine the lease at the same points. In each case it was provided that six months' notice should be given, and the landlord

THE EFFECT OF EXERCISING A BREAK CLAUSE 85

considered that for the purposes of the break clause, time was of the essence. The landlord gave notice purporting to invoke the review clause, but gave it less than six months before the review date. The Court of Appeal held that the presumption raised by *United Scientific* that time was not of the essence, was displaced by the fact that the review provision and the break provision were clearly interrelated. Time was of the essence for both provisions, and the landlord's notice of intention to review the rent was accordingly out of time and ineffective.

Other examples include: 8–007

(i) *Al Saloom v Shirley James Travel Service Ltd* (1981) 42 P. & C.R. 181—In that case, there was a clause which provided that the lessee should have the right to give not less than six months' notice in writing prior to the expiration of the third year of the term to determine the lease and a further provision that, subject to the lessee's right of determination, the lessor should have the right, on giving to the lessee not more than 12 months' nor less than six months' notice in writing prior to the expiration of the third year of the term, to review the yearly rent for the time being payable thereunder. Waller L.J. said, at p.185: ". . . both provisions about break and rent review in this case were in the same clause and closely allied to each other. The words 'not less than six months' notice in writing prior to the expiration of the third year of the term' were used for both break and rent review. Whether the word 'interrelated', 'correlated' or 'associated' is used, the implication of the use of the same phrase in the same clause is overwhelming . . . I have no doubt that in both cases here time was of the essence . . ."

(ii) *Coventry City Council v J Hepworth & Sons* (1983) 46 P. & C.R. 170 (CA)—In this case, a 42-year lease of business premises granted in 1953 contained a rent review clause, with a provision that the landlord should give notice in writing on or before December 31, 1974, together with a provision entitling the tenant to break the lease on March 31, 1975 should he so wish. The landlord failed to give the required notice before December 31, 1974, and took no further action over the rent review in the belief that they were out of time. Following the decision in *United Scientific*, they sought to implement the rent review clause, arguing that time was not after all of the essence. The Court of Appeal held that the combined effect of the requirement for a landlord's trigger notice and the corresponding right for the tenant to break the lease, did amount to contra indications in the lease such as to displace the presumption that time was not of the essence. The landlord was accordingly debarred from operating the clause.

(iii) *William Hill (Southern) Ltd v Govier* [1984] 1 E.G.L.R. 121— Here, a 40-year lease of office premises contained a rent review clause and a tenant's break clause. The relevant review date was December 25, 1982 and the relevant part of the review clause provided that, if the landlord and the tenant failed to agree the reviewed rent nine months before the review date, then either party could within a further period of one month refer the question of the amount of rent to a chartered survey. The tenant's break clause was operable by at least three months' previous written notice to expire on December 25, 1982. No steps to agree a reviewed rent or to refer the matter for determination were taken prior to the review date. The tenant argued that time was of the essence for the reference to the chartered surveyor and that the right to review was lost. Mr Edward Evans-Lombe QC, sitting as a Deputy High Court Judge, held that on the true construction of the lease, the rent review clause and the break clause were linked in a way which indicated an intention by the parties that the tenant should know whether the landlord was seeking an increase in rent, and, accordingly, time was of the essence of the provision requiring a reference to a chartered surveyor within the month succeeding the commencement of the ninth month before the review date, and the right to review had been lost.

(iv) *Central Estates Ltd v Secretary of State for the Environment* (1996) 72 P. & C.R. 482 (CA)—The subject lease provided that either party might determine the lease at the end of the 21st year by six months' previous written notice; further, that either party might require a rent review in the 14th, 21st, 28th and 35th year by serving a notice in writing 12 months in advance of the following period. There was therefore an interrelation of the break clause and the rent review procedure in respect of the 21st year with September 29, 1991 being the latest date for service of notice requiring rent review and March 29, 1992 for service of notice determining the lease. The plaintiff wrote to the defendant on April 14, 1992 giving notice of a rent review to take effect on September 29, 1992. The defendant refused to accept the notice as being out of time. The plaintiff issued proceedings for a declaration that time was not of the essence and that the letter of April 14, 1992 was valid and effective. The plaintiff was successful at trial, but on appeal the Court of Appeal held that the presumption that the timetable specified in a rent review clause for completion of the various steps for determining the rent payable in respect of the period following the review date is not of the essence, was displaced. Time was held to be of the essence if the timetable laid down by the lease allowed a period after the service of the rent review notice in which to consider whether or not to serve a break notice. For, if time was not of the essence, the period allowed for the service of the break notice (as to which time was of the essence) was eliminated or eroded.

## THE EFFECT OF EXERCISING A BREAK CLAUSE

It should be recalled, however, that it is not in every case where a rent **8–008** review clause is associated with an option to determine that time is of the essence of the rent review clause. Rather, in this scenario, there is a rebuttable presumption that time is to be of the essence. So, in *Coventry City Council v J Hepworth & Sons Ltd* (1983) 46 P. & C.R. 170, at p.176, Lawton L.J. said:

> ". . . where you have a triggering off of a rent review provision started by the landlord, followed by an option given to the tenant to break the lease if he so wishes, then time is to be presumed to be of the essence of the agreement, unless there are contra-indications."

Likewise in *Metrolands Investments Ltd v Dewhurst Ltd* (1986) 52 **8–009** P. & C.R. 232, at p.244, Slade L.J. said:

> ". . . in a case where a lease contains a break clause as well as a rent review clause and the timetables of the two clauses are closely interlocked, the interrelation of the two causes is *likely* to suffice as a contra-indication sufficient to rebut the ordinary presumption—though everything must depend on the wording of the particular lease." (Emphasis as in original.)

In *Metrolands* itself, the lease under consideration had an unusual **8–010** feature. The event in the rent review clause as to which the tenant contended that time was of the essence was the *actual obtaining* of an arbitrator's decision in relation to the new rent. It was readily conceivable, therefore, that the landlord might have acted with irreproachable promptness and diligence in setting in motion the rent review arbitration machinery provided for by the lease, but that, without any fault whatever on the landlord's part, the arbitrator's decision might not have been obtained until after the specified date. Further, any potential hardship to the tenant which might otherwise have arisen through tardy action by the landlord in initiating the rent review could be eliminated or, at least, substantially mitigated by the tenant initiating such action itself. For these reasons, the ordinary presumption that, where a rent review clause is associated with a break clause, time is of the essence of the rent review clause, was rebutted.

The ordinary presumption was also rebutted in *Edwin Woodhouse* **8–011** *Trustee Co Ltd v Sheffield Brick Co Plc* [1984] 1 E.G.L.R. 130. In that case, a lease provided for a rent review on December 25, 1982. The reviewed rent was to be:

> "such sum or amount as the parties shall agree as being or (failing agreement at least six months next before [the rent review date]) as a Valuer appointed by the parties or (failing appointment at least two months next before [the rent review date]) nominated at the request of either party by the President . . . shall determine as being the yearly rental value of the demised premises . . ."

His Honour Judge Finlay QC (sitting as a Deputy Judge of the High Court) held that, on a true construction of the lease, there were no clear terms which indicated that the landlord was under a duty to serve anything in the nature of a trigger notice in order to set the rent review in motion. Nor was it possible to find within the lease anything which imposed on the landlord any such duty. The consequence of this was that time was not of the essence in relation to any implied obligation upon the landlord to serve a notice to bring into operation the rent review provisions of the lease.

(d) *The landlord's entitlement to claim double rent*

8–012  Insofar as is relevant, s.1 of the Landlord & Tenant Act 1730 provides:

"In case any Tenant ... for any Term ... shall wilfully hold over any Lands ... after the determination of such term ... and after Demand made, and Notice in Writing given, for delivering the Possession thereof, by his ... Landlords ... then and in such Case such Person ... so holding over, shall, for and during the Time he ... shall so hold over, or keep the Person ... intitled, out of Possession of the said Lands ... Pay to the Person ... so kept out of Possession ... at the Rate of double the yearly Value of the Lands ... for so long as the same are detained, to be recovered in any of His Majesty's Courts of Record, by Action of Debt ...."

8–013  Section 1 of the Landlord & Tenant Act 1730 is to be read together with s.18 of the Distress for Rent Act 1737 which, insofar as is relevant, provides:

"And whereas great inconveniences have happened and may happen to landlords, whose tenants have power to determine their leases, by giving notice to quit the premises by them that hold them, and yet refusing to deliver up the possession, when the landlord has agreed with another tenant for the same; be it further enacted ... that ... in case any tenant ... shall give notice of his ... intention to quit the premises ... at a time mentioned in such notice, and shall not accordingly deliver up the possession thereof at the time in such notice contained; that then the said tenant ... shall from thenceforward pay to their landlord ... double the rent ... which he ... should otherwise have paid; to be levied, sued for and recovered at the same times and in the same manner, as the single rent ... before the giving of such notice could be levied, sued for or recovered; and such double rent ... shall continue to be paid, during all the time such tenant ... shall continue in possession as aforesaid."

8–014  In *Oliver Ashworth (Holdings) Ltd v Ballard (Kent) Ltd* [2000] Ch. 12 (CA), the Court of Appeal considered the question whether in circumstances where a landlord asserts that a break notice is invalid and treats the lease as continuing, and the tenant remains in occupation beyond the period specified in the break notice, the landlord is entitled to double rent under s.18 of the Distress for Rent Act 1737. Answering this question in the negative, the Court of Appeal held that, having regard to the 1737 Act as a whole, including the preamble and recitals, read with the related Landlord & Tenant Act 1730, a landlord's entitlement to double rent under s.18 arose only where the tenant held over as a trespasser after serving a valid notice to quit and the landlord treated him as a trespasser. As was said by Laws L.J., at pp.38–39:

> "Reading the Acts of 1730 and 1737 as a whole including the latter's preamble and recitals, it is to my mind entirely clear that the legislature was concerned only to compensate landlords for the potential loss of rent arising where a tenant holds over against the landlords' insistence that he should comply with his own notice to quit".

## 2 As regards an underlessee

(a) *Where the tenant exercises the break clause*
In *Pennell v Payne* [1995] Q.B. 192, at p.197, Simon Brown L.J. said:  **8–015**

> "At common law, the general rule is that, when the head tenancy comes to an end, any sub-tenancy derived out of it also automatically and simultaneously comes to an end."

This general rule does not apply in cases of surrender and merger. See **8–016** s.139 of the Law of Property Act 1925 and the speech of Lord Denning in *St Marylebone Property Co Ltd v Fairweather* [1963] A.C. 510, at p.546.

In *Pennell*, Simon Brown L.J. held, at pp.202H–203A, that a tenant's **8–017** upwards notice to quit had the effect of bringing to an end any subtenancy granted by the tenant. He also added, at pp.199H–200A, that:

> "A tenant's exercise of his right to determine a lease under a break clause is precisely equivalent to his determining a periodic tenancy by notice to quit: in each case a term which would otherwise have continued by operation of law is being voluntarily determined."

From this, it can be divined that the exercise of a break clause by the **8–018** tenant does not have the same effect as a surrender and, accordingly, on termination by a head tenant under a break clause, any sub-tenancy derived out of the head lease also ends. This point is reiterated in the speech of Lord Millett in *Barrett v Morgan* [2000] 2 A.C. 264, at pp.270–272.

In *PW & Co v Milton Gate Investments Ltd* [2004] Ch. 142, at paras **8–019** 58–85, Neuberger J. (as he then was) held that it is not possible to contract out of the rule in *Pennell* (viz. a sub-tenancy cannot survive the determination of a head lease unless the head lease is determined by a consensual arrangement not provided for by the terms of the head lease itself).

**8–020** The rigour of the rule in *Pennell* may be mitigated by the fact that the sub-tenant can, in an appropriate case, sue the tenant for breach of the express/implied covenant for quiet enjoyment, in circumstances where the tenant has exercised a break clause and brought the sub-tenancy to an end.

(b) *Where the landlord exercises the break*

**8–021** In a similar fashion to the exercise of a tenant's break clause, on the termination of a head lease on the exercise of a landlord's break clause, any underlease created by the head tenant automatically falls with it.

**8–022** As a matter of practice, an intended undertenant should always inspect the head lease because, where there is no break clause in the underlease, the superior landlord's termination of the head lease does not make the head tenant liable to the undertenant for breach of the express/implied covenant for quiet enjoyment. In this regard, see *Kelly v Rogers* [1892] 1 Q.B. 910, at p.912 in which an underlessee sued the head tenant for breach of his covenant for quiet enjoyment after the superior landlord forfeited the head lease for non payment of rent. Lopes L.J. said:

> "In order to maintain an action on a covenant for quiet enjoyment in the present form, it is necessary to shew some act of interruption by the defendant or some person claiming by, through, or under him, against whose act he covenants. The plaintiff is unable to prove any such act here. The only act of interruption was by the superior landlord. I think it clear that this is not within the covenant."

Chapter 9

# Business Tenancies

**1 Introduction**

Recent statistics (from the British Property Federation) indicate that about three commercial property leases in every ten incorporate a break clause, and this proportion is increasing. This chapter is concerned with all those leases where the Landlord and Tenant Act 1954 ("the 1954 Act") Pt II applies, and has not been excluded. Various questions arise, both in relation to existing leases incorporating break clauses, and where applications are made for the renewal of leases where the landlord or the tenant seeks the inclusion of a break clause. These questions are reviewed in the following sections.  **9–001**

**2 A landlord's break notice and the 1954 Act**

Section 24(1) of the 1954 Act begins, "A tenancy to which this part of this Act applies shall not come to an end unless terminated in accordance with the provisions of this part of this Act . . . ." Thus, if the landlord serves a break notice, which successfully determines the contractual term of a lease, the tenant will remain entitled to occupy the demised premises, subject to the 1954 Act applying thereto. If the landlord wishes to determine the tenant's continuation of the tenancy then it will need to serve a notice pursuant to s.25 of the 1954 Act.  **9–002**

Although (as explained in Ch.1) at common law a notice to quit is a different creature to a break notice, the 1954 Act treats the two in the same way. Thus, by s.69(1) of the 1954 Act, "'Notice to quit' means a notice to terminate a tenancy (whether a periodical tenancy or a tenancy for a term of years certain) given in accordance with the provisions (whether express or implied) of that tenancy".  **9–003**

Whether it was possible for a landlord to operate a break clause and serve a s.25 notice, using one document, was considered by the Court of  **9–004**

Appeal in *Scholl Manufacturing Ltd v Clifton (Slim-Line) Ltd* [1967] Ch. 41. In that case the Court of Appeal decided that if a single notice satisfied both the contractual requirements of a lease and the requirements of s.25 of the 1954 Act, then that notice was valid for those purposes. *Scholl* has been applied since, including by the Court of Appeal in *Blunden v Frogmore Investments Ltd* [2002] 2 E.G.L.R. 29. In *Scholl* the Court of Appeal (including Harman L.J.) observed that Harman J. (as he then was) was correct to decide that a notice could operate as a valid break notice, but not as a valid s.25 Notice. (See Harman J.'s decision in *Weinbergs Weatherproofs v Radcliffe Paper Mills Co* [1958] Ch. 437).

**9–005** If a landlord serves a single notice, that seeks to serve as both a break notice and a s.25 notice, then the court will look at the particular notice that has been served, and ask itself whether the notice is valid in whole or in part, or entirely invalid. If a single notice is invalid as a break notice then the s.25 notice portion will be bound to be ineffective, because the fixed term of the lease will continue and therefore the date for expiry of the s.25 notice will be premature. Thus the prudent course is normally to serve separate documents, serving one as the break notice and the other as the s.25 notice. If these two documents are served at the same time then the court will infer that they were served in the correct order. This point arose in *Keith Bailey Rogers & Co v Cubes Ltd* (1975) 31 P. & C.R. 412. On p.416 of his judgment Templeman J. said:

"When a landlord has power to serve two notices in sequence, notice exercising the break clause followed by notice under Section 25, and he launches both notices on the same day, it is to be assumed that the notices were delivered in the correct sequence and it is not necessary to pester the postman to see which notice was delivered first."

**9–006** All of the above comments assume that the landlord for the purposes of the 1954 Act is the same person as the landlord who is to serve the break notice. This will not necessarily be the case, because the landlord for the purposes of the 1954 Act has a special meaning (see s.44 of the 1954 Act).

**9–007** Furthermore the above text also assumes that the notice or notices seek to determine the lease in its entirety, i.e. extending to all the premises the subject of the lease. Although the common law permits a notice determining part of the premises demised by a lease, the 1954 Act does not similarly provide. A s.25 notice must relate to the entire premises that are demised by a lease. This inconsistency produced an injustice in the case of *Southport Old Links Ltd v Naylor* [1985] 1 E.G.L.R. 66. In that case the lease of a golf course contained a break clause in relation to the course itself, but not the club house. The landlord served a valid break notice, relating to the course. However its s.25 notice, which related to the course but not to the club house, was found by the Court of Appeal to be invalid. As Oliver L.J. said, at p.67:

"There is simply no machinery in the [1954] Act for determining a business tenant's tenancy of a part, or separate parts, of a holding, leaving the tenancy of the remainder to continue and putting the tenant in the position of seeking a new lease— or, I suppose, new leases—of the parts of the holding in respect of which his tenancy has been determined."

Notably, Oliver L.J. added, at p.69, that the 1954 Act may be "defective" in not making provision for this situation. However, the Law Commission, after reviewing the position, has decided not to recommend a change in the law. Presently, therefore, if a landlord is desirous of achieving what the landlord in *Southport Old Links* was not able to achieve, then great care must be taken to ensure that the lease is drafted appropriately, e.g. by including a provision to the effect that the exercise of the break clause in relation to part of the demise creates a separate and distinct tenancy of that part for a term of years expiring upon the date specified in the break notice (which tenancy can then properly be terminated by a notice under s.25 of the 1954 Act).

## 3 The inclusion of a landlord's break notice in a new lease

For various reasons, including harmonising lease expiry, where site assembly for future development is concerned, landlords quite often seek to include a break clause in a new lease that is granted pursuant to the 1954 Act. Such a clause is often referred to as a "redevelopment break clause", although it may not be conditional upon the landlord establishing a future intent or desire to redevelop. Instead it may be unfettered in scope, e.g. operable at any time on, say, six months' prior notice.   9–008

The courts have considered when, and in what terms, such a landlord's break clause should be included in a new lease on several occasions. The reasoning in the cases contains subtly different nuances. It is worth examining some of the more important cases chronologically, as follows:   9–009

- (i) *Adams v Green* [1978] 2 E.G.L.R. 46—This case concerned an application for a new lease of a shop occupied as a confectioner and tobacconist. The landlord and the tenant agreed on a term of 14 years, but the landlord, who owned the row of all 12 shops, sought the inclusion of a break clause exercisable on two years' prior notice. This was on the basis that the row of shops was "rather elderly", and that the landlord wanted to preserve a future right to redevelop. Seven other shops had already been let with two year break clauses. The County Court Judge refused the landlord's request for a break clause, but the Court of Appeal acceded to it, on the basis that it was exercisable in the event of a subsequent redevelopment. Stamp L.J., who delivered the main judgment, said as follows:

> "It was no part of the policy — and I underline the word 'policy' — of the 1954 Act to give security of tenure to a business tenant at the expense of preventing redevelopment
>
> . . .
>
> and if the break clause is included the tenant will nevertheless be protected by the terms of the Act itself from the effect of any notice not given bona fide for the purpose for which it is intended, but if the tenancy is determined by a notice it will be open to the tenant to apply for a new tenancy, and the then landlords, in order to sustain an objection to granting a new tenancy, would have to prove the intention to redevelop."

(ii) *J H Edwards & Sons Ltd v Central London Commercial Estates Ltd* [1984] 2 E.G.L.R. 103—This case concerned two shops in Tottenham Court Road, London. The landlord wished to cater for the possibility of future redevelopment by including break clauses in the new leases of the shops. The County Court Judge refused the landlord's request. Again the Court of Appeal disagreed and incorporated break clauses. Fox L.J. said:

> "If it is likely that the superior landlord for the time being may wish to develop the property, then (since it is not the policy of the 1954 Act to inhibit development) he should not be saddled with a lease which may prevent such development. In that connection a present intention to redevelop immediately is not necessary: (see Adams v Green . . . . Amika Motors v Colebrook Holdings Limited . . . .). Accordingly it seems to me that it must be wrong in principle, in the present case, to order the grant of new leases for such substantial periods of 12 and 10 years respectively without development 'break' clauses
>
> . . .
>
> In considering what would be proper leases in the circumstances of this case I think that the predominant considerations are two. First, that so far as reasonable the lease should not prevent the superior landlord from using the premises for the purposes of development. Secondly, that a reasonable degree of security of tenure should be provided for the tenant. Those considerations are to some degree in conflict. The function of the Court is to strike a reasonable balance between them in all the circumstances of the case
>
> . . .

I also bear in mind that it is not the purpose of the Act to give a tenant saleable assets but rather to protect him in the conduct of his business . . ."

(iii) *Becker v Hill Street Properties Ltd* [1990] 2 E.G.L.R. 78—This case concerned a dentist seeking a new lease of his surgery that occupied part of a building in Upper Wimpole Street, London. The landlords had acquired the whole of the building at an auction, with the potential for a profitable residential conversion. The County Court Judge refused the landlord's request for a break clause, but instead granted the tenant a lesser term of four and one-half years, until the dentist anticipated retiring. Although the Court of Appeal considered that the Judge had misdirected himself they upheld his conclusion.

(iv) *Davy's of London (Wine Merchants) Ltd v City of London Corporation* [2004] 3 E.G.L.R. 39—This case was an appeal from the County Court, involving further evidence, that was heard by Lewison J. (as he then was). After reviewing various authorities the Judge said at para.68:

> "I must of course balance the redevelopment aspirations of the landlords against the business interests of the tenant; not allowing the latter to frustrate the former. Any tenant running a serious business needs to plan ahead. It is not much consolation to a businessman to be told that if the landlord is not ready to redevelop, the break clause will not be exercised. The uncertainty paralyses business planning. Of course, when the break clause comes to be exercised, Davy's will be entitled to put the landlords to proof of their intentions. The changes both to the substantive provisions of the 1954 Act and to the procedure of the Court should mean that proceedings for the grant of a new tenancy (or for termination of a tenancy without renewal) will be less protracted than in the past."

In *Davy's,* the Judge also pointed out, at para.21 of his judgment, that:

> "The case was presented to the Judge, and the appeal was presented to me, on the basis that the Court was exercising a discretion under Section 35 of the Act, rather than reaching a decision under Section 33. The difference between the two is that the former requires the Court, in reaching its decision, to have regard to the terms of the current tenancy. The latter does not, and it leaves the question of reasonableness at large. I do not have to decide which of the two is the applicable section; but it is fair to say that the cases do not speak with one voice."

The issue as to whether s.33 or s.35 governs the question as to the inclusion of a break clause remains unresolved at the present time.

9–010 It appears to follow from the above cases that a judge should not make a decision that prevents a development being carried out. However, depending on the particular circumstances, the judge might decide that a development should be delayed. The stronger the landlord's present evidence regarding development, the more likely it is that a break clause will be incorporated that is operable at an early stage.

### 4 The inclusion of a tenant's break clause in a new lease

9–011 Perhaps surprisingly, there is no reported case dealing with the situation discussed in this section. The comments of the authors must inevitably, therefore, be somewhat speculative. However it is suggested that, in the event of a conflict between the tenant wishing for an early break clause, and the landlord opposing the same, the court is more likely to side with the tenant rather than the landlord. The principal basis for this observation is the approach of the Deputy High Court Judge (H.H.J. Micklem) in *CBS United Kingdom Ltd v London & Scottish Properties Ltd* [1985] 2 E.G.L.R. 125. That case concerned an application for the new tenancy of factory premises, where the main issue was the length of the term to be granted. The tenant sought a substantially shorter term than the landlord. The case was notable for the representation of tenant and landlord, being respectively Lord Neuberger and Lord Justice Lewison, when practising at the Bar. After reviewing the arguments put before him, the Deputy High Court Judge concluded that since the purpose of the 1954 Act was to protect the tenant, it was logical that the protection should extend for no longer than the tenant sought.

9–012 For completeness it might be observed that a Circuit Judge at the Colchester and Clacton County Court appeared unimpressed by the decision in *CBS* (see *Ganton House Investments v Crossman Investments* [1995] 1 E.G.L.R. 239). However, it is submitted that the reasoning in the *CBS* case is more persuasive. Of course if the tenant is overly ambitious in requesting a very short term, or a particularly short break clause, then different considerations might apply.

### 5 A tenant cannot break a lease and then seek a new lease under the 1954 Act

9–013 If a lease incorporates a tenant's break clause and is within the protection of the 1954 Act, a tenant might be tempted to break the lease and then apply (per a s.26 request) for a new lease. The temptation could be strong if the passing rent was higher than the market rent, and the tenant wished to achieve a rent reduction. However strong the temptation, the tenant should resist it. The Court of Appeal decided in *Garston v Scottish Widows Fund* [1998] 1 W.L.R. 1583 that if a tenant broke a lease, then that tenant could not serve a s.26 request seeking a new lease. As Nourse L.J. said, at p.1589:

> "One of the main purposes of Part II of the Act of 1954 is to enable business tenants, where there is no good reason for their eviction, to continue in occupation after the expiration of their contractual tenancies. It is not a purpose of the Act to enable a business tenant who has chosen to determine his contractual tenancy to continue in occupation on terms different from those of that tenancy."

**6 The position of sub-tenants**

If a head lease ends, because of the operation of a break clause, any underlease carved out of the head lease also ends. See *Barrett v Morgan* [2000] 2 A.C. 264. However, if the 1954 Act applies to the underlease, then the undertenant can serve a s.26 request seeking a new tenancy.

**9–014**

Chapter 10

# Agricultural Tenancies

As regards lettings of agricultural land, the common law relating to the relationship of landlord and tenant is modified by statute, in particular, the Agricultural Holdings Act 1986 ("the 1986 Act") and the Agricultural Tenancies Act 1995 ("the 1995 Act"). The 1986 Act applies only to agricultural holdings, as defined by s.1 thereof. The 1986 Act also applies only to an agreement entered into before September 1, 1995. Save for limited exceptions, any agricultural tenancy created on or after September 1, 1995 will be a farm business tenancy governed by the 1995 Act. As may be expected, these statutes restrict the manner in which a contract for an agricultural tenancy or a farm business tenancy (as the case may be) can be determined. 10–001

## 1 Termination of contracts for agricultural tenancies

The 1986 Act is a consolidating Act which repeals and replaces the Agricultural Holdings Act 1948, the Agricultural Holdings (Notices to Quit) Act 1977, the Agricultural Holdings Act 1984 and other amending statutes. Certain provisions in the Agricultural Act 1947 and the Agricultural (Miscellaneous Provisions) Act 1954 remain in force. The 1986 Act has been supplemented by the Agricultural Act 1986 and amended by the Agricultural Holdings (Amendment) Act 1990. The 1986 Act applies to tenancies of agricultural holdings whenever created, agreements whenever created, agreements whenever made and other things whenever done but, in general, and subject to exceptions, that Act does not apply in relation to a tenancy beginning on or after September 1, 1995. See s.98(1) of the 1986 Act and s.4(1) of the 1995 Act. 10–002

An "agricultural holding" is defined in s.1(1) of the 1986 Act as the aggregate of the land (whether agricultural land or not) comprised in a contract of tenancy which is a contract for an agricultural tenancy, not being a contract under which the land is let to the tenant during his continuance in any office, appointment or employment held under the 10–003 landlord. The phrase "contract for an agricultural tenancy" is defined in s.1(2) as follows:

> "a contract of tenancy relating to any land is a contract for an agricultural tenancy if, having regard to—
> (a) the terms of the tenancy,
> (b) the actual or contemplated use of the land at the time of the conclusion of the contract and subsequently, and
> (c) any other relevant circumstances,
>
> the whole of the land comprised in the contract, subject to such exceptions only as do not substantially affect the character of the tenancy, is let for use as agricultural land."

**10-004** One of the principal features of the 1986 Act is the security of tenure it offers agricultural tenants. As regards security of tenure, the scheme of the 1986 Act is based upon there being a tenancy from year to year. So, s.2 imposes restrictions on letting agricultural lend for lesser periods of time than from year to year; and s.3 provides for tenancies for two years or more to continue from year to year. Importantly, for present purposes, s.25 controls the length of the notice to quit which can be given to a tenant from year to year; and s.26 imposes restrictions on the operation of a notice to quit. These latter provisions will be considered more fully in the following paragraphs.

**10-005** Section 25(1) of the 1986 Act requires that a notice to quit an agricultural holding is invalid if it expires before the expiry of 12 months from the end of the current year of tenancy. This rule applies to notices to quit the whole or part of an agricultural holding (s.31) and despite any contractual provisions to the contrary (s.25(1)). It applies equally to notices by tenants as well as notices by landlords. See *Flather v Hood* (1928) 44 T.L.R. 698 (a decision on s.25(1) of the Agricultural Holdings Act 1923). The effect of this provision is "merely a fetter" on the right of the landlord or the tenant to give a valid notice to quit in all cases except those specified in the proviso. See *Gladstone v Bower* [1960] 12 Q.B. 384, at p.394, per Pearce L.J.

**10-006** Section 25(1) of the 1986 Act also extends to break notices. So much is clear from the decision of the House of Lords in *Edell v Dulieu* [1924] A.C. 38, at p.41, where Viscount Cave L.C. said that a "notice to quit" within the meaning of s.28 of the Agriculture Act 1920 (containing almost identical provisions to s.25 of the 1986 Act) "includes a notice purporting to terminate the tenancy". Similarly, in *Gladstone v Bower* [1960] 1 Q.B. 170, at p.177, Diplock J. said that s.25(1) of the Agricultural Holdings Act 1923 (again, almost identical in terms to s.25 of the 1986 Act) "applies to any tenancy where the tenant's leasehold interest is determinable by notice, such as determination under a 'break' clause in a lease for a fixed-term." Thus, if a party to a contract for an agricultural tenancy wishes to exercise a break clause then, subject to certain statutory exceptions (set out in para.10–008), and notwithstanding any provision to the contrary in the contract of tenancy of the holding, a break notice will be invalid if it purports to terminate the tenancy before the expiry of 12 months from the end of the then current year of tenancy.

**10–007** The requirement for 12 months' notice can be waived by the recipient of the notice. In *Elsden v Pick* [1980] 1 W.L.R. 898, the landlord accepted the tenant's notice to quit which gave less than 12 months' notice. The landlord was allowed to obtain an order for possession when the tenant later attempted to rely on the invalidity of his own notice. As Shaw L.J. said, at p.906C, the relevant statutory provisions do not prohibit, as between landlord and tenant, a waiver of the requisite term of notice.

**10–008** There are a limited number of statutory exceptions from the time limit laid down by s.25(1) of the 1986 Act. Thus, s.25(1) does not apply:

(i) Where the tenant is insolvent (s.25(2)(a)).

(ii) To a notice given in pursuance of a provision in the contract of tenancy authorising the resumption of possession of the holding or some part of it for some specified purpose other than the use of land for agriculture (s.25(2)(b)).

(iii) To a notice given by a tenant to a sub-tenant (s.25(2)(c)).

(iv) Where the tenancy is one which by virtue of s.149(6) Law of Property Act 1925 has taken effect at a term of 90 years determinable by one month's notice expiring on a quarter day, following a relevant death or marriage (s.25(2)(d)).

(v) Where on a reference under s.12 of the 1986 Act with respect to an agricultural holding, the arbitrator determines that the rent payable in respect of the holding shall be increased, a notice to quit the holding by the tenant at least six months before it purports to take effect shall not be invalid by virtue of s.25(1) if it purports to terminate the tenancy at the end of the year of the tenancy beginning with the date as from which the increase of rent is effective (s.25(3)).

(vi) Where the Agricultural Land Tribunal has, on an application with respect to an agricultural holding under para.9 of Pt II of Sch.3 to the 1986 Act (i.e. bad husbandry), granted a certificate specifying a minimum period of notice for termination of the tenancy (not being a period of less than two months) and directed that the period shall apply instead of the period of notice required in accordance with s.25(1) (Section 25(5)).

(vii) In relation to a tenancy entered into before March 25, 1947, to a notice to quit given by the Secretary of State under the provisions of the tenancy where possession is required for naval, military or air force purposes or to a notice given by a corporation carrying on a railway, dock, canal, water or other undertaking, or by a government department or local authority, for certain specified purposes (s.98(2) and para.4 of Sch.12).

(viii) Where an arbitrator has specified a date for the termination of the tenancy by notice to quit under art.7 of the Agricultural Holdings (Arbitration on Notices) Order 1987 (SI 1987/710).

**10–009** It should be observed that s.25(2)(b) of the 1986 Act refers to "some specified purpose" which is distinct from a "specific purpose". A general provision allowing the landlord to break the contract for agricultural tenancy and to resume possession "for any non-agricultural purpose" is common and falls within the exception. See, for example, *Paddock Investments Ltd v Lory* [1975] 2 E.G.L.R. 5, where a lease of agricultural land contained a power for the landlord to resume possession of any portion of the land "for the purpose of development only under the Agricultural Holdings Act 1948" upon giving the tenant at least two months' notice.

**10–010** As well as ensuring compliance with the requirements of s.25(1) of the 1986 Act, where a party seeks to exercise a break clause contained in the contract for an agricultural holding, care should be taken that the break notice also complies with any other contractual and common law requirements (i.e. relating to the form and content of the notice, the persons who may give and receive the notice, the service of notice, etc). These latter requirements are considered elsewhere in this work. However, in any case where the landlord seeks to exercise a break clause in a contract for an agricultural tenancy, and none of the Cases in Pt I of Sch.3 of the 1986 Act apply, then he should make it clear and unambiguous on the face of the break notice that he intends to terminate the tenancy subject to s.26(1) of the 1986 Act (on which see para.10–011), irrespective of any breaches by the tenant. See *Cowan v Wrayford* [1953] 1 W.L.R. 1340, at p.1343, per Somervell L.J. (concerning s.24 of the Agricultural Holdings Act 1948).

**10–011** Section 26(1) of the 1986 Act contains an important restriction on the ability of a landlord to break a contract for an agricultural tenancy. Thus, where notice to quit an agricultural holding or part of an agricultural holding is given to the tenant, and not later than one month from the giving of the notice to quit the tenant serves on the landlord a counter-notice in writing requiring that s.26(1) shall apply to the notice to quit, then, subject to s.26(2), the notice to quit shall not have effect unless, on an application by the landlord, the Agricultural Land Tribunal consent to its operation. Under s.27(1) of the 1986 Act, the Agricultural Land Tribunal shall consent under s.26 to the operation of a notice to quit an agricultural holding or part of an agricultural holding if, but only if, they are satisfied as to one or more of the matters mentioned in s.27(3), being a matter or matters specified by the landlord in his application for their consent.

The matters mentioned in s.27(3) are: 10–012

(i) That the carrying out of the purpose for which the landlord proposes to terminate the tenancy is desirable in the interests of good husbandry as respects the land to which the notice relates, treated as a separate unit (s.27(3)(a)).

(ii) That the carrying out of the purpose is desirable in the interests of sound management of the estate of which the land to which the notice relates forms part or which that land constitutes (s.27(3)(b)).

(iii) That the carrying out of the purpose is desirable for the purposes of agricultural research, education, experiment or demonstration, or for the purposes of the enactments relating to smallholdings (s.27(3)(c)).

(iv) That the carrying out of the purpose is desirable for the purposes of the enactments relating to allotments (s.27(3)(d)).

(v) That greater hardship would be caused by withholding than by giving consent to the operation of the notice (s.27(3)(e)).

(vi) That the landlord proposes to terminate the tenancy for the purpose of the land being used for a use, other than for agriculture, not falling within Case B (s.27(3)(f)).

Further, even if the Agricultural Land Tribunal are satisfied as mentioned in s.27(1) of the 1986 Act, the Tribunal shall withhold consent under s.26 to the operation of the notice to quit if in all the circumstances it appears to them that a fair and reasonable landlord would not insist on possession (s.27(2)). The Agricultural Land Tribunal may also impose conditions on any consent under s.26 to ensure that the land to which the notice to quit relates will be used for the purpose for which the landlord proposes to terminate the tenancy (s.27(4)). 10–013

It should be noted that an agricultural tenant possesses certain statutory rights to claim compensation on termination of his lease under ss.60–78 of the 1986 Act. Compensation is payable to a tenant of an agricultural holding under the 1986 Act when, inter alia, his tenancy is "terminated". By s.96 of the 1986 Act, "termination" is defined as meaning the cesser of the contract of tenancy by reason of effluxion of time or from any other cause. It is clear that this covers the situation where either the landlord or the tenant has given notice to quit or a break notice. In *Re Disraeli Agreement* [1939] 1 Ch. 382 (a case concerning the tenant's right to compensation under the Agricultural Holdings Act 1923), a contract for an agricultural tenancy contained a proviso that the landlord could resume possession of any portion of the land so leased in case it was required for building purposes without compensation, but with a proportionate reduction in the rent attributable to the area so taken 10–014 by the landlord. Cross J. held that this proviso deprived the tenant of its right to compensation for disturbance and, thus, was rendered invalid. See also *Coates v Diment* [1951] 1 All E.R. 890 and *Parry v 1,000,000 Pigs Ltd* [1980] 260 E.G. 281.

## 2 Termination of a farm business tenancy

**10–015** The 1995 Act introduced a new code applicable to "farm business tenancies" as defined in s.1(1) thereof. One of the principal features of the 1995 Act is that the tenant has virtually no security of tenure other than that bargained for with the landlord. Unlike the position under the 1986 Act, there is little interference with the parties' common law rights to bring their tenancy to an end, or with the general law on notices to quit/ break notices. Save for limited exceptions, a tenancy beginning before September 1, 1995 cannot be a farm business tenancy because the statute is not retrospective.

**10–016** For the purposes of the 1995 Act, a tenancy is a "farm business tenancy" if (a) it meets the "business conditions" together with either the "agriculture condition" or the "notice conditions", and (b) it is not a tenancy which, by virtue of s.2 of the 1995 Act cannot be a farm business tenancy (s.1(1)). The "business conditions" are: (a) that all or part of the land comprised in the tenancy is farmed for the purposes of a trade or business, and (b) that, since the beginning of the tenancy, all or part of the land so comprised has been so farmed (s.1(2)). The "agriculture condition" is that, having regard to: (a) the terms of the tenancy, (b) the use of the land comprised in the tenancy, (c) the nature of any commercial activities carried out on that land, and (d) any other relevant circumstances, the character of the tenancy is primarily or wholly agricultural (s.1(3)). The "notice conditions" are: (a) that, on or before the relevant day (i.e. the earlier of the day on which the parties enter into the farm business tenancy or the beginning of the tenancy), the landlord and the tenant each gave the other a written notice (i) identifying (by name or otherwise) the land to be comprised in the tenancy or proposed tenancy, and (ii) containing a statement to the effect that the person giving the notice intends that the tenancy or proposed tenancy is to be, and remain, a farm business tenancy, and (b) that, at the beginning of the tenancy, having regard to the terms of the tenancy and any other relevant circumstances, the character of the tenancy was primarily or wholly agricultural (s.1(4)).

**10–017** A tenant under a farm business tenancy has only limited statutory security of tenure, unlike the case of a tenant of an agricultural holding; and it is common for fixed-term farm business tenancies to contain break clauses permitting one or other or both of the parties to determine the tenancy before its term date.

**10–018** A farm business tenancy for a term of more than two years shall, instead of terminating on the term date, continue (as from that date) as a tenancy from year to year, but otherwise on the terms of the original tenancy so far as applicable, unless at least 12 months before the term date (i.e. in relation to a fixed-term tenancy, the date fixed for the expiry of the term) a written notice has been given by either party to the other of his intention to terminate the tenancy (s.5(1)). This provision has effect notwithstanding any agreement to the contrary (s.5(4)). The requirement of notice to terminate does not apply to a tenancy for a term of two years exactly nor to a tenancy of less than two years (both of which will expire by effluxion of time under the common law).

Where a farm business tenancy is a tenancy from year to year, a notice to quit the holding or part of the holding shall (notwithstanding any provision to the contrary in the tenancy) be invalid unless: (a) it is in writing; (b) it is to take effect at the end of a year of the tenancy; and (c) it is given at least 12 months before the date on which it is to take effect (s.6(1)). Section 6(1) does not apply in relation to a counter-notice given under s.140(2) of the Law of Property Act 1925 (apportionment of conditions on severance of reversion, s.6(3)). Where, by virtue of s.5(1) of the 1995 Act, a farm business tenancy for a term of more than two years is to continue (as from the date fixed for the expiry of the term) as a tenancy from year to year, a notice to quit which complies with s.6(1) and which is to take effect on the first anniversary of the term date shall not be invalid merely because it is given before the date fixed for the expiry of the term (s.6(2)). These requirements apply equally to notices given by landlords as they do to notices from tenants. They only apply when the farm business tenancy is a tenancy from year to year, and not, for example, where the tenancy is month to month or quarter to quarter. See *Land Settlement Association v Carr* [1944] K.B. 657 concerning the Agricultural Holdings Act 1923 in which the contract of tenancy was for a period of 364 days. **10–019**

Section 7 of the 1995 Act is of particular relevance where a farm business tenancy of more than two years contains a break clause. It provides that, where a farm business tenancy is a tenancy for a term of more than two years, any notice to quit the holding or part of the holding given in pursuance of any provision of the tenancy shall (notwithstanding any provision to the contrary in the tenancy) be invalid unless it is in writing and is given at least 12 months before the date on which it is to take effect (s.7(1)). This provision does not apply in relation to a counter-notice given by the tenant under s.140(2) of the Law of Property Act 1925 (apportionment of conditions on severance of reversion) (s.7(2)) and does not apply to a tenancy which, by virtue of s.149(6) of the Law of Property Act 1925 (lease for life or lives or for a term determinable with life or lives or on the marriage of, or formation of a civil partnership by, the lessee), takes effect as such a term of years as is mentioned in that provision (s.7(3)). Obviously a break notice given pursuant to a break clause within the farm business tenancy will also need to comply with any other contractual and/or common law requirements. **10–020**

It may be noted that s.36(1) of the 1995 Act contains its own provisions as to the service of any notice or other document which is required **10–021** or authorised to be given under that Act (s.36(1)). Any such notice or other document is duly given to a person if it is delivered to him; it is left at his proper address; or it is given to him in a manner authorised by a written agreement made, at any time before the giving of the notice, between him and the person giving the notice (s.36(2)). Transmission by fax is insufficient (s.36(3)). Further, where (a) a notice or other document to which this section applies is to be given to a landlord under a farm business tenancy and an agent or servant of his is responsible for the control of the management of the holding, or (b) such a document is to be given to a tenant under a farm business tenancy and an agent or servant of his is responsible for the carrying on of a business on the holding, the notice or document is duly given if it is given to that agent or servant (s.36(5)).

10–022 In a similar manner to the position under the 1986 Act, the tenant under a farm business tenancy is entitled, on the termination of the tenancy, to obtain from his landlord compensation in respect of certain matters. See s.16(1) of the 1995 Act. Under s.38(1), "termination" is defined as meaning the cesser of the tenancy by reason of effluxion of time or from any other cause. This is apt to include the termination of a farm business tenancy upon exercise of a break clause.

10–023 From a practical perspective, a landlord can avoid the restrictions imposed by ss.5–7 of the 1995 Act: (i) by entering into a farm business tenancy for a fixed-term of two years or less, and/or (ii) by not allowing a fixed-term tenancy of more than two years to lapse and, thereby, to become a tenancy from year to year.

Chapter 11

# Residential Tenancies

This chapter will consider the position under:  **11–001**

(i) Rent Act 1977 protected tenancies;
(ii) Assured tenancies;
(iii) Assured shorthold tenancies; and
(iv) Contractual tenancies without any statutory security of tenure.

## 1 Termination of Rent Act protected tenancies

A "protected tenancy" is a contractual tenancy satisfying the definition **11–002** contained in s.1 of the Rent Act 1977 ("the 1977 Act"), namely that it is a tenancy under which a dwelling-house (which may be a house or part of a house) is let as a separate dwelling. Such a tenancy is a protected tenancy unless it is prevented from being so by one of the exceptions contained in ss.4–16 and 24(3) of the 1977 Act. A "statutory tenancy" arises after the termination of the protected tenancy if the protected tenant occupies the dwelling-house previously subject to the protected tenancy as his residence; see s.2(1) of the 1977 Act. Since January 15, 1989, it has not been possible to create a Rent Act protected tenancy.

The effect of these provisions is to make a distinction between: (i) a **11–003** protected tenant who is in possession of a dwelling-house under a contractual tenancy (but still enjoys the protection of the 1977 Act); and (ii) a statutory tenant whose only right to occupy the dwelling-house is given to him by the 1977 Act. The statutory tenancy will arise immediately upon the determination of the protected tenancy (provided, of course, that the tenant continues to occupy the dwelling-house as his residence). Thus, termination of a protected tenancy by operation of a break clause will not, of itself, give the landlord a right to go to court for an order for possession. The landlord of a Rent Act tenant is not entitled, even after termination of the protected tenancy, to recover possession against the will of the tenant in the exercise of his common law rights.

**11–004** Here, two points may be observed:

(i) It is not possible to contract out of the 1977 Act, whether in respect of rent, the recovery of possession or any other matter. See, for example, *Foster v Robinson* [1951] 1 K.B. 149 (a decision under the Increase of Rent and Mortgage Interest (Restrictions) Act 1920).

(ii) Section 3(1) of the 1977 Act provides that a person who retains possession of a dwelling-house as a statutory tenant must observe and is entitled to the benefit of all the terms and conditions of the original contract of tenancy so far as they are consistent with the provisions of the 1977 Act. In other words, the terms of the statutory tenancy are generally the same as the terms of the protected tenancy. However, terms of the original contractual tenancy which are inconsistent with the provisions of the 1977 Act (e.g. a term of the original tenancy that it is terminable on notice) are not carried over into the statutory tenancy. So, in *Shuter v Hersh* [1922] 1 K.B. 438 (another case concerning the Increase of Rent and Mortgage Interest (Restrictions) Act 1920), Scrutton L.J. observed, at p.450, that the statutory tenancy continues "whether or not a notice to quit is given".

**11–005** If a landlord is desirous of determining a protected tenancy by operation of a break clause, the landlord must comply with all common law and contractual requirements and, further, ensure that he complies with the obligations laid down by the relevant provisions of the Protection from Eviction Act 1977 and that the break notice contains the material prescribed by the Notices to Quit (Prescribed Information) Regulations 1980. As to these, see paras 11–019—11–020 below.

**11–006** Once the protected tenancy has been terminated, the landlord can only recover possession of the dwelling-house by obtaining an order for possession from the court. Section 98 of the 1977 Act provides that, subject to the provisions of Pt VII thereof, a court is not to make an order for possession of a dwelling-house currently let on a protected tenancy or a statutory tenancy unless it considers it reasonable to make such an order and either: (i) the court is satisfied that suitable alternative accommodation is available for the tenant or will be available when the order in question takes effect; or (ii) the circumstances are specified in any of the cases in Pt I of Sch.15 to the 1977 Act.

## 2 Termination of assured tenancies

**11–007** Part I of the Housing Act 1988 ("the 1988 Act") came into force on January 15, 1989 and introduced two new types of tenancy, namely, the assured tenancy and the assured shorthold tenancy. Subject to certain exceptions in Sch.1 of the 1988 Act (e.g. tenancies where the rent is over £100,000.00 per annum), an assured tenancy is a tenancy under which a dwelling-house is let as a separate dwelling if and so long as: (a) the tenant or, in the case of joint tenants, each of the joint tenants is an individual; and (b) the tenant or, in the case of joint tenants, at least one of the tenants occupies the dwelling-house as his only or principal term; and (c) the tenancy does not fall within one or more of the specific exceptions; see s.1(1) of the 1988 Act.

An assured tenancy cannot be brought to an end by the landlord except by: (a) the execution of an order obtained from the court for possession of the dwelling-house under s.7 or s.21; (b) obtaining an order of the court under s.6A (a demotion order); or (c) the exercise of the power held by the landlord in fixed-term tenancies to determine tenancy in certain circumstances; see s.5(1) of the 1988 Act. Under s.45(1) of the 1988 Act, a fixed-term tenancy is any tenancy other than a periodic tenancy. It follows, therefore, that a landlord may terminate a fixed-term assured tenancy by operating a break clause. **11–008**

However, under s.5(2) of the 1988 Act, if an assured tenancy which is a fixed-term tenancy comes to an end otherwise than by virtue of (i) an order of the court of the kind mentioned in ss.5(1)(a) or (b) or any other order of the court; or (ii) a surrender or other action on the part of the tenant, then, subject to s.7, the tenant shall be entitled to remain in possession of the dwelling-house let under that tenancy and, subject to s.5(4), his right to possession shall depend upon a periodic tenancy arising by virtue of s.5(2). Thus, a statutory periodic tenancy will arise where a fixed-term tenancy is terminated under a break clause. **11–009**

Under s.5(3) of the 1988 Act, the statutory periodic tenancy: **11–010**

(i) takes effect in possession immediately on the coming to an end of the fixed-term tenancy;

(ii) is deemed to have been granted by the person who was the landlord under the fixed-term tenancy immediately before it came to an end to the person who was then the tenant under that tenancy;

(iii) comprises the same dwelling-house as was let under the fixed-term tenancy;

(iv) is one under which the periods of the tenancy are the same as those for which rent was last payable under the fixed-term tenancy; and

(v) is otherwise on the same terms as the fixed-term tenancy immediately before it came to an end, except that any term which makes provision for determination by the landlord or the tenant shall not have effect while the tenancy remains an assured tenancy. So, for example, a break clause contained in the original fixed-term contractual tenancy will not be carried over into the statutory periodic tenancy.

**11–011** The court cannot make an order for possession of a dwelling-house let on an assured tenancy except on one or more of the 16 statutory grounds in Sch.2 to the 1988 Act. Of these, Grounds 1—8 are mandatory grounds for possession (i.e. if the court is satisfied that any of these grounds is established, it must make an order for possession); and Grounds 9—16 are discretionary grounds for possession (i.e. if the court is satisfied that any of these grounds is established, it may make an order for possession if it considers it reasonable to do so); see s.7(4) of the 1988 Act.

**11–012** It should be observed that the 1988 Act does not place restrictions on the tenant's right to terminate the tenancy in any manner which would be valid at common law. Thus, a tenant's break clause will be effective to determine a fixed-term assured tenancy.

### 3 Termination of assured shorthold tenancies

**11–013** By operation of s.19A of the 1988 Act, any assured tenancy which: (a) is entered into on or after the day on which that section came into force (i.e. February 28, 1997) otherwise than pursuant to a contract made before that date; or (b) comes into being by virtue of s.5 of the 1988 Act on the coming to an end of an assured tenancy which was itself entered into on or after February 29, 1997 (otherwise than pursuant to a contract made before that date), is an assured shorthold tenancy unless it falls within one of the exceptions found in Sch.2A to the 1988 Act.

**11–014** Apart from the general statutory grounds for possession applicable to assured tenancies, in the case of assured shorthold tenancies, s.21 of the 1988 Act provides further mandatory grounds for possession. So far as fixed-term assured shorthold tenancies are concerned, under s.21(1) of the 1988 Act, on or after the coming to an end of the fixed term, a court shall make an order for possession of the dwelling-house if it is satisfied: (a) that the shorthold tenancy has come to an end and no further assured tenancy (whether shorthold or not) is for the time being in existence, other than an assured shorthold periodic tenancy (whether statutory or not); and (b) the landlord or, in the case of joint landlords, at least one of them has given to the tenant not less than two months' notice in writing stating that he requires possession of the dwelling-house. Where an order for possession under s.21(1) is made in relation to a dwelling-house let under an assured shorthold tenancy, the order may not be made so as to take effect earlier than six months after the beginning of the tenancy (s.21(5)).

**11–015** It is thought that, during the fixed term of an assured shorthold tenancy, a landlord can successfully claim possession relying on s.21 of the 1988 Act if there is a contractual break clause in the tenancy allowing the landlord to recover possession before the expiry of the term. Further, if there is a break clause allowing the landlord to terminate the tenancy on giving notice within the fixed term, then, depending on the wording used in the tenancy agreement itself, service of a notice pursuant to s.21(1) of the 1988 Act may be sufficient to activate the break: see *Fawaz v Aylward* (1997) 29 H.L.R. 408.

**11–016** In *Fawaz* the plaintiff landlords granted the defendant tenant an assured shorthold tenancy of a property for a term of one year. Clause 7 of the tenancy agreement provided that: "The landlord or the tenant may determine the tenancy hereby created at or at any time after the end of the first 6 months of the tenancy provided one month's prior notice in writing of such desire is given to the other party." On February 13, 1996, the landlords served on the tenant a notice pursuant to s.21(1) of the 1988 Act requiring possession of the dwelling after April 14, 1996. Upon expiry of the notice, the landlords brought proceedings for possession of the property. The tenant defended the claim on the basis that the notice served on him had not validly determined the term of the tenancy in accordance with cl.7 of the tenancy agreement. The judge held at first instance that the notice was sufficient both to determine the tenancy and to comply with s.21(1), and made an order for possession. The tenant appealed to the Court of Appeal.

**11–017** Dismissing the appeal, Cazalet J. said, at p.412:

"Here the notice specified a specific date within the time span of clause 7, the break clause of the tenancy agreement. The notice states itself to be an exercise of the right to obtain possession. On the face of the notice possession is required: it is not a possible exercise of such a right. Further the document is clearly a notice to determine the tenancy

. . .

I consider that the notice served by the [landlords] was clear and unambiguous. It indicated in terms that possession of the premises was required. In my view the judge was right to hold, as he did, that it was a valid notice both under clause 7 of the tenancy agreement and under section 21(1)(b). The requirement of possession was only consistent with the determination of the fixed term of the tenancy agreement, with due notice being given under clause 7 – one month – and in respect of section 21(1)(b) – not less than two months."

## 4 Termination of contractual tenancies without any statutory security of tenure

**11–018** Before a landlord can succeed in obtaining a possession order against an unprotected tenant who lacks any security of tenure (e.g. where the annual passing rent exceeds the assured shorthold tenancy threshold of £100,000.00) or a Rent Act protected tenant, he must ensure that the contractual fixed term has come to an end. Here, consideration should be given to the effect of s.5 of the Protection from Eviction Act 1977 ("the 1977 Act").

**11–019** Section 5(1) of the 1977 Act provides that no notice by a landlord or a tenant to quit any premises let (whether before or after the commencement of this Act) as a dwelling shall be valid unless: (a) it is in writing and contains such information as may be prescribed, and (b) it is given not less than four weeks before the date on which it is to take effect. The 'prescribed information' to be included in such a notice to quit is contained in the Schedule to the Notices to Quit etc (Prescribed Information) Regulations 1988.

**11–020** Whether this provision applies in the case of a fixed-term tenancy containing a break clause exercisable by the service of a break notice depends on what is meant by the phrase "notice to quit". If "notice to quit" is apt to cover a break notice then, in the case of any tenancy to which s.5 of the 1977 Act applies, a break notice must comply with the requirements of ss.5(1)(a) and (b) (as well as any other contractual and common law requirements). There is no authority on this point, although it is thought that this construction of s.5 of the 1977 Act is the correct one, particularly in light of *Edell v Dulieu* [1924] A.C. 38 and *Gladstone v Bower* [1960] 1 Q.B. 170 (on the meaning of "notice to quit" in s.28 of the Agriculture Act 1920 and s.25(1) of the Agricultural Holdings Act 1923). See Ch.10, paras 10–005 and 10–006.

# Chapter 12

# Drafting Break Clauses

**1 General remarks**

The proportion of commercial leases incorporating break clauses is now about 30 per cent. They are included at the behest of landlords, of tenants, or both of them. They are included for many reasons. For tenants, break clauses introduce flexibility. For landlords, they can assist with site assembly, particularly where a major development might be in prospect. **12–001**

Whatever the immediate or long term estate management benefit that is sought to be gained from break clauses it is important to remember that the presence of a break clause in a lease can have economic influences. Thus the presence of such a clause is likely to affect the value of a landlord's reversion. In addition, with any lease that incorporates provisions for rent review, the presence of a break clause is likely to affect the rent payable on review. This means that if a break clause is incorporated in a lease, the rent review provisions should be examined to consider the valuation consequences that the break clause may have on the reviewed rent. A key point will be whether or not the break clause is incorporated in the hypothetical lease. This point should be addressed by the inclusion of express wording in the clause of the lease that deals with the rent reviews. **12–002**

The Code for Leasing Business Premises (2007) recommends that "the only pre-conditions to tenants exercising any break clauses should be that they are up to date with the main rent, give up occupation and leave behind no continuing sub-leases. Disputes about the state of the premises, or what has been left behind or removed, should be settled later (like with normal lease expiry)". However in practice this recommendation is often not followed. Since the Code has no statutory force the parties to a lease are free to draft break clauses in any way they wish, and there is plenty of scope for parties and their advisers to use their negotiating and drafting skills to gain an advantage. Quite often this advantage is not obvious until the break clause falls to be operated. **12–003**

**12–004** Broadly speaking those acting for parties seeking the benefit of break clauses should strive to achieve clauses that are as simple as possible whereas those who will be the recipient of break notices should strive to make break clauses as complicated and as qualified as possible.

## 2 Matters to address when drafting a break clause

**12–005** The specific matters to be considered in the course of drafting a break clause include:

(i) Who is to have the benefit of the clause? If the benefit of a tenant's break clause is to be personal to the tenant, then can the tenant re-acquire the benefit by an assignment from an assignee?

(ii) If the benefit of the break clause is given to joint landlords or joint tenants, then each will need to authorise the operation of the clause, unless the clause gives one party express authority to operate the clause on behalf of the others.

(iii) When is the break clause to be exercisable? Is it to be at any time (a 'rolling break'), at any time after a specified date, or operative on one or more specified dates?

(iv) If the break notice is to expire in the middle of a rental period, the legal adviser will want to consider whether or not to include an apportionment provision.

(v) What pre-conditions are to be specified as necessary before the break clause can be exercised? When are the pre-conditions to be satisfied? (At the time of service of the break notice, when it expires, or both?)

(vi) How is the break notice to be served? Are there any particular persons that have to be served, e.g. someone who is not the landlord or the tenant?

(vii) Should the break notice be in any particular form (for example on paper of a particular colour)? And, should the break notice contain any particular words?

(viii) When a lease is granted to a tenant who is given an option to determine, and the tenant sublets to a third party, it is essential for the tenant to reserve a right to terminate the sub-lease otherwise he cannot effectively terminate the head lease without possibly incurring liability in damages to the superior landlord (for breach of the covenant to yield up vacant possession) and/or to the third party (for breach of the covenant for quiet enjoyment). A head tenant's right to terminate the sublease can be

# DRAFTING BREAK CLAUSES

made conditional upon the head tenant's desire to end the head lease by means of the following type of wording: "The power of the landlord [i.e. the headlessor] to terminate this lease is exercisable only if the landlord desires to terminate the superior lease under which he holds."

(ix) In the case of business tenancies, the draftsman should be aware of the incidence of compensation under s.37 of the Landlord and Tenant Act 1954. If, for example, the landlord has the right to break the lease at the expiry of the 14th year of the term, rather than at the expiry of, say, the 12th year of the term, the tenant's right to compensation on quitting may be halved.

(x) Also, in the case of business tenancies, the draftsman may want to consider whether the lease should contain an express provision to the effect that service of a notice under s.25 of the Landlord and Tenant Act 1954 shall be sufficient notice for the purposes of exercising a landlord's break clause. If the break clause relates only to part of the demise, particular care must be taken to bear in mind the points mentioned at para.9–007.

Some break clause precedents for landlords and tenants are included in Appendices 1–4. **12–006**

Chapter 13

# Practical Advice as to the Exercise of Break Clauses and Disputes as to Their Exercise

**1 Points for the tenant when exercising a break clause**

(a) *Preconditions*

A tenant or its adviser, before exercising a break clause, should draw up a list of all the pre-conditions that need to be satisfied. If any work to the premises is required, then efforts should be made to engage with the landlord as to the extent of any work that is sought by the landlord. Any such work should then be carried out well before the deadline prescribed by the break clause. Once the work has been carried out, the landlord should be invited to confirm that he is satisfied with the work.  **13–001**

If the landlord declines to engage with the tenant on any work that is needed then the tenant will need to get its own advice (probably from a surveyor) as to the work that is needed. This work should then be undertaken well before the break date.  **13–002**

If there are other pre-conditions, then they will need to be satisfied; whether they involve the provision of vacant possession, the payment of rent or other sums, or whatever. If there is a dispute between landlord and tenant as to the amount that is payable (e.g. a dispute over the quantum of service charges) or a dispute over the period for which payment is due (e.g. because it is not clear whether the tenant should pay a full quarters rent, or only a proportion) then the prudent course is to pay the maximum amount alleged by the landlord to be payable. However that payment should be made under protest and with a reservation of the right to claim back the overpayment (see para.7–048).  **13–003**

(b) *The break notice itself*

13–004 A copy of the break notice should be prepared in draft, ensuring it complies with all the requirements, and mirrors the language, of the lease. There are no prizes for creative drafting. The notice should be checked to ensure that it identifies the correct recipient(s). If there is any conceivable doubt as to who the landlord might be then a Land Registry search should be undertaken and/or recent rent demand notices examined. A good many negligence cases have resulted from service of a notice on the wrong landlord, either because there has been a simple change of landlord or because that landlord has granted a concurrent or overriding lease, inserting an intermediate landlord between the original landlord and the tenant.

13–005 If at all possible, the draft break notice should be independently checked by a colleague. A considerable number of cases on break notices have arisen because solicitors have made a mistake in its drafting and are litigating in the hope that the courts will rule that the mistake is not fatal to the operation of the break clause.

(c) *Service of the break notice*

13–006 The provisions in the lease referring to service of a break notice should be carefully checked. Plainly, these provisions should be followed. If in doubt, copies of the break notice should be sent to various possible addresses, each without prejudice to the validity of the others. Evidence as to service should be preserved until it is no longer relevant. Furthermore, if possible, an acknowledgement as to receipt of the break notice should be obtained from the landlord.

**2 Points for the landlord on receiving a tenant's break notice**

(a) *Pre-conditions in a tenant's break clause*

13–007 Until the Court of Appeal's decision in *Fitzroy House Epworth Street (No. 1) Ltd v Financial Times Ltd* [2006] 1 W.L.R. 2207 there was a belief, amongst many landlords and their advisers, that they had a duty to act reasonably, and to co-operate with a tenant who had served or was going to serve a break notice. It was believed that this assistance extended to saying what money was owed by the tenant, or what work was needed to ensure compliance with a condition in the break clause. That belief was fostered by the decision in *Commercial Union Life Insurance Co Ltd v Label Ink Ltd* (2001) L. & T.R. 380. However that decision has now been over-ruled by *Fitzroy*. Unless the word "reasonably" appears in a break clause, thereby expressly requiring the landlord to act reasonably, then compliance with pre-conditions in a break clause requires a purely objective assessment. For example, if the pre-condition is whether "the tenant has materially complied with all its obligations under this lease . . .", as was the case in *Fitzroy*, then this simply involves asking whether the tenant has complied with its obligations, and if not whether the non-compliance is material.

If a landlord declines to answer any questions from the tenant, who is seeking assistance as to what the landlord requires to achieve compliance, this should not be a factor in deciding whether there has been material compliance. Thus, the advice to be given to a landlord, assuming that he wants the lease to continue, is not to render advice or assistance to the tenant. If advice is given it is likely to amount to a representation, which if relied upon by the tenant, could create an estoppel. If the landlord declines to assist the tenant with its enquiries, then the tenant is likely to have to indulge in "overkill", by doing more work to the premises than is probably needed.

**13–008**

(b) *The tenant's break notice*
The landlord should check the following:

**13–009**

(i) that the notice has been served by the proper party, and on the proper party;

(ii) that the notice has been served in time; and

(iii) that the content of the notice fully complies with the break clause.

Since the landlord does not need to act reasonably there is no obligation upon him to point out to the tenant any flaws in the notice or other defect in the purported exercise of the break clause. Indeed in those cases where only one opportunity is afforded to the tenant to break the lease, and the landlord wishes to retain the tenant, then it would be commercial folly for the landlord to say anything. Silence is golden.

**13–010**

## 3 Points for the landlord when exercising a break clause

(a) *Preconditions*
A landlord or his advisor, before exercising a break clause, should draw up a list of any pre-conditions that need to be satisfied. In comparison with the tenant's break clause, in which pre-conditions requiring compliance with all or some of the tenant's covenants are commonplace, pre-conditions to a landlord's break clause are less common.

**13–011**

One type of condition that is not unusual is the "redevelopment" condition. If a landlord has fettered his right to an absolute break, with wording referring to a development, then he needs to carefully assess exactly what the language of the break clause requires. If the wording of the clause "mirrors" the language of s.30(1)(f) of the 1954 Act, there is a potential trap. Section 30(1)(f) only requires the landlord to show his intention at the time of the hearing. Introducing the language of s.30(1)(f) into a break clause will normally require showing the intention at the break date or (depending upon the drafting) on the date when the notice

**13–012**

is served. If the clause only refers to a "desire" to develop, then this creates a far lower evidential hurdle than "intends". See, further, paras 6–022–6–024 and 7–057–7–060.

(b) *The break notice itself*
13–013 A copy of the break notice should be prepared in draft, ensuring that it complies with all the requirements, and mirrors the language, of the lease. As with tenants break notices, there are no prizes for creative drafting.
13–014 The notice should be checked to ensure that it identifies the correct recipient(s). If possible, the draft break notice should be independently checked by a colleague.

(c) *Service of the break notice*
13–015 The provisions in the lease referring to service of a break notice should be carefully checked and followed. If in doubt, copies of the break notice should be sent to various possible addresses, each without prejudice to the validity of the others.
13–016 Evidence as to service should be preserved until it is no longer relevant. If possible an acknowledgement as to receipt of the break notice should be obtained from the tenant.

## 4 Points for the tenant on receiving a landlord's break notice

(a) *Preconditions in a landlord's break clause*
13–017 The law relating to pre-conditions in a tenant's break clause applies here. Thus, compliance with any pre-condition requires a purely objective assessment, unless the language of the clause itself introduces a subjective element.

(b) *The landlord's break notice*
13–018 The tenant should check the following:

(i) that the notice has been served by the proper party, and on the proper party;

(ii) that the notice has been served in time; and

(iii) that the content of the notice fully complies with the break clause.

13–019 As with the tenant's break notice, there is no obligation upon the tenant to point out to the landlord any flaws in the notice, or other defect in the purported exercise of the break clause.

## 5 Litigation tactics—the tenant's exercise of a break clause

If a tenant has sought to exercise a break, but there is a dispute as to whether that exercise has been successful, then failing a negotiated settlement between the parties, litigation is needed to break the deadlock. For practical reasons the claimant is often the landlord. This is because the tenant will have vacated the premises and stopped paying rent. There will normally be no reason for the tenant to incur the costs of litigation. In contrast, the landlord will still be demanding rent, which the tenant will not be paying. In addition, there may be pressure from third parties to cause the landlord to wish to break the impasse. A common situation is the rating authority pressing the landlord for payment of rates, on the basis that the tenant has informed the authority that its lease has come to an end. Litigating against the tenant may be a necessary step in order to prove to the rating authority that the landlord is contending that the lease is still alive, and that it is the tenant that remains liable for rates. Production of the claim form in the relevant Magistrates Court is normally successful in persuading Magistrates to adjourn proceedings. **13–020**

If the landlord issues proceedings then it has a choice as to the content of that claim. It can be just for unpaid rent, and other monies that are due pursuant to the lease. This has the advantage of simplicity, since the Particulars of Claim need only recite the lease, the obligations to pay and the failure to effect payment. The drawback, however, is that the tenant's defence will then allege that the lease is broken, perhaps merely referring to the break notice. The landlord will then need to serve a Reply which explains why the break was ineffective. In turn, the tenant may need to serve a Rejoinder, which explains why the break is effective. This elongates the pleadings stage of the case, and is also rather 'messy' procedurally. In order to speed up the pace of the litigation, in addition to the landlord claiming unpaid monies pursuant to the lease, it is possible to claim a declaration that the lease remains unbroken. The Particulars of Claim served by the landlord will then refer to the details of the dispute regarding the break, and say why the tenant's contentions (which have presumably already been identified in correspondence) are wrong. An example of a landlord's Particulars of Claim that embodies claims both for unpaid monies and declaratory relief appears as a precedent in Appendix 5. **13–021**

## 6 Litigation tactics—the landlord's exercise of a break clause

If the landlord has sought to exercise a break clause, whether it be pursuant to an unconditional break or a redevelopment clause, and the tenant disputes the validity of that break, either the landlord or the tenant **13–022** could initiate litigation. In practice the landlord is normally the claimant, because the tenant is content to remain in occupation. Furthermore, the maximum commercial advantage for the tenant is often gained by inactivity. This forces the landlord not only to issue proceedings but also to try to have these expedited. If the landlord does initiate proceedings, then its Particulars of Claim will normally seek declaratory relief (that the lease has been broken) plus possession of the premises.

**13–023** The tenant may decide to initiate proceedings, seeking a declaration that its lease remains effective, where it is the tenant's desire to seek to achieve clarity as to its position. Plainly, if there remains a doubt as to whether a lease has been successfully broken, then the tenant is unable to make any long term plans for its business in the relevant premises.

## Appendix 1

# Break Clause for the Landlord–On One or More Specified Dates

1.1 The following definitions apply:  A1–001

Break Date(s) — [Either insert a specific date or dates, or cross refer to other date(s) in the Lease, e.g. the day before a rent review date(s)].
Break Notice — Notice in the form set out in the Schedule hereto.

1.2 The Landlord may terminate this Lease by serving a Break Notice on the Tenant at least [Insert Period] months before the specified Break Date.

1.3 [A Break Notice shall only be effective if, at the Break Date the Landlord desires/intends to demolish/develop/refurbish all (or a part) of the Premises].

1.4 [Subject to Clause 1.3], following service of a Break Notice, this Lease shall terminate on the Break Date.

1.5 Termination of this Lease on the Break Date shall not affect any other right or remedy that either party may have in relation to any earlier breach of this Lease.

**The schedule—the form of the landlord's break notice**

To [Insert Name and Address of Tenant]  A1–002

Re: A lease date [Insert Date] of premises at [Insert Address of Premises] ("the Lease").

We refer to Clause [Insert Clause Number] of the Lease. By this notice the Landlord hereby exercises its right to terminate the Lease pursuant to the above Clause on [Insert the Break Date].

........................................

[On behalf of, and with the authority of] the Landlord

Appendix 2

# Break Clause for the Landlord– Incorporating a Rolling Break

1.1 In this Clause, the following definitions apply:

Break Date — the date stated in the Break Notice on which this Lease shall terminate.

Break Notice — Notice in the form set out in the Schedule hereto.

1.2 Subject to the provisions in the remainder of this Clause, the Landlord may terminate this Lease at any time by serving a Break Notice on the Tenant at least [Insert Period] before the Break Date.

1.3 The Break Notice must specify the Break Date, but shall not specify as the break date any date which is earlier than date [Insert the earliest Break Date].

1.4 [The Break Notice shall only be effective if, at the Break Date, the Landlord desires/intends to demolish/develop/refurbish/all (or a part) of the Premises].

1.5 Subject to Clause 1.4, following service of a Break Notice, this Lease shall terminate on the Break Date.

1.6 Termination of this Lease on the Break Date shall not affect any other right or remedy that either party may have in relation to any earlier breach of this Lease.

**The schedule—the form of the landlord's break notice**

To [Insert Name and Address of Tenant]

Re: Lease dated [Insert Date] of premises at [Insert Address of Premises] ("the Lease").

We refer to Clause [Insert Clause Number] of the Lease. By this notice the Landlord exercises its right to terminate the Lease pursuant to the above Clause on [Insert the Break Date].

........................................

[On behalf of, and with the authority of] the Landlord

Appendix 3

# Break Clause for the Tenant–On One or More Specified Dates

1.1 The following definitions apply: A3–001

    Break Date(s) — [Either insert a specific date or dates, or cross refer to other date(s) in the Lease, e.g. the day before a rent review date(s)].

    Break Notice — Notice in the form set out in the Schedule hereto.

1.2 The Tenant may terminate this Lease by serving a Break Notice on the Landlord at least [Insert Period] months before the specified Break Date.

1.3 [The right to serve a Break Notice is personal to the original Tenant, provided the term of this Lease has never been assigned].

1.4 A Break Notice shall only be effective if, at the Break Date:

    (i) The Tenant has paid all rent and other monies due under the Lease.
    (ii) Vacant possession of the whole of the Premises is given.
    (iii) There is no [material] [substantial] breach of any of the Tenant covenants in the Lease [relating to the state of repair and condition of the premises] [relating to, and say what particular covenant(s) must be complied with].
    (iv) The Tenant pays, on or before the Break Date, the sum of [insert the sum].

1.5 Subject to Clause 1.4, following service of a Break Notice, this Lease shall terminate on the Break Date.

1.6 Termination of this Lease on the Break Date shall not affect any other right or remedy that either party may have in relation to any earlier breach of this Lease.

**The schedule—the form of the tenant's break notice**

**A3–002** To [Insert Name and Address of Landlord]

Re: A lease dated [Insert Date] of premises at [Insert Address of Premises] ("the Lease").

We refer to Clause [Insert Clause Number] of the Lease. By this notice the Tenant hereby exercises its right to terminate the Lease pursuant to the above Clause on [Insert the Break Date].

......................................

[On behalf of, and with the authority of] the Tenant

Appendix 4

# Break Clause for the Tenant– Incorporating a Rolling Break

1.1 In this Clause, the following definitions apply:

Break Date — the date stated in the Break Notice on which this Lease shall terminate.
Break Notice — Notice in the form set out in the Schedule hereto.

1.2 Subject to the provisions in the remainder of this Clause, the Tenant may terminate this Lease at any time by serving a Break Notice on the Landlord at least [Insert Period] before the Break Date.

1.3 [The right to serve the Break Notice is personal to the original Tenant, provided that the term of this Lease has never been assigned].

1.4 The Break Notice must specify the Break Date, but shall not specify as the Break Date any date which is earlier than [Insert the earliest Break Date].

1.5 The Break Notice shall only be effective if:

(i) The Tenant has paid all rent and other monies due under the Lease.
(ii) Vacant possession of the whole of the Premises is given.
(iii) There is no [material] [substantial] breach of any of the Tenant covenants in the Lease [relating to the state of repair and condition of the premises] [relating, and say what particular covenant(s) must be complied with].
(iv) The Tenant pays, on or before the Break Date, the sum of [Insert the sum].

1.6 Subject to Clause 1.5, following service of a Break Notice, this Lease shall terminate on the Break Date.

1.7 Termination of this Lease on the Break Date shall not affect any other right or remedy that either party may have in relation to any earlier breach of this Lease.

**The schedule—the form of tenant's break notice**

A4–002  To [Insert Name and Address of Landlord]

Re: Lease dated [Insert Date] of premises at [Insert Address of the Premises] ("the Lease").

We refer to Clause [Insert Clause Number] of the Lease. By this notice the Tenant exercises its right to terminate the Lease pursuant to the above Clause on [Insert the Break Date].

........................................

[On behalf of, and with the authority of] the Tenant

Appendix 5

# Particulars of Claim
# Landlord's Claim for Declaration, Etc

<u>IN THE HIGH COURT OF JUSTICE</u>   <u>Claim No.</u>

<u>CHANCERY DIVISION</u>

B E T W E E N:

ABC LIMITED

<u>Claimant</u>

-and-

XYZ LIMITED

<u>Defendant</u>

---
PARTICULARS OF CLAIM
---

1. By a lease dated [date] ("the Lease"), made between the Claimant **A5–001** of the first part, and the Defendant of the second part, the Claimant demised to the Defendant the premises known as and situate at [insert name and address of premises] ("the Demised Premises") for a term commencing from [date] and expiring on

[date], subject to earlier determination pursuant to [clause number], and otherwise subject to the covenants on the part of the Defendant therein contained.

2. By the Lease, the Defendant covenanted to pay to the Claimant:

    (i) The yearly rent of [amount] per annum by equal quarterly payments in advance on the usual quarter days ([clause number]).

    (ii) Interest, payable and calculated pursuant to [clause number].

3. Further, by the Lease, the Defendant covenanted with the Claimant as follows:

    (i) At all times during the term to keep in good and substantial repair and condition the Demised Premises ([clause number]).

    (ii) In [date] and every fifth year thereafter and also in the last six months of the term (howsoever determined) in a good and workmanlike manner to prepare and decorate or otherwise treat as appropriate all interior and exterior parts of the Demised Premises required to be so treated ([clause number]).

4. At clause [number] of the Lease there was a tenant's break clause ("the Break Clause") in the following terms:

[If the Tenant (here meaning XYZ Limited) wishes to terminate this Lease on [date] and shall give to the Landlord not less than 12 months' notice in writing of that wish and shall up to the time of such determination pay the rents reserved by and materially perform and observe the covenants contained in this Lease then upon the expiry of such notice the Term shall immediately cease and determine.]

5. On or about [date] a company called DEF Limited served a notice ("the Notice") upon the Claimant, as Landlord, purportedly pursuant to the Break Clause.

6. In order for the Lease to terminate on [date], pursuant to the Notice, it was not only necessary for the Defendant (as opposed to DEF Limited) to serve the Notice, but it was also necessary for the Defendant, up to [date], to pay the rents reserved by, and materially perform and observe the covenants contained in, the Lease.

7. As mentioned in paragraph 5 above, the Defendant did not serve the Notice.

8. Further, the Defendant failed to pay to the Claimant the rents reserved by the Lease up to [date]:

LANDLORD'S CLAIM FOR DECLARATION 133

## PARTICULARS OF SUMS UNPAID A5–002

[Insert particulars]

9. Further, the Defendant did not materially perform and observe the covenants contained in the Lease up to [date]:

## PARTICULARS OF MATERIAL NON-PERFORMANCE & OBSERVANCE A5–003

[Insert particulars]

10. By reason of the foregoing matters, the Break Clause was not validly exercised and the Lease continues.
11. Further, pursuant to clause [clause number] of the Lease, the Defendant is liable to pay to the Claimant the sums set out in paragraph 8 above.
12. Further, the Claimant is entitled to interest upon the aforegoing monies, pursuant to clause [clause number] of the Lease or, alternatively, pursuant to Section 35A of the Senior Courts Act 1981.

AND the Claimant claims:

(1) A declaration that the Lease has not been determined by the operation of the Break Clause and that the said Lease remains in full force and effect.

(2) [The sums set out in paragraph 8 above].

(3) Interest as aforesaid.

(4) Costs, pursuant to clause [number] of the Lease.

(5) Further or other relief.

STATEMENT OF TRUTH

Etc.

# Appendix 6

# Defence and Counterclaim In Response to Landlord's Claim for Declaration, Etc.

IN THE HIGH COURT OF JUSTICE

CHANCERY DIVISION

B E T W E E N:

Claim No.

ABC LIMITED

Claimant

-and-

XYZ LIMITED

Defendant

---

DEFENCE & COUNTERCLAIM

---

DEFENCE

1. The Defendant joins issue with the Claimant's claim and, save as is expressly admitted or not admitted herein, every allegation in

A6–001

the Claim Form and the Particulars of Claim is denied as if separately set out and traversed.

2. Save where is otherwise stated to the contrary:
   (i) References herein to paragraph numbers are references to the numbered paragraphs in the Particulars of Claim.
   (ii) Definitions used in the Particulars of Claim are adopted herein.
3. Paragraphs 1–3 are admitted.
4. As to paragraph 4, whereas it is admitted that the Notice was served by DEF Limited, it is averred that, at all material times:
   (i) DEF Limited had general authority to act on the Defendant's behalf in connection with all matters concerning the Lease, including the service of the Notice.
   (ii) The Claimant knew that DEF Limited was so authorised.
5. Paragraph 5 is admitted.
6. Paragraph 6 is denied for the reasons set out above. The Notice was served by DEF Limited for and on behalf of the Defendant.
7. Paragraph 7 is denied. The Defendant has paid the rent in full up to [date].

### PARTICULARS OF SUMS PAID

**A6–002** [Insert particulars]

8. Paragraph 8 is denied. It is averred that:
   (i) On [date], Mr [name], of DEF Limited, acting on behalf of the Defendant, had a meeting at the Demised Premises with Mr [name], acting on behalf of the Claimant. At the meeting, the parties agreed what works needed to be carried out in and upon the Demised Premises in order for the Break Clause validly to be exercised ("the Agreed Works").
   (ii) Over the course of [dates], in reliance upon the forgoing agreement, the Agreed Works were carried out in and upon the Demised Premises by the Defendant.
   (iii) On [date], DEF Limited, on behalf of the Defendant, wrote to the Claimant, inviting it to inspect the Demised Premises and to confirm that it was satisfied that the works had been carried out.
   (iv) Thereafter, despite receiving the said letter, the Claimant said nothing to indicate to the Defendant that it required any further work to be carried out to the Demised Premises.

# RESPONSE TO LANDLORD'S CLAIM

9. Paragraph 9 is denied. For the reasons aforesaid, the Break Clause was validly exercised and the Lease terminated on [date].
10. For the reasons given in paragraph 7 above, paragraph 10 is denied.
11. It is further denied that the Claimant is entitled to the interest claimed or any interest.

## COUNTERCLAIM

A6–003

12. Paragraphs 3–10 herein are repeated.

AND the Defendant counterclaims:

(1) A declaration that the Lease was determined by the operation of the Break Clause on [date].

(2) Costs.

(3) Further or other relief.

STATEMENT OF TRUTH

Etc.

# Appendix 7

# Relevant Provisions of the Landlord and Tenant Act 1730

**[I] Persons holding over Lands, &c. after Expiration of Leases, to pay double the yearly Value.**

In case any Tenant or Tenants for any Term of Life, Lives or Years, or other Person or Persons, who are or shall come into Possession of any Lands, Tenements or Hereditaments, by, from or under, or by Collusion with such Tenant or Tenants, shall wilfully hold over any Lands, Tenements or Hereditaments, after the Determination of such Term or Terms, and after Demand made, and Notice in Writing given, for delivering the Possession thereof, by his or their Landlords or Lessors, or the Person or Persons to whom the Remainder or Reversion of such Lands, Tenements or Hereditaments shall belong, his or their Agent or Agents thereunto lawfully authorized; then and in such Case such Person or Persons so holding over, shall, for and during the Time he, she and they shall so hold over, or keep the Person or Persons intitled, out of Possession of the said Lands, Tenements, and Hereditaments, as aforesaid, pay to the Person or Persons so kept out of Possession, their Executors, Administrators or Assigns, at the Rate of double the yearly Value of the Lands, Tenements and Hereditaments so detained, for so long time as the same are detained, to be recovered in any of his Majesty's Courts of Record, by Action of Debt.

Appendix 8

# Relevant Provisions of the Distress for Rent Act 1737

**18 Tenants holding after the time they notify for quitting, to pay double rent.**

And whereas great inconveniences have happened and may happen to landlords whose tenants have power to determine their leases, by giving notice to quit the premisses by them holden, and yet refusing to deliver up the possession when the landlord hath agreed with another tenant for the same: from and after the said twenty fourth day of June one thousand seven hundred and thirty eight, in case any tenant or tenants shall give notice of his, her, or their intention to quit the premisses by him, her, or them holden, at a time mentioned in such notice, and shall not accordingly deliver up the possession thereof at the time in such notice contained, that then the said tenant or tenants, his, her, or their executors or administrators, shall from thenceforward pay to the landlord or landlords, lessor or lessors, double the rent or sum which he, she, or they should otherwise have paid, to be levied, sued for, and recovered at the same times and in the same manner as the single rent or sum, before the giving such notice, could be levied, sued for, or recovered; and such double rent or sum shall continue to be paid during all the time such tenant or tenants shall continue in possession as aforesaid.

Appendix 9

# Relevant Provisions of the Law of Property Act 1925

**63 All estate clause implied.** A9–001

(1) Every conveyance is effectual to pass all the estate, right, title, interest, claim, and demand which the conveying parties respectively have, in, to, or on the property conveyed, or expressed or intended so to be, or which they respectively have power to convey in, to, or on the same.

(2) This section applies only if and as far as a contrary intention is not expressed in the conveyance, and has effect subject to the terms of the conveyance and to the provisions therein contained.

(3) This section applies to conveyances made after the thirty-first day of December, eighteen hundred and eighty-one.

**140 Apportionment of conditions on severance.** A9–002

(1) Notwithstanding the severance by conveyance, surrender, or otherwise of the reversionary estate in any land comprised in a lease, and notwithstanding the avoidance or cesser in any other manner of the term granted by a lease as to part only of the land comprised therein, every condition or right of re-entry, and every other condition contained in the lease, shall be apportioned, and shall remain annexed to the severed parts of the reversionary estate as severed, and shall be in force with respect to the term whereon each severed part is reversionary, or the term in the part of the land as to which the term has not been surrendered, or has not been avoided or has not otherwise ceased, in like manner as

if the land comprised in each severed part, or the land as to which the term remains subsisting, as the case may be, had alone originally been comprised in the lease.

(2) In this section "right of re-entry" includes a right to determine the lease by notice to quit or otherwise; but where the notice is served by a person entitled to a severed part of the reversion so that it extends to part only of the land demised, the lessee may within one month determine the lease in regard to the rest of the land by giving to the owner of the reversionary estate therein a counter notice expiring at the same time as the original notice.

(3) This section applies to leases made before or after the commencement of this Act and whether the severance of the reversionary estate or the partial avoidance or cesser of the term was effected before or after such commencement:

> Provided that, where the lease was made before the first day of January eighteen hundred and eighty-two nothing in this section shall affect the operation of a severance of the reversionary estate or partial avoidance or cesser of the term which was effected before the commencement of this Act.

## 142 Obligation of lessor's covenants to run with reversion.

(1) The obligation under a condition or of a covenant entered into by a lessor with reference to the subject-matter of the lease shall, if and as far as the lessor has power to bind the reversionary estate immediately expectant on the term granted by the lease, be annexed and incident to and shall go with that reversionary estate, or the several parts thereof, notwithstanding severance of that reversionary estate, and may be taken advantage of and enforced by the person in whom the term is from time to time vested by conveyance, devolution in law, or otherwise; and, if and as far as the lessor has power to bind the person from time to time entitled to that reversionary estate, the obligation aforesaid may be taken advantage of and enforced against any person so entitled.

(2) This section applies to leases made before or after the commencement of this Act, whether the severance of the reversionary estate was effected before or after such commencement:

> Provided that, where the lease was made before the first day of January eighteen hundred and eighty-two, nothing in this

section shall affect the operation of any severance of the reversionary estate effected before such commencement.

This section takes effect without prejudice to any liability affecting a covenantor or his estate.

### 196 Regulations respecting notices.

A9–004

(1) Any notice required or authorised to be served or given by this Act shall be in writing.

(2) Any notice required or authorised by this Act to be served on a lessee or mortgagor shall be sufficient, although only addressed to the lessee or mortgagor by that designation, without his name, or generally to the persons interested, without any name, and notwithstanding that any person to be affected by the notice is absent, under disability, unborn, or unascertained.

(3) Any notice required or authorised by this Act to be served shall be sufficiently served if it is left at the last-known place of abode or business in the United Kingdom of the lessee, lessor, mortgagee, mortgagor, or other person to be served, or, in case of a notice required or authorised to be served on a lessee or mortgagor, is affixed or left for him on the land or any house or building comprised in the lease or mortgage, or, in case of a mining lease, is left for the lessee at the office or counting-house of the mine.

(4) Any notice required or authorised by this Act to be served shall also be sufficiently served, if it is sent by post in a registered letter addressed to the lessee, lessor, mortgagee, mortgagor, or other person to be served, by name, at the aforesaid place of abode or business, office, or counting-house, and if that letter is not returned by the postal operator (within the meaning of the Postal Services Act 2000) concerned undelivered; and that service shall be deemed to be made at the time at which the registered letter would in the ordinary course be delivered.

(5) The provisions of this section shall extend to notices required to be served by any instrument affecting property executed or coming into operation after the commencement of this Act unless a contrary intention appears.

(6) This section does not apply to notices served in proceedings in the court.

**A9–005 205 General definitions.**

>    (1) In this Act unless the context otherwise requires, the following expressions have the meanings hereby assigned to them respectively, that is to say:—
>
>    . . .
>
>    (ii) "Conveyance" includes a mortgage, charge, lease, assent, vesting declaration, vesting instrument, disclaimer, release and every other assurance of property or of an interest therein by any instrument, except a will; "convey" has a corresponding meaning; and "disposition" includes a conveyance and also a devise, bequest, or an appointment of property contained in a will; and "dispose of" has a corresponding meaning;
>
>    . . .

# Appendix 10

# Relevant Provisions of the Landlord and Tenant Act 1954

**24 Continuation of tenancies to which Part II applies and grant of new tenancies.**    A10–001

(1) A tenancy to which this Part of this Act applies shall not come to an end unless terminated in accordance with the provisions of this Part of this Act; and, subject to the following provisions of this Act either the tenant or the landlord under such a tenancy may apply to the court for an order for the grant of a new tenancy—

    (a) if the landlord has given notice under section 25 of this Act to terminate the tenancy, or
    (b) if the tenant has made a request for a new tenancy in accordance with section 26 of this Act.

. . .

**25 Termination of tenancy by the landlord.**    A10–002

(1) The landlord may terminate a tenancy to which this Part of this Act applies by a notice given to the tenant in the prescribed form specifying the date at which the tenancy is to come to an end (hereinafter referred to as "the date of termination"):

    Provided that this subsection has effect subject to the provisions of section 29B(4) of this Act and the provisions of Part IV of this Act as to the interim continuation of tenancies pending the disposal of applications to the court.

(2) Subject to the provisions of the next following subsection, a notice under this section shall not have effect unless it is given

not more than twelve nor less than six months before the date of termination specified therein.

(3) In the case of a tenancy which apart from this Act could have been brought to an end by notice to quit given by the landlord—

    (a) the date of termination specified in a notice under this section shall not be earlier than the earliest date on which apart from this Part of this Act the tenancy could have been brought to an end by notice to quit given by the landlord on the date of the giving of the notice under this section; and

    (b) where apart from this Part of this Act more than six months' notice to quit would have been required to bring the tenancy to an end, the last foregoing subsection shall have effect with the substitution for twelve months of a period six months longer than the length of notice to quit which would have been required as aforesaid.

(4) In the case of any other tenancy, a notice under this section shall not specify a date of termination earlier than the date on which apart from this Part of this Act the tenancy would have come to an end by effluxion of time.

. . .

## A10–003 26 Tenant's request for a new tenancy.

(1) A tenant's request for a new tenancy may be made where the current tenancy is a tenancy granted for a term of years certain exceeding one year, whether or not continued by section twenty-four of this Act, or granted for a term of years certain and thereafter from year to year.

(2) A tenant's request for a new tenancy shall be for a tenancy beginning with such date, not more than twelve nor less than six months after the making of the request, as may be specified therein:

    Provided that the said date shall not be earlier than the date on which apart from this Act the current tenancy would come to an end by effluxion of time or could be brought to an end by notice to quit given by the tenant.

(3) A tenant's request for a new tenancy shall not have effect unless it is made by notice in the prescribed form given to the landlord and sets out the tenant's proposals as to the property to be

comprised in the new tenancy (being either the whole or part of the property comprised in the current tenancy), as to the rent to be payable under the new tenancy and as to the other terms of the new tenancy.

...

## 30 Opposition by landlord to application for new tenancy. A10–004

(1) The grounds on which a landlord may oppose an application under [section 24(1) of this Act, or make an application under section 29(2) of this Act], of this Act are such of the following grounds as may be stated in the landlord's notice under section 25 of this Act or, as the case may be, under subsection (6) of section 26 thereof, that is to say—

...

(f) that on the termination of the current tenancy the landlord intends to demolish or reconstruct the premises comprised in the holding or a substantial part of those premises or to carry out substantial work of construction on the holding or part thereof and that he could not reasonably do so without obtaining possession of the holding;

(g) subject as hereinafter provided, that on the termination of the current tenancy the landlord intends to occupy the holding for the purposes, or partly for the purposes, of a business to be carried on by him therein, or as his residence.

...

## 33 Duration of new tenancy. A10–005

Where on an application under this Part of this Act the court makes an order for the grant of a new tenancy, the new tenancy shall be such tenancy as may be agreed between the landlord and the tenant, or, in default of such an agreement, shall be such a tenancy as may be determined by the court to be reasonable in all the circumstances, being, if it is a tenancy for a term of years certain, a tenancy for a term not exceeding fifteen years, and shall begin on the coming to an end of the current tenancy.

**A10–006  35 Other terms of new tenancy.**

(1) The terms of a tenancy granted by order of the court under this Part of this Act (other than terms as to the duration thereof and as to the rent payable thereunder) [including, where different persons own interests which fulfil the conditions specified in different parts of s.44(1) of this Act, terms as to the apportionment of the rent,] shall be such as may be agreed between the landlord and the tenant or as, in default of such agreement, may be determined by the court; and in determining those terms the court shall have regard to the terms of the current tenancy and to all relevant circumstances . . .

**A10–007  69 Interpretation.**

(1) In this Act the following expressions have the meanings hereby assigned to them respectively, that is to say:—

. . .

"notice to quit" means a notice to terminate a tenancy (whether a periodical tenancy or a tenancy for a term of years certain) given in accordance with the provisions (whether express or implied) of that tenancy . . .

Appendix 11

# Relevant Provisions of the Recorded Delivery Service Act 1962

**1 Recorded delivery service to be an alternative to registered post.**  A11–001

(1) Any enactment which requires or authorises a document or other things to be sent by registered post (whether or not it makes any other provision in relation thereto) shall have effect as if it required or, as the case may be, authorised that thing to be sent by registered post or the recorded delivery service; and any enactment which makes any other provision in relation to the sending of a document or other thing by registered post or to a thing so sent shall have effect as if it made the like provision in relation to the sending of that thing by the recorded delivery service or, as the case may be, to a thing sent by that service.

. . .

# Appendix 12

# Relevant Provisions of the Rent Act 1977

**1 Protected tenants and tenancies.**     A12–001

Subject to this Part of this Act, a tenancy under which a dwelling-house (which may be a house or part of a house) is let as a separate dwelling is a protected tenancy for the purposes of this Act.

Any reference in this Act to a protected tenant shall be construed accordingly.

**2 Statutory tenants and tenancies.**     A12–002

(1) Subject to this Part of this Act—
   (a) after the termination of a protected tenancy of a dwelling-house the person who, immediately before that termination, was the protected tenant of the dwelling-house shall, if and so long as he occupies the dwelling-house as his residence, be the statutory tenant of it; and
   (b) Part I of Schedule 1 to this Act shall have effect for determining what person (if any) is the statutory tenant of a dwelling-house [or, as the case may be, is entitled to an assured tenancy of a dwelling-house by succession] at any time after the death of a person who, immediately before his death, was either a protected tenant of the dwelling-house or the statutory tenant of it by virtue of paragraph (a) above.

(2) In this Act a dwelling-house is referred to as subject to a statutory tenancy when there is a statutory tenant of it.

(3) In subsection (1)(a) above and in Part 1 of Schedule 1, the phrase "if and so long as he occupies the dwelling-house as his residence" shall be construed as it was immediately before the commencement of this Act (that is to say, in accordance with section 3(2) of the Rent Act 1968).

(4) A person who becomes a statutory tenant of a dwelling-house as mentioned in subsection (1)(a) above is, in this Act, referred to as a statutory tenant by virtue of his previous protected tenancy.

(5) A person who becomes a statutory tenant as mentioned in subsection 1(b) above is, in this Act, referred to as a statutory tenant by succession.

## 3 Terms and conditions of statutory tenancies.

(1) So long as he retains possession, a statutory tenant shall observe and be entitled to the benefit of all the terms and conditions of the original contract of tenancy, so far as they are consistent with the provisions of this Act.

(2) It shall be a condition of a statutory tenancy of a dwelling-house that the statutory tenant shall afford to the landlord access to the dwelling-house and all reasonable facilities for executing therein any repairs which the landlord is entitled to execute.

(3) Subject to section 5 of the Protection from Eviction Act 1977 (under which at least 4 weeks' notice to quit is required), a statutory tenant of a dwelling-house shall be entitled to give up possession of the dwelling-house if, and only if, he gives such notice as would have been required under the provisions of the original contract of tenancy, or, if no notice would have been so required, on giving not less than 3 months' notice.

(4) Notwithstanding anything in the contract of tenancy, a landlord who obtains an order for possession of a dwelling-house as against a statutory tenant shall not be required to give to the statutory tenant any notice to quit.

(5) Part II of Schedule 1 to this Act shall have effect in relation to the giving up of possession of statutory tenancies and the changing of statutory tenants by agreement.

## 98 Grounds for possession of certain dwelling-houses.

(1) Subject to this Part of this Act, a court shall not make an order for possession of a dwelling-house which is for the time being let on a protected tenancy or subject to a statutory tenancy unless the court considers it reasonable to make such an order and either—

    (a) the court is satisfied that suitable alternative accommodation is available for the tenant or will be available for him when the order in question takes effect, or

    (b) the circumstances are as specified in any of the Cases in Part I of Schedule 15 to this Act.

. . .

# Appendix 13

# Relevant Provisions of the Protection from Eviction Act 1977

**5 Validity of notices to quit.**

(1) Subject to subsection (1B) below no notice by a landlord or a tenant to quit any premises let (whether before or after the commencement of this Act) as a dwelling shall be valid unless—

    (a) it is in writing and contains such information as may be prescribed, and

    (b) it is given not less than 4 weeks before the date on which it is to take effect.

(1A) Subject to subsection (1B) below, no notice by a licensor or a licensee to determine a periodic licence to occupy premises as a dwelling (whether the licence was granted before or after the passing of this Act) shall be valid unless—

    (a) It is in writing and contains such information as may be prescribed, and

    (b) It is given not less than 4 weeks before the date on which it is to take effect.

(1B) Nothing in subsection (1) or subsection (1A) above applies to—

    (a) premises let on an excluded tenancy which is entered into on or after the date on which the Housing Act 1988 came into force unless it is entered into pursuant to a contract made before that date; or

    (b) premises occupied under an excluded licence.

(2) In this section "prescribed" means prescribed by regulations made by the Secretary of State by statutory instrument, and a statutory instrument containing any such regulations shall be subject to annulment in pursuance of a resolution of either House of Parliament.

(3) Regulations under this section may make different provision in relation to different descriptions of lettings and different circumstances.

Appendix 14

# Relevant Provisions of the Agricultural Holdings Act 1986

**1 Principal definitions.**

(1) In this Act "agricultural holding" means the aggregate of the land (whether agricultural land or not) comprised in a contract of tenancy which is a contract for an agricultural tenancy, not being a contract under which the land is let to the tenant during his continuance in any office, appointment or employment held under the landlord.

**A14–001**

(2) For the purposes of this section, a contract of tenancy relating to any land is a contract for an agricultural tenancy if, having regard to—

   (a) the terms of the tenancy,
   (b) the actual or contemplated use of the land at the time of the conclusion of the contract and subsequently, and
   (c) any other relevant circumstances,

the whole of the land comprised in the contract, subject to such exceptions only as do not substantially affect the character of the tenancy, is let for use as agricultural land.

(3) A change in user of the land concerned subsequent to the conclusion of a contract of tenancy which involves any breach of the terms of the tenancy shall be disregarded for the purpose of determining whether a contract which was not originally a contract for an agricultural tenancy has subsequently become one unless it is effected with the landlord's permission, consent or acquiescence.

(4) In this Act "agricultural land" means—

   (a) land used for agriculture which is so used for the purposes of a trade or business, and

(b) any other land which, by virtue of a designation under section 109(1) of the Agriculture Act 1947, is agricultural land within the meaning of that Act.

(5) In this Act "contract of tenancy" means a letting of land, or agreement for letting land, for a term of years or from year to year; and for the purposes of this definition a letting of land, or an agreement for letting land, which, by virtue of subsection (6) of section 149 of the Law of Property Act 1925, takes effect as such a letting of land or agreement for letting land as is mentioned in that subsection shall be deemed to be a letting of land or, as the case may be, an agreement for letting land, for a term of years.

**2 Restriction on letting agricultural land for less than from year to year.**

A14–002

(1) An agreement to which this section applies shall take effect, with the necessary modifications, as if it were an agreement for the letting of land for a tenancy from year to year unless the agreement was approved by the Minister before it was entered into.

(2) Subject to subsection (3) below, this section applies to an agreement under which—

   (a) any land is let to a person for use as agricultural land for an interest less than a tenancy from year to year, or
   (b) a person is granted a licence to occupy land for use as agricultural land,

if the circumstances are such that if his interest were a tenancy from year to year he would in respect of that land be the tenant of an agricultural holding.

(3) This section does not apply to an agreement for the letting of land, or the granting of a licence to occupy land—

   (a) made (whether or not it expressly so provides) in contemplation of the use of the land only for grazing or mowing (or both) during some specified period of the year, or
   (b) by a person whose interest in the land is less than a tenancy from year to year and has not taken effect as such a tenancy by virtue of this section.

(4) Any dispute arising as to the operation of this section in relation to any agreement shall be determined by arbitration under this Act.

**3 Tenancies for two years or more to continue from year to year unless terminated by notice.**

A14–003

(1) Subject to section 5 below, a tenancy of an agricultural holding for a term of two years or more shall, instead of terminating on

the term date, continue (as from that date) as a tenancy from year to year, but otherwise on the terms of the original tenancy so far as applicable, unless—

(a) not less than one year nor more than two years before the term date a written notice has been given by either party to the other of his intention to terminate the tenancy, or

(b) section 4 below applies.

(2) A notice given under subsection (1) above shall be deemed, for the purposes of this Act, to be a notice to quit.

(3) This section does not apply to a tenancy which, by virtue of subsection (6) of section 149 of the Law of Property Act 1925, takes effect as such a term of years as is mentioned in that subsection.

(4) In this section "term date", in relation to a tenancy granted for a term of years, means the date fixed for the expiry of that term.

## 25 Length of notice to quit.

(1) A notice to quit an agricultural holding or part of an agricultural holding shall (notwithstanding any provision to the contrary in the contract of tenancy of the holding) be invalid if it purports to terminate the tenancy before the expiry of twelve months from the end of the then current year of tenancy. **A14–004**

(2) Subsection (1) above shall not apply—

(a) where the tenant is insolvent,

(b) to a notice given in pursuance of a provision in the contract of tenancy authorising the resumption of possession of the holding or some part of it for some specified purpose other than the use of the land for agriculture,

(c) to a notice given by a tenant to a sub-tenant,

(d) where the tenancy is one which, by virtue of subsection (6) of section 149 of the Law of Property Act 1925, has taken effect as such a term of years as is mentioned in that subsection.

(3) Where on a reference under section 12 above with respect to an agricultural holding the arbitrator determines that the rent payable in respect of the holding shall be increased, a notice to quit the holding given by the tenant at least six months before it purports to take effect shall not be invalid by virtue of subsection (1) above if it purports to terminate the tenancy at the end of the year of the tenancy beginning with the date as from which the increase of rent is effective.

(4) On an application made to the Tribunal with respect to an agricultural holding under paragraph 9 of Part II of Schedule 3 to

this Act, the Tribunal may, if they grant a certificate in accordance with the application—

(a) specify in the certificate a minimum period of notice for termination of the tenancy (not being a period of less than two months), and
(b) direct that that period shall apply instead of the period of notice required in accordance with subsection (1) above;

and in any such case a notice to quit the holding which states that the Tribunal have given a direction under this subsection shall not be invalid by virtue of subsection (1) above if the notice given is not less than the minimum notice specified in the certificate.

(5) A notice to quit within subsection (3) or (4) above shall not be invalid by virtue of any term of the contract of tenancy requiring a longer period of notice to terminate the tenancy, and a notice to quit within subsection (4) above shall not be invalid by reason of its terminating at a date other than the end of a year of the tenancy.

### 26 Restriction on operation of notices to quit.

(1) Where—

(a) notice to quit an agricultural holding or part of an agricultural holding is given to the tenant, and
(b) not later than one month from the giving of the notice to quit the tenant serves on the landlord a counter-notice in writing requiring that this subsection shall apply to the notice to quit,

then, subject to subsection (2) below, the notice to quit shall not have effect unless, on an application by the landlord, the Tribunal consent to its operation.

(2) Subsection (1) above shall not apply in any of the Cases set out in Part I of Schedule 3 to this Act; and in this Act "Case A", "Case B" (and so on) refer severally to the Cases set out and so named in that Part of that Schedule.

(3) Part II of that Schedule shall have effect in relation to the Cases there specified.

### 27 Tribunal's consent to operation of notice to quit.

(1) Subject to subsection (2) below, the Tribunal shall consent under section 26 above to the operation of a notice to quit an agricultural holding or part of an agricultural holding if, but only if, they are satisfied as to one or more of the matters mentioned in

subsection (3) below, being a matter or matters specified by the landlord in his application for their consent.

(2) Even if they are satisfied as mentioned in subsection (1) above, the Tribunal shall withhold consent under section 26 above to the operation of the notice to quit if in all the circumstances it appears to them that a fair and reasonable landlord would not insist on possession.

(3) The matters referred to in subsection (1) above are—

   (a) that the carrying out of the purpose for which the landlord proposes to terminate the tenancy is desirable in the interests of good husbandry as respects the land to which the notice relates, treated as a separate unit;
   (b) that the carrying out of the purpose is desirable in the interests of sound management of the estate of which the land to which the notice relates forms part or which that land constitutes;
   (c) that the carrying out of the purpose is desirable for the purposes of agricultural research, education, experiment or demonstration, or for the purposes of the enactments relating to smallholdings;
   (d) that the carrying out of the purpose is desirable for the purposes of the enactments relating to allotments;
   (e) that greater hardship would be caused by withholding than by giving consent to the operation of the notice;
   (f) that the landlord proposes to terminate the tenancy for the purpose of the land's being used for a use, other than for agriculture, not falling within Case B.

(4) Where the Tribunal consent under section 26 above to the operation of a notice to quit, they may impose such conditions as appear to them requisite for securing that the land to which the notice relates will be used for the purpose for which the landlord proposes to terminate the tenancy.

(5) Where, on an application by the landlord, the Tribunal are satisfied that, by reason of any change of circumstances or otherwise, any condition imposed under subsection (4) above ought to be varied or revoked, they shall vary or revoke the condition accordingly.

(6) Where—

   (a) on giving consent under section 26 above to the operation of a notice to quit the Tribunal imposed a condition under subsection (4) above, and
   (b) it is proved on an application to the Tribunal on behalf of the Crown that the landlord has acted in contravention of

the condition or has failed within the time allowed by the condition to comply with it,

the Tribunal may by order impose on the landlord a penalty of an amount not exceeding two years' rent of the holding at the rate at which rent was payable immediately before the termination of the tenancy, or, where the notice to quit related to a part only of the holding, of an amount not exceeding the proportion of the said two years' rent which it appears to the Tribunal is attributable to that part.

(7) The Tribunal may, in proceedings under this section, by order provide for the payment by any party of such sum as the Tribunal consider a reasonable contribution towards costs.

(8) A penalty imposed under subsection (6) above shall be a debt due to the Crown and shall, when recovered, be paid into the Consolidated Fund.

(9) An order under subsection (6) or (7) above shall be enforceable in the same manner as a judgment or order of the county court to the like effect.

**A14–007**   **60 Right to, and measure of, compensation for disturbance.**

(1) This section applies where the tenancy of an agricultural holding terminates by reason—

(a) of a notice to quit the holding given by the landlord, or
(b) of a counter-notice given by the tenant under section 32 above after the giving to him of such a notice to quit part of the holding as is mentioned in that section,

and the tenant quits the holding in consequence of the notice or counter-notice.

. . .

**A14–008**   **96 Interpretation.**

(1) In this Act, unless the context otherwise requires—

. . .

"termination", in relation to a tenancy, means the cesser of the contract of tenancy by reason of effluxion of time or from any other cause;

. . .

Appendix 15

# Relevant Provisions of the Housing Act 1988

**5 Security of tenure.**

(1) An assured tenancy cannot be brought to an end by the landlord except by—   **A15–001**

  (a) obtaining—

    (i) an order of the court for possession of the dwelling-house under section 7 or 21, and

    (ii) the execution of the order,

  (b) obtaining an order of the court under section 6A (demotion order), or

  (c) in the case of a fixed term tenancy which contains power for the landlord to determine the tenancy in certain circumstances, by the exercise of that power,

and, accordingly, the service by the landlord of a notice to quit is of no effect in relation to a periodic assured tenancy.

(1A) Where an order of the court for possession of the dwelling-house is obtained, the tenancy ends when the order is executed.

(2) If an assured tenancy which is a fixed term tenancy comes to an end otherwise than by virtue of—

  (a) an order of the court of the kind mentioned in subsection (1)(a) or (b) or any other order of the court, or

  (b) a surrender or other action on the part of the tenant,

then, subject to section 7 and Chapter II below, the tenant shall be entitled to remain in possession of the dwelling-house let under that tenancy and, subject to subsection (4) below, his right to possession shall depend upon a periodic tenancy arising by virtue of this section.

(3) The periodic tenancy referred to in subsection (2) above is one—
   (a) taking effect in possession immediately on the coming to an end of the fixed term tenancy;
   (b) deemed to have been granted by the person who was the landlord under the fixed term tenancy immediately before it came to an end to the person who was then the tenant under that tenancy;
   (c) under which the premises which are let are the same dwelling-house as was let under the fixed term tenancy;
   (d) under which the periods of the tenancy are the same as those for which rent was last payable under the fixed term tenancy; and
   (e) under which, subject to the following provisions of this Part of this Act, the other terms are the same as those of the fixed term tenancy immediately before it came to an end, except that any term which makes provision for determination by the landlord or the tenant shall not have effect while the tenancy remains an assured tenancy.

(4) The periodic tenancy referred to in subsection (2) above shall not arise if, on the coming to an end of the fixed term tenancy, the tenant is entitled, by virtue of the grant of another tenancy, to possession of the same or substantially the same dwelling-house as was let to him under the fixed term tenancy.

(5) If, on or before the date on which a tenancy is entered into or is deemed to have been granted as mentioned in subsection (3)(b) above, the person who is to be the tenant under that tenancy—
   (a) enters into an obligation to do any act which (apart from this subsection) will cause the tenancy to come to an end at a time when it is an assured tenancy, or
   (b) executes, signs or gives any surrender, notice to quit or other document which (apart from this subsection) has the effect of bringing the tenancy to an end at a time when it is an assured tenancy,

the obligation referred to in paragraph (a) above shall not be enforceable or, as the case may be, the surrender, notice to quit or other document referred to in paragraph (b) above shall be of no effect.

(5A) Nothing in subsection (5) affects any right of pre-emption—
   (a) which is exercisable by the landlord under a tenancy in circumstances where the tenant indicates his intention to dispose of the whole of his interest under the tenancy, and
   (b) in pursuance of which the landlord would be required to pay, in respect of the acquisition of that interest, an amount representing its market value.

# HOUSING ACT 1988

"Dispose" means dispose by assignment or surrender, and "acquisition" has a corresponding meaning.

(6) If, by virtue of any provision of this Part of this Act, Part I of Schedule 1 to this Act has effect in relation to a fixed term tenancy as if it consisted only of paragraphs 11 and 12, that Part shall have the like effect in relation to any periodic tenancy which arises by virtue of this section on the coming to an end of the fixed term tenancy.

(7) Any reference in this Part of this Act to a statutory periodic tenancy is a reference to a periodic tenancy arising by virtue of this section.

## 21 Recovery of possession on expiry or termination of assured shorthold tenancy.

(1) Without prejudice to any right of the landlord under an assured shorthold tenancy to recover possession of the dwelling-house let on the tenancy in accordance with Chapter I above, on or after the coming to an end of an assured shorthold tenancy which was a fixed term tenancy, a court shall make an order for possession of the dwelling-house if it is satisfied—

   (a) that the assured shorthold tenancy has come to an end and no further assured tenancy (whether shorthold or not) is for the time being in existence, other than [an assured shorthold periodic tenancy (whether statutory or not)]; and

   (b) the landlord or, in the case of joint landlords, at least one of them has given to the tenant not less than two months' notice [in writing ] stating that he requires possession of the dwelling-house.

(2) A notice under paragraph (b) of subsection (1) above may be given before or on the day on which the tenancy comes to an end; and that subsection shall have effect notwithstanding that on the coming to an end of the fixed term tenancy a statutory periodic tenancy arises.

(3) Where a court makes an order for possession of a dwelling-house by virtue of subsection (1) above, any statutory periodic tenancy which has arisen on the coming to an end of the assured shorthold tenancy shall end (without further notice and regardless of the period) in accordance with section 5(1A).

(4) Without prejudice to any such right as is referred to in subsection (1) above, a court shall make an order for possession of a

dwelling-house let on an assured shorthold tenancy which is a periodic tenancy if the court is satisfied—

(a) that the landlord or, in the case of joint landlords, at least one of them has given to the tenant a notice [in writing] stating that, after a date specified in the notice, being the last day of a period of the tenancy and not earlier than two months after the date the notice was given, possession of the dwelling-house is required by virtue of this section; and

(b) that the date specified in the notice under paragraph (a) above is not earlier than the earliest day on which, apart from section 5(1) above, the tenancy could be brought to an end by a notice to quit given by the landlord on the same date as the notice under paragraph (a) above.

(4A) Where a court makes an order for possession of a dwelling-house by virtue of subsection (4) above, the assured shorthold tenancy shall end in accordance with section 5(1A).

(5) Where an order for possession under subsection (1) or (4) above is made in relation to a dwelling-house let on a tenancy to which section 19A above applies, the order may not be made so as to take effect earlier than—

(a) in the case of a tenancy which is not a replacement tenancy, six months after the beginning of the tenancy, and

(b) in the case of a replacement tenancy, six months after the beginning of the original tenancy.

(5A) Subsection (5) above does not apply to an assured shorthold tenancy to which section 20B (demoted assured shorthold tenancies) applies.

(6) In subsection (5)(b) above, the reference to the original tenancy is—

(a) where the replacement tenancy came into being on the coming to an end of a tenancy which was not a replacement tenancy, to the immediately preceding tenancy, and

(b) where there have been successive replacement tenancies, to the tenancy immediately preceding the first in the succession of replacement tenancies.

(7) For the purposes of this section, a replacement tenancy is a tenancy—

(a) which comes into being on the coming to an end of an assured shorthold tenancy, and

(b) under which, on its coming into being—

(i) the landlord and tenant are the same as under the earlier tenancy as at its coming to an end, and

(ii) the premises let are the same or substantially the same as those let under the earlier tenancy as at that time.

Appendix 16

# Relevant Provisions of the Landlord and Tenant (Covenants) Act 1995

**3 Transmission of benefit and burden of covenants.**

(1) The benefit and burden of all landlord and tenant covenants of a tenancy — **A16–001**

    (a) shall be annexed and incident to the whole, and to each and every part, of the premises demised by the tenancy and of the reversion in them, and

    (b) shall in accordance with this section pass on an assignment of the whole or any part of those premises or of the reversion in them.

(2) Where the assignment is by the tenant under the tenancy, then as from the assignment the assignee—

    (a) becomes bound by the tenant covenants of the tenancy except to the extent that—

        (i) immediately before the assignment they did not bind the assignor, or

        (ii) they fall to be complied with in relation to any demised premises not comprised in the assignment; and

    (b) becomes entitled to the benefit of the landlord covenants of the tenancy except to the extent that they fall to be complied with in relation to any such premises.

(3) Where the assignment is by the landlord under the tenancy, then as from the assignment the assignee—

    (a) becomes bound by the landlord covenants of the tenancy except to the extent that—

(i) immediately before the assignment they did not bind the assignor, or

(ii) they fall to be complied with in relation to any demised premises not comprised in the assignment; and

(b) becomes entitled to the benefit of the tenant covenants of the tenancy except to the extent that they fall to be complied with in relation to any such premises.

(4) In determining for the purposes of subsection (2) or (3) whether any covenant bound the assignor immediately before the assignment; any waiver or release of the covenant which (in whatever terms) is expressed to be personal to the assignor shall be disregarded.

(5) Any landlord or tenant covenant of a tenancy which is restrictive of the user of land shall, as well as being capable of enforcement against an assignee, be capable of being enforced against any other person who is the owner or occupier of any demised premises to which the covenant relates, even though there is no express provision in the tenancy to that effect.

(6) Nothing in this section shall operate—

(a) in the case of a covenant which (in whatever terms) is expressed to be personal to any person, to make the covenant enforceable by or (as the case may be) against any other person; or

(b) to make a covenant enforceable against any person if, apart from this section, it would not be enforceable against him by reason of its not having been registered under the Land Registration Act 2002 or the Land Charges Act 1972.

(7) To the extent that there remains in force any rule of law by virtue of which the burden of a covenant whose subject matter is not in existence at the time when it is made does not run with the land affected unless the covenantor covenants on behalf of himself and his assigns, that rule of law is hereby abolished in relation to tenancies.

## 28 Interpretation.

(1) In this Act (unless the context otherwise requires)—

. . .

"covenant" includes term, condition and obligation, and references to a covenant (or any description of covenant) of a tenancy include a covenant (or a covenant of that description) contained in a collateral agreement;

"landlord" and "tenant", in relation to a tenancy, mean the person for the time being entitled to the reversion expectant on the term of the tenancy and the person so entitled to that term respectively;

"landlord covenant", in relation to a tenancy, means a covenant falling to be complied with by the landlord of premises demised by the tenancy;

. . .

"tenant covenant", in relation to a tenancy, means a covenant falling to be complied with by the tenant of premises demised by the tenancy.

. . .

# Appendix 17

# Relevant Provisions of the Agricultural Tenancies Act 1995

**1 Meaning of "farm business tenancy".**

(1) A tenancy is a "farm business tenancy" for the purposes of this Act if—    **A17–001**
    (a) it meets the business conditions together with either the agriculture condition or the notice conditions, and
    (b) it is not a tenancy which, by virtue of section 2 of this Act cannot be a farm business tenancy.

(2) The business conditions are—
    (a) that all or part of the land comprised in the tenancy is farmed for the purposes of a trade or business, and
    (b) that, since the beginning of the tenancy, all or part of the land so comprised has been so farmed.

(3) The agriculture condition is that, having regard to—
    (a) the terms of the tenancy,
    (b) the use of the land comprised in the tenancy,
    (c) the nature of any commercial activities carried on on that land, and
    (d) any other relevant circumstances,
the character of the tenancy is primarily or wholly agricultural.

(4) The notice conditions are—
    (a) that, on or before the relevant day, the landlord and the tenant each gave the other a written notice—
        (i) identifying (by name or otherwise) the land to be comprised in the tenancy or proposed tenancy, and

(ii) containing a statement to the effect that the person giving the notice intends that the tenancy or proposed tenancy is to be, and remain, a farm business tenancy, and

(b) that, at the beginning of the tenancy, having regard to the terms of the tenancy and any other relevant circumstances, the character of the tenancy was primarily or wholly agricultural.

(5) In subsection (4) above "the relevant day" means whichever is the earlier of the following—

(a) the day on which the parties enter into any instrument creating the tenancy, other than an agreement to enter into a tenancy on a future date, or
(b) the beginning of the tenancy.

. . .

## 5 Tenancies for more than two years to continue from year to year unless terminated by notice.

A17–002

(1) A farm business tenancy for a term of more than two years shall, instead of terminating on the term date, continue (as from that date) as a tenancy from year to year, but otherwise on the terms of the original tenancy so far as applicable, unless at least twelve months [. . .] before the term date a written notice has been given by either party to the other of his intention to terminate the tenancy.

(2) In subsection (1) above "the term date", in relation to a fixed term tenancy, means the date fixed for the expiry of the term.

(3) For the purposes of section 140 of the Law of Property Act 1925 (apportionment of conditions on severance of reversion), a notice under subsection (1) above shall be taken to be a notice to quit.

(4) This section has effect notwithstanding any agreement to the contrary.

## 6 Length of notice to quit.

A17–003

(1) Where a farm business tenancy is a tenancy from year to year, a notice to quit the holding or part of the holding shall (notwithstanding any provision to the contrary in the tenancy) be invalid unless—

(a) it is in writing,
(b) it is to take effect at the end of a year of the tenancy, and

(c) it is given at least twelve months [. . .] before the date on which it is to take effect.

(2) Where, by virtue of section 5(1) of this Act, a farm business tenancy for a term of more than two years is to continue (as from the term date) as a tenancy from year to year, a notice to quit which complies with subsection (1) above and which is to take effect on the first anniversary of the term date shall not be invalid merely because it is given before the term date, and in this subsection "the term date" has the meaning given by section 5(2) of this Act.

(3) Subsection (1) above does not apply in relation to a counter-notice given by the tenant by virtue of subsection (2) of section 140 of the Law of Property Act 1925 (apportionment of conditions on severance of reversion).

## 7 Notice required for exercise of option to terminate tenancy or resume possession of part.

(1) Where a farm business tenancy is a tenancy for a term of more than two years, any notice to quit the holding or part of the holding given in pursuance of any provision of the tenancy shall (notwithstanding any provision to the contrary in the tenancy) be invalid unless it is in writing and is given at least twelve months before the date on which it is to take effect. **A17–004**

(2) Subsection (1) above does not apply in relation to a counter-notice given by the tenant by virtue of subsection (2) of section 140 of the Law of Property Act 1925 (apportionment of conditions on severance of reversion).

(3) Subsection (1) above does not apply to a tenancy which, by virtue of subsection (6) of section 149 of the Law of Property Act 1925 (lease for life or lives or for a term determinable with life or lives or on the marriage of, or formation of a civil partnership by, the lessee), takes effect as such a term of years as is mentioned in that subsection.

## 16 Tenant's right to compensation for tenant's improvement.

(1) The tenant under a farm business tenancy shall, subject to the provisions of this Part of this Act, be entitled on the termination of the tenancy, on quitting the holding, to obtain from his landlord compensation in respect of any tenant's improvement. **A17–005**

. . .

### 36 Service of notices.

(1) This section applies to any notice or other document required or authorised to be given under this Act.

(2) A notice or other document to which this section applies is duly given to a person if—

  (a) it is delivered to him,
  (b) it is left at his proper address, or
  (c) it is given to him in a manner authorised by a written agreement made, at any time before the giving of the notice, between him and the person giving the notice.

(3) A notice or other document to which this section applies is not duly given to a person if its text is transmitted to him by facsimile or other electronic means otherwise than by virtue of subsection (2)(c) above.

(4) Where a notice or other document to which this section applies is to be given to a body corporate, the notice or document is duly given if it is given to the secretary or clerk of that body.

(5) Where—

  (a) a notice or other document to which this section applies is to be given to a landlord under a farm business tenancy and an agent or servant of his is responsible for the control of the management of the holding, or
  (b) such a document is to be given to a tenant under a farm business tenancy and an agent or servant of his is responsible for the carrying on of a business on the holding,

the notice or document is duly given if it is given to that agent or servant.

(6) For the purposes of this section, the proper address of any person to whom a notice or other document to which this section applies is to be given is—

  (a) in the case of the secretary or clerk of a body corporate, the registered or principal office of that body, and
  (b) in any other case, the last known address of the person in question.

(7) Unless or until the tenant under a farm business tenancy has received—

  (a) notice that the person who before that time was entitled to receive the rents and profits of the holding ("the original landlord") has ceased to be so entitled, and

(b) notice of the name and address of the person who has become entitled to receive the rents and profits,

any notice or other document given to the original landlord by the tenant shall be deemed for the purposes of this Act to have been given to the landlord under the tenancy.

## 38 Interpretation.

(1) In this Act, unless the context otherwise requires—

. . .

"termination", in relation to a tenancy, means the cesser of the tenancy by reason of effluxion of time or from any other cause.

. . .

# Appendix 18

# *Finch v Underwood* (1875—1876) L.R. 2 Ch.D. 310 at 314—316

JAMES L.J.: —

*Judgment, James, L.J.*

I am of opinion that this decree cannot be affirmed. The case is one of condition precedent; it is not a case of forfeiture, and none of the considerations applicable to forfeiture apply to it. A renewal of a lease is a privilege to which the tenant is to be entitled in certain circumstances and on certain terms. The covenant here was that on the request of either of the tenants the landlord would (the covenants of the lease having been duly kept) grant a renewed lease to the two. I am of opinion that the lessor is entitled to say that, as there were two tenants in the original lease who entered into joint and several covenants, and his agreement was in terms to grant the renewed lease to the two subject to the same covenants, he is entitled to have the joint and several covenants of the two in the renewed lease. We need not enter into the question how the case would stand if one of the lessees had died; they are both living, and it is impossible to say that one of them, the other not choosing to join, can, under the terms of this covenant, require a lease to be granted to himself. The lease which the lessor agreed to grant is not the same kind of lease as is asked for by this bill.

**A18–001**

I think, moreover, that the Plaintiff, if otherwise entitled to a lease, would have lost that right by breach of the covenants to repair. No doubt every property must at times be somewhat out of repair, and a tenant must have a reasonable time allowed to do what is necessary: but where it is required as a condition precedent to the granting a new lease that the lessee's covenants shall have been performed, the lessee who comes to claim the new lease must shew that at that time the property is in such a state as the covenants require it to be. He can easily send in his builder, get a report of what repairs are necessary, and do them before he applies for the lease. There is no hardship in requiring this of him, and I think he is not entitled to excuse himself by saying that the want of repair is trifling. The answer to that is, "No matter; your bargain was to leave the property in thorough repair." If he has not fulfilled his legal bargain, which is also his bargain in equity, he cannot sustain his claim for a lease. The case of *Hare* v. *Burges* (1), on which the Vice-Chancellor relied, was not a case of condition precedent, and the only point decided was that there were in that case no equitable grounds for declining to enforce a contract which was good at law. The decree must be reversed, and the bill dismissed with costs.

MELLISH L.J.: —

**A18–002**  I am of the same opinion. The tenant must take the covenant to renew as he finds it; if it contains conditions precedent he must comply with them before he can claim the benefit of it, and if he has not done so a Court of Equity cannot relieve him. Under the terms of the covenant in the present case the lease is to be granted only in case the covenants and agreements on the part of the tenants shall have been duly observed and performed. What does that mean? I think it does not mean that the tenants must have strictly observed and performed the covenants all through the term, for the expression is, "shall have been duly observed and performed;" and I think that this is satisfied if they have been so observed and performed that there is no existing right of action under them at the time when the lease is applied for. In the present case the landlord alleged the premises to be out of repair, and sent in his surveyor, who certified that the interior required repairs to the amount of £45. The Plaintiff's surveyor does not deny the accuracy of any one of the items of dilapidation set forth by the Defendant's surveyor, but estimates the cost of repairing them at £20; and another witness for the Plaintiff states his readiness to repair them for £13 10s. It is clear, then, that at the time of applying for the lease there was an existing breach of the covenant to repair for which an action would lie. In a case like this, if a tenant wishes to claim the benefit of such a covenant he should send in his surveyor to see what repairs are needed, and should effect the repairs which the surveyor certifies to be requisite. The Court would be inclined to give credit to a survey thus honestly made, and would lean towards holding the condition precedent to have been complied with. But in the present case it is admitted that there was an existing breach of the covenant to repair.

. . .

# Appendix 19

# United Scientific Holdings Ltd v Burnley Borough Council [1978] A.C. 904 at 928—929, 945—946, and 951

March 23, 1977.  Lord Diplock—

. . .

Both in the Court of Chancery and in the courts of common law the rules that have been developed about particular stipulations not being of the essence of the contract or not being "conditions precedent" applied to synallagmatic contracts only. They did not apply to unilateral or "if contracts," of which the example most germane to the instant appeals is an option. As pointed out by Lord Denning M.R. in *United Dominions Trust (Commercial) Ltd. v. Eagle Aircraft Services Ltd.* [1968] 1 W.L.R. 74, 81 where speaking of options to purchase real or personal property or to renew a lease, he said:

> 'In point of legal analysis, the grant of an option in such cases, is an irrevocable offer (being supported by consideration so that it cannot be revoked). In order to be turned into a binding contract, the offer must be accepted in exact compliance with its terms. The acceptance must correspond with the offer.'

Exact compliance with the terms of the offer in an "if contract" had been required in courts of equity as well as in courts of common law: see *Weston v. Collins* (1865) 12 L.T. 4; *Finch v. Underwood* (1876) 2 Ch.D. 310. A rationale of the distinction which was drawn between the two kinds of contracts in courts of equity is that equity was concerned with the performance of contracts into which parties had already entered. It did not force any person to enter into a contract with another.

Again I will refrain from repeating the more elaborate juristic analysis of the distinction between the two types of contract that I attempted in the *United Dominions Trust* case [1968] 1 W.L.R. 74, 83–84. A more practical business explanation why stipulation as to the time by which an option to acquire an interest in property should be exercised by the grantee must be punctually observed, is that the grantor, so long as the option remains open, thereby submits to being disabled from disposing of his proprietary interest to anyone other than the grantee, and this without any guarantee that it will be disposed of to the grantee. In accepting such a fetter upon his powers of disposition of his property, the grantor needs to know with certainty the moment when it has come to an end.

My Lords, although a lease is a synallagmatic contract it may also contain a clause granting to the tenant an option to obtain a renewal of the lease upon the expiration of the term thereby granted. Such a clause provides a classic instance of an option to acquire a leasehold interest in futuro, and it is well established that a stipulation as to the time at which notice to exercise the option must be given is of the essence of the option to renew. Although your Lordships have not been referred to any direct authority upon the converse case of a "break clause" granting to the tenant an option to determine his interest in the property and his contractual relationship with the landlord prematurely at the end of a stated period of the full term of years granted by the lease, there is a practical business reason for treating time as of the essence of such a clause, which is similar to that applicable to an option to acquire property. The exercise of this option by the tenant will have the effect of depriving the landlord of the existing source of income from his property and the evident purpose of the stipulation as to notice is to leave him free thereafter to enter into a contract with a new tenant for a tenancy commencing at the date of surrender provided for in the break clause.

. . .

**A19–002** LORD SIMON OF GLAISDALE—

. . .

(3) The law does not purport to bring parties into a relationship of contractual obligation which they themselves have failed to create. This is the true ground of decision in those cases where a stipulation as to time is contained in an option. An option is a type of unilateral contract. When, as is usual, it is supported by consideration it constitutes an irrevocable offer which turns into a bilateral contract by an acceptance in strict compliance with its terms: see Lord Denning M.R. in United Dominions Trust (Commercial) Ltd. v. Eagle Aircraft Services Ltd. [1968] 1 W.L.R. 74, 81C. It is apt to be misleading to say that time is of the essence of an option, since that may give the impression of a bilateral contractual term. The legal reality is that this type of unilateral contract never matures into a bilateral contract at all unless the option is exercised in time. But, as Diplock L.J. pointed out in the *United Dominions Trust* case (p. 84G), it is quite possible to have this sort of unilateral obligation

in an otherwise bilateral contract. An option in a lease to terminate or to renew the tenancy or to purchase the reversion will be such a term. In each such case the parties, on the exercise of the option, are brought into a new legal relationship. It was argued on behalf of the tenants in the instant appeals that the rent review clauses were also such unilateral terms. I cannot agree. The operation of the rent review clauses does not at all change the relationship of the parties, which remains that of landlord and tenant throughout the currency of the lease whether or not the machinery of the rent review clauses is operated. It was envisaged from the outset that the rent would be reviewed during the currency of the leases: the clauses merely provided machinery for determination of the new rent, which in more stable conditions might have been stipulated in advance. Moreover, the clauses went to the very basis of the consideration moving from the landlords: in a period of inflation the latter would not have granted leases for such long terms without inclusion of rent review clauses — and certainly the initial rent would in each case have been much higher without those clauses. To put it the other way round, the rent review clauses were integral parts of the consideration moving from the tenants, whereby they acquired a long term of years at an initial rent lower than it would otherwise have been. Rent review clauses cannot be considered as severable terms of unilateral obligation. However, where a rent review clause is associated with a true option (a "break" clause, for example), it is a strong indication that time is intended to be of the essence of the rent review clause — if not absolutely, at least to the extent that the tenant will reasonably expect to know what new rent he will have to pay before the time comes for him to elect whether to terminate or renew the tenancy (cf. *Samuel Properties (Developments) Ltd. v. Hayek* [1972] 1 W.L.R. 1296). That situation stands in significant contrast with those in the instant appeals.

. . .

LORD SALMON— A19–003

. . .

Options to determine or to renew are not agreements to determine or renew. They are no more than irrevocable offers (kept open for good consideration) to do so providing the tenant complies with certain conditions usually before a certain date. If the tenant complies with the conditions in time he thereby accepts the offer. The offer plus the acceptance constitutes a fresh agreement determining or renewing the lease as the case may be (see the *United Dominion Trust* case [1968] 1 W.L.R. 74, Lord Denning M.R. at p. 81). The same is true, mutatis mutandis, of an option to acquire the reversion. Neither equity nor the common law would ever intervene to make a contract for the parties. Anything which falls short of a complete acceptance of the offer is of no effect except sometimes as a counter-offer.

. . .

# Appendix 20

# Bass Holdings Ltd v Morton Music Ltd [1988] 1 Ch. 493 at 517—520

KERR L.J.

...

This brings me to the classification of breaches of covenants by reference to the time of their occurrence and subsistence, on which the present issues turn. As explained below, there is clearly a long standing conveyancing practice, going back more than two centuries, whereby tenants' options in leases are made subject to provisos dealing with the observance of the tenants' covenants, similar to the option in the present case, whether the option be for a new lease as here, or for premature termination of an existing lease (a "break" option), or for the purchase of the freehold. In all such cases the provisos link the required observance of the covenants to a point of time in the nature of a terminus ad quem. This may be either the date of the exercise of the option as here, or the date of the expiry of the option, or – in cases of options for renewals or for the purchase of the freehold – the date of the expiry of the lease. For present purposes the particular date referred to in the proviso ("the operative date") does not matter. What matters is whether the breach (or breaches) of covenant on which the plaintiffs rely as precluding the exercise of the option has only occurred in the past, so that its effect is spent by the operative date in question, or whether there is still a breach – or at any rate a cause of action based upon a breach, whether for forfeiture or damages or both – which subsists on the operative date. I will refer to the breaches of covenant in these two situations respectively as "spent breaches" and "subsisting breaches". The present appeal is concerned exclusively with spent breaches.

In my view the position on the authorities and on the issues raised by the present case can be summarised as follows.

(1) The first question is whether, on the true construction of the proviso in question, the absence of any material breaches of covenant by the

defendants is a *condition precedent* to the exercise of the option, as well as the giving of the requisite notice purporting to exercise the option. Generally, and admittedly in the present case, the proviso contains a double condition precedent, viz. (i) the absence of any material breaches of covenants and (ii) compliance with the requirement as to notice.

(2) That, however, leaves the crucial question whether the condition precedent (i), that there must be no material breaches of covenant by the defendants, applies to spent as well as to subsisting breaches. This question is covered by dicta in numerous cases, going back in particular to *Grey v. Friar* (1854) 4 H.L.Cas. 565, and by the decision of Clauson J. in *Simons v. Associated Furnishers Ltd.* [1931] 1 Ch. 379. The upshot of these authorities is that spent breaches will not destroy the tenant's right to exercise the option, but subsisting breaches will. As shown by the passages to which I refer below, the reasoning is in effect as follows. First, it must be accepted that absolute and precise compliance by the tenant with every single covenant throughout the period of the lease prior to the operative date is virtually impossible of attainment. If this were required as a condition precedent, then the option would in practice be worthless or merely at the mercy of the landlord. Therefore the parties cannot have intended that the absence of spent breaches should be a condition precedent. Secondly, however, it is natural and sensible that the landlord should require the tenant not to be in breach of any covenant on the operative date and that all outstanding claims for breach of covenant should have been previously satisfied, so that the lease is then effectively clear. The proviso is therefore to be construed as intended to apply to subsisting breaches, with the result that the relevant condition precedent is the absence of any subsisting breach.

(3) The only suggestion that spent breaches might be able to preclude the exercise of the option is to be found in the judgment of Griffiths L.J. in *Bassett v. Whiteley* (1982) 45 P. & C.R. 87. But this lies in a different line of authority, as explained below, and cannot properly be applied to the present case.

(4) Subject to the question whether the wording of any particular proviso imposes a condition precedent to the exercise of the option, which was the issue in *Grey v. Friar*, 4 H.L.Cas. 565, the precise words used in such provisos in relation to the observance of the covenants have played no part in the conclusions summarised in (2) above. While it would of course be possible to formulate a proviso which is sufficiently explicit to cause spent breaches to preclude the exercise of the option, there appears to be no reported case in which this was so; and the wording of the proviso in the present case is in a form similar to, and effectively indistinguishable from, the formulations adopted in all the cases subsequent to *Grey v. Friar*. Accordingly, in mentioning some of these cases below, it would serve no purpose to set out the precise terms of the particular provisos.

(5) The reasoning summarised in (2) above, which has led to the generally accepted conclusion that the condition precedent imposed by provisos like the present was intended to apply only to subsisting

breaches, is of course particularly cogent in relation to "break" options. In such cases it will obviously be of great importance to the landlord that the demised land or premises should be surrendered to him free from any subsisting breaches of covenant. In cases of options for renewals it may also be of some importance to the landlord that the slate should be clean before the new lease takes effect. In cases of options to buy the freehold, the absence of subsisting breaches may be less important to the landlord. However, the authorities suggest no distinction between these types of option in relation to the conclusions summarised in (2) above. Admittedly, *Grey v. Friar* in 1854, 4 H.L.Cas. 565, and *Porter v. Shephard* (1796) 6 Durn. & E. 665, which was followed in *Grey v. Friar*, both involved "break" options. But their reasoning has been followed and applied in relation to tenants' options generally. Accordingly, there is nowadays no reason for imposing any different or special construction on the familiar forms of provisos governing any particular type of tenants' option, such as the option for a further lease in the present case.

(6) Strong arguments can admittedly be raised in extreme cases against the construction that the effect of the condition precedent is to be limited to the absence of subsisting breaches. For instance, what about a tenant who has persistently broken his covenants and only puts matters right just before the operative date? As mentioned below, this troubled Griffiths L.J. in *Bassett v. Whiteley*, 45 P. & C.R. 87, albeit in a different context. But it must also be borne in mind that the condition requiring the absence of any subsisting breach on the operative date involves not only that any breach should have ceased, but also that there should be no subsisting cause of action in respect of any breach. Thus, a landlord may perhaps take advantage of the latter condition, in order to defeat a tenant's option, by postponing any claim for forfeiture or damages in respect of an earlier breach until after the operative date. Anomalies on both sides are inevitable on any construction. But the consensus to be found in the authorities is that the anomaly which must be rejected as too great to be acceptable is that any spent breach should disqualify.

(7) The upshot, in cases such as the present, is that we are nowadays dealing with what has become a standard conveyancing formula imposing a condition precedent concerning the absence of (material) breaches of covenant in relation to the exercise of virtually any tenants' option in leases. The unanimous consensus on the authorities in relation to a proviso such as the present is as summarised in (2) above, viz. that the condition applies to subsisting breaches and not to spent breaches. There is no reported case in which any tenant's option has been defeated by a spent breach, and virtually none in which this has even been suggested. In these circumstances it is in my view of great importance that this accepted long standing interpretation of provisos such as the present should be respected and upheld, since it must have been relied upon and applied in countless transactions.

(8) Up to this point my conclusions accord entirely with those of the judge. But I regret that at this juncture there comes a parting of the ways

between our views. He points out, entirely correctly, that the jurisprudence leading to the accepted interpretation which I have summarised above, that spent breaches are irrelevant to the exercise of tenants' options, has been concerned throughout with spent breaches of positive covenants, such as failures to pay rent, to repair, etc. The issue has never arisen in the context of a spent breach of a negative covenant. Admittedly, none of the authorities contains any suggestion that there is any difference between breaches of positive and negative covenants for present purposes, whether the breaches be spent or subsisting. But the judge nevertheless concluded that there was a material difference between them. He appears to have based this on the consideration that a breach of a positive covenant can be remedied in the sense, or to the extent, of belated performance. In effect, the tenant can take some positive action to put things right. But a breach of a negative covenant, albeit "spent" in the sense in which I have used this term, is irremediable. It cannot be undone, any more than Omar Khayam's "moving finger ... having writ," or an indelible stain on the tenant's escutcheon. The judge accordingly concluded that while the defendants' failure to pay the rent and water rates did not disqualify them from exercising the option, their applications for planning permission without the plaintiffs' consent did have this effect. The reason was that the former were breaches of positive covenants whereas the latter were breaches of a negative covenant. The judge therefore granted the plaintiffs' application for a declaration that the defendants' option had not been validly exercised.

(9) With all due respect, I cannot agree with this analysis or with the conclusion to which it leads. It is not based on any commercial or other practical consideration. Its effect would be entirely fortuitous. Thus, as mentioned at the beginning of this judgment, many of the covenants in this lease in common form contain both positive and negative obligations in one provision, and other obligations to the same or similar effect have been expressed in the form of both positive and negative covenants. I do not see on what realistic grounds it could be said that the intention of the parties was that spent breaches of positive covenants should be irrelevant, but that any breach of any negative covenant, albeit equally "spent" in its practical effect, should disqualify.

. . .

## Appendix 21

# *Hounslow London Borough Council v Pilling* [1993] 1 W.L.R. 1242 at 1246–1247

NOURSE L.J.

. . .

What was decided in [Hammersmith and Fulham London Borough Council v Monk [1992] 1 AC 478] was that a contractual periodic tenancy held by two or more joint tenants continued only so long as they all agreed to its continuation, so that, in the absence of any contrary term in the agreement, the tenancy was determinable by a notice to quit given by one joint tenant without the concurrence of the other or others. There the tenancy was terminable by four weeks' notice to expire on a Monday and it was in fact determined by what Lord Bridge of Harwich, at p. 482A–B, called "an appropriate notice". He said, at p. 483:

> "Thus the application of ordinary contractual principles leads me to expect that a periodic tenancy granted to two or more joint tenants must be terminable at common law by an appropriate notice to quit given by any one of them whether or not the others are prepared to concur."

. . .

In my judgment . . . the decision of the House of Lords in *Monk*'s case is distinguishable . . . All that that case decided was that the continuation of a periodic joint tenancy beyond the end of each period of it depends on the joint will of the tenants, so that if one of them gives notice determining it at the end of a period it does not continue. Here the notice purported to determine the tenancy not at the end of a period but in the middle of one. On the assumption, which I certainly make, that clause 14 permitted notice to be given for an immediate determination, the effect of Miss Doubtfire's letter of 6 December and the council's acceptance of it was to determine the tenancy on 9 December and not on 16 December. I therefore agree with Mr. Luba that the notice was not a notice to quit, but one operating a break clause in the tenancy agreement. Such a notice could not be given by one only of the joint tenants: see *In re Viola's Indenture of Lease* [1909] 1 Ch. 244.

. . .

Appendix 22

# *Union Eagle Ltd v Golden Achievement Ltd* [1997] A.C. 514 at 523

Lord Hoffmann

...

The fact is that the purchaser was late. Any suggestion that relief can be obtained on the ground that he was only slightly late is bound to lead to arguments over how late is too late, which can be resolved only by litigation. For five years the vendor has not known whether he is entitled to resell the flat or not. It has been sterilised by a caution pending a final decision in this case. In his dissenting judgment, Godfrey J.A. said that the case 'cries out for the intervention of equity'. Their Lordships think that, on the contrary, it shows the need for a firm restatement of the principle that in cases of rescission of an ordinary contract of sale of land for failure to comply with an essential condition as to time, equity will not intervene.

...

*Solicitors: Hugh Cartright & Amin; Edwin Coe.*

S.S.

# Appendix 23

# *Mannai Investment Co Ltd v Eagle Star Life Assurance Co Ltd* [1997] A.C. 749 at 767–769, 773–775, and 780–782

LORD STEYN

. . .

On reflection I have come to the conclusion that the question of the construction of the notices should be answered by holding that the notices were effective to determine the leases. I will first summarise my analysis of the problem before I explain why I feel unable to accept the attractively presented arguments of counsel for the landlord.

The reasons for my conclusion can be stated in the form of numbered propositions.

(1) This is not a case of a contractual right to determine which prescribes as an indispensable condition for its effective exercise that the notice must contain specific information. After providing for the form of the notice ('in writing'), its duration ('not less than six months') and service ('on the landlord or its solicitors'), the only words in clause 7(13) relevant to the content of the notice are the words 'notice to expire on the third anniversary of the term commencement date determine this lease'. Those words do not have any customary meaning in a technical sense. No terms of art are involved. and neither side has suggested that anything should be implied into the language. That is not surprising since the tests governing the implication of terms could not conceivably be satisfied. The language of clause 7(13) must be given its ordinary meaning. A notice simply expressed to determine the lease on the third anniversary of the commencement date would therefore have been effective. The principle is that that is certain which the context renders certain: *Sunrose Ltd. v. Gould* [1962] 1 W.L.R. 20.

(2) The question is not how the landlord understood the notices. The construction of the notices must be approached objectively. The issue is

how a reasonable recipient would have understood the notices. and in considering this question the notices must be construed taking into account the relevant objective contextual scene. The approach in *Reardon Smith Line Ltd. v. Yngvar Hansen-Tangen (trading as H. E. Hansen-Tangen)* [1976] 1 W.L.R. 989, which deals with the construction of commercial contracts, is by analogy of assistance in respect of unilateral notices such as those under consideration in the present case. Relying on the reasoning in Lord Wilberforce's speech in the *Reardon Smith* case, at pp. 996D–997D, three propositions can be formulated. First, in respect of contracts and contractual notices the contextual scene is always relevant. Secondly, what is *admissible* as a matter of the rules of evidence under this heading is what is arguably relevant. But admissibility is not the decisive matter. The real question is what evidence of surrounding circumstances may ultimately be allowed to influence the question of interpretation. That depends on what meanings the language read against the objective contextual scene will let in. Thirdly, the inquiry is objective: the question is what reasonable persons, circumstanced as the actual parties were, would have had in mind. It follows that one cannot ignore that a reasonable recipient of the notices would have had in the forefront of his mind the terms of the leases. Given that the reasonable recipient must be credited with knowledge of the critical date and the terms of clause 7(13) the question is simply how the reasonable recipient would have understood such a notice. This proposition may in other cases require qualification. Depending on the circumstances a party may be precluded by an estoppel by convention from raising a contention contrary to a common assumption of fact or law (which could include the validity of a notice) upon which they have acted: *Norwegian American Cruises A/S (formerly Norwegian American Lines A/S) v. Paul Mundy Ltd.* [1988] 2 Lloyd's Rep. 343. Such an issue may involve subjective questions. That is, however, a different issue and not one relevant to this appeal. I proceed therefore to examine the matter objectively.

(3) It is important not to lose sight of the purpose of a notice under the break clause. It serves one purpose only: to inform the landlord that the tenant has decided to determine the lease in accordance with the right reserved. That purpose must be relevant to the construction and validity of the notice. Prima facie one would expect that if a notice unambiguously conveys a decision to determine a court may nowadays ignore immaterial errors which would not have misled a reasonable recipient.

(4) There is no justification for placing notices under a break clause in leases in a unique category. Making due allowance for contextual differences, such notices belong to the general class of unilateral notices served under contractual rights reserved, e.g. notices to quit, notices to determine licences and notices to complete: *Delta Vale Properties Ltd. v. Mills* [1990] 1 W.L.R. 445, 454E-G. To those examples may be added notices under charter parties, contracts of affreightment, and so forth. Even if such notices under contractual rights reserved contain errors they may be valid if they are 'sufficiently clear and unambiguous to leave a

reasonable recipient in no reasonable doubt as to how and when they are intended to operate': the *Delta* case, at p. 454E-G, *per* Slade L.J. and adopted by Stocker and Bingham L.JJ.; see also *Carradine Properties Ltd. v. Aslam* [1976] 1 W.L.R. 442, 444. That test postulates that the reasonable recipient is left in no doubt that the right reserved is being exercised. It acknowledges the importance of such notices. The application of that test is principled and cannot cause any injustice to a recipient of the notice. I would gratefully adopt it.

(5) That brings me to the application of this test. The facts are simple. Crediting a reasonable recipient with knowledge of the terms of the lease and third anniversary date (13 January), I venture to suggest that it is obvious that a reasonable recipient would have appreciated that the tenant wished to determine the leases on the third anniversary date of the leases but wrongly described it as the 12th instead of the 13th. The reasonable recipient would not have been perplexed in any way by the minor error in the notices. The notices would have achieved their intended purpose.

. . .

Counsel for the tenant invited the House in his case and in his reply to say that *Hankey v. Clavering* was wrongly decided. I am content to say that it no longer represents the law. Like Lord Hoffmann I would hold that the correct test for the validity of a notice is that posed by Goulding J. in *Carradine Properties Ltd. v. Aslam* [1976] 1 W.L.R. 442, 444: 'Is the notice quite clear to a reasonable tenant reading it? Is it plain that he cannot be misled by it?''

. . .

LORD HOFFMANN. My Lords, the appellant was tenant under two 10-year leases of offices in Jermyn Street, each of which contained in clause 7(13) a right to terminate at the end of the third year in the following terms:

A23–002

'The tenant may by serving not less than six months' notice in writing on the landlord or its solicitors such notice to expire on the third anniversary of the term commencement date determine this lease and upon the expiry of such notice this lease shall cease and determine and have no further effect . . .'

After the grant of the leases the market rents of offices in the West End fell sharply. On 24 June 1994 the tenant served on the landlord two notices, each of which read as follows: 'Pursuant to clause 7(13) of the lease we as tenant hereby give notice to you to determine the lease on 12 January 1995.' It is agreed that the third anniversary of the commencement date was actually 13 January 1995. The question is whether notwithstanding this mistake the notices were effective to terminate the leases.

This might seem a straightforward question, particularly when it is remembered that such notices, operating, as they do, unilaterally to alter the rights of the parties, must comply strictly with the terms of the lease. The Court of Appeal held that the notice was ineffective on the simple

H  ground that '12 January' could not mean '13 January'. In so doing, they followed (as in my view they were bound to do) the decision of the Court of Appeal in *Hankey v. Clavering* [1942] 2 K.B. 326 which in turn had followed the decision of the Court of Queen's Bench in *Cadby v. Martinez*, 11 A. & E. 720. In that case, the notice said Midsummer instead of Lady Day. It seemed obvious to Lord Denman C.J. that there was no way in which it could be construed to refer to Lady Day and he merely observed,
A  at p. 726, that 'in [no case] has a proviso or covenant in a deed been held to be satisfied by a notice inconsistent with the terms of it'.

And yet, my Lords, the case is by no means straightforward. The clause does not require the tenant to use any particular form of words. He must use words which unambiguously convey a particular meaning, namely an intention to terminate the lease on 13 January. In *Hankey v. Clavering* [1942] 2 K.B. 326, where the notice to quit said '21 December'
B  instead of '25 December,' Lord Greene M.R. said, at pp. 328, 330, 'the whole thing was obviously a slip' on the part of the landlord but that the notice was invalid 'however much the recipient might guess, or however certain he might be' that it was a mere slip. So even if the recipient was certain that the landlord actually wanted to terminate his tenancy on the right date, which was 25 December, so that the necessary intention was
C  unambiguously communicated, the notice was bad. One is bound to be left with a feeling that something has gone wrong here. Common sense cannot produce such a result; it must be the result of some rule of law. If so, what is that rule and is it correct?

I propose to begin by examining the way we interpret utterances in everyday life. It is a matter of constant experience that people can convey their meaning unambiguously although they have used the wrong words.
D  We start with an assumption that people will use words and grammar in a conventional way but quite often it becomes obvious that, for one reason or another, they are not doing so and we adjust our interpretation of what they are saying accordingly. We do so in order to make sense of their utterance: so that the different parts of the sentence fit together in a coherent way and also to enable the sentence to fit the background of facts which
E  plays an indispensable part in the way we interpret what anyone is saying. No one, for example, has any difficulty in understanding Mrs. Malaprop. When she says 'She is as obstinate as an allegory on the banks of the Nile', we reject the conventional or literal meaning of allegory as making nonsense of the sentence and substitute 'alligator' by using our background knowledge of the things likely to be found on the banks of the Nile and choosing one which sounds rather like 'allegory'.
F  Mrs. Malaprop's problem was an imperfect understanding of the conventional meanings of English words. But the reason for the mistake does not really matter. We use the same process of adjustment when people have made mistakes about names or descriptions or days or times because they have forgotten or become mixed up. If one meets an acquaintance and he
G  says 'And how is Mary?' it may be obvious that he is referring to one's wife, even if she is in fact called Jane. One may even, to avoid embarrassment,

answer 'Very well, thank you' without drawing attention to his mistake. The message has been unambiguously received and understood.

If one applies that kind of interpretation to the notice in this case, there will also be no ambiguity. The reasonable recipient will see that in purporting to terminate pursuant to clause 7(13) but naming 12 January 1995 as the day upon which he will do so, the tenant has made a mistake. He will reject as too improbable the possibility that the tenant meant that unless he could terminate on 12 January, he did not want to terminate at all. He will therefore understand the notice to mean that the tenant wants to terminate on the date on which, in accordance with clause 7(13), he may do so, i.e. 13 January.

Why, then, do cases like *Hankey v. Clavering* [1942] 2 K.B. 326 arrive at a different answer? I want first to deal with two explanations which seem to me obviously inadequate. First, it is sometimes said that the examples which I have given from ordinary life are concerned with what the speaker meant to say. He may subjectively have intended to say something different from what he actually said and it may be possible, by the kind of reasoning which I have described, to divine what his subjective intentions were. But the law is not concerned with subjective intentions. All that matters is the objective meaning of the words which he has used.

It is of course true that the law is not concerned with the speaker's subjective intentions. But the notion that the law's concern is therefore with the 'meaning of his words' conceals an important ambiguity. The ambiguity lies in a failure to distinguish between the meanings of words and the question of what would be understood as the meaning of a person who uses words. The meaning of words, as they would appear in a dictionary, and the effect of their syntactical arrangement, as it would appear in a grammar, is part of the material which we use to understand a speaker's utterance. But it is only a part; another part is our knowledge of the background against which the utterance was made. It is that background which enables us, not only to choose the intended meaning when a word has more than one dictionary meaning but also, in the ways I have explained, to understand a speaker's meaning, often without ambiguity, when he has used the wrong words.

When, therefore, lawyers say that they are concerned, not with subjective meaning but with the meaning of the language which the speaker has used, what they mean is that they are concerned with what he would objectively have been understood to mean. This involves examining not only the words and the grammar but the background as well. So, for example, in *Doe d. Cox v. Roe*, 4 Esp. 185 the landlord of a public house in Limehouse gave notice to quit 'the premises which you hold of me ... commonly called ... The Waterman's Arms'. The evidence showed that the tenant held no premises called The Waterman's Arms; indeed, there were no such premises in the parish of Limehouse. But the tenant did hold premises of the landlord called The Bricklayer's Arms. By reference to the background, the notice was construed as referring to The Bricklayer's Arms. The meaning was objectively clear to a reasonable recipient, even though the landlord had used the wrong name. We therefore will in due course have to answer the question: if, as long ago as 1803, the background could be used to show that a person who speaks of The Waterman's Arms means The Bricklayer's Arms, why can it not show that a person who speaks of 12 January means 13 January?

The immediate point, however, is that the fact that the law does not have regard to subjective meaning is no explanation of the way *Hankey v. Clavering* [1942] 2 K.B. 326 was decided. There was no need to resort to subjective meaning: the notice would objectively have been understood to mean that the landlord wanted to terminate the tenancy on the day on which he was entitled to do so.

. . .

There can, I think, be no question of anyone having acted in reliance on the principle of construction used in *Hankey v. Clavering* [1942] 2 K.B. 326. The consequence of such a construction is only to allow one party to take an unmeritorious advantage of another's verbal error, an adventitious bonus upon which no one could have relied. In this respect, the case for rejecting the old authorities is at least as strong as it was in *Sudbrook Trading Estate Ltd. v. Eggleton* [1983] 1 A.C. 444, in which this House overruled cases going back to the early 19th century on the construction of contracts for sale at a valuation.

Nor do I think that a decision overruling the old cases will create uncertainty as to what the law is. In fact I think that the present law is uncertain and that only a decision of this House, either adopting or rejecting the *Hankey v. Clavering* rule of construction, will make it certain. So, for example, in *Carradine Properties Ltd. v. Aslam* [1976] 1 W.L.R. 442, 444, Goulding J. said that the test for the validity of a notice was: 'Is the notice quite clear to a reasonable tenant reading it? Is it plain that he cannot be misled by it?' and he went on to say that the reasonable tenant must be taken to know the terms of the lease. This test was approved by the Court of Appeal in *Germax Securities Ltd. v. Spiegal* (1978) 37 P. & C.R. 204, 206 and, as will be apparent from what I have already said, I think that it was the right test to adopt. It is, however, absolutely impossible to reconcile the application of such a test with the decision in *Hankey v. Clavering*, in which no reasonable tenant who knew the terms of the lease could possibly have mistaken the landlord's meaning. It is therefore not surprising that in *Micrografix v. Woking 8 Ltd.* [1995] 2 E.G.L.R. 32 Jacob J. felt free to dismiss *Hankey v. Clavering* as 'much distinguished' and to ignore it, or that Rattee J. in *Garston v. Scottish Widows' Fund and Life Assurance Society* [1996] 1 W.L.R. 834 should be puzzled as to why the Court of Appeal in this case considered, as I think rightly, that they were bound by *Hankey v. Clavering*.

In my view, therefore, the House should say unequivocally that the test stated by Goulding J. in *Carradine Properties Ltd. v. Aslam* [1976] 1 W.L.R. 442 was right and that Hankey v. Clavering and the earlier cases should no longer be followed. The notice should be construed against the background of the terms of the lease. Interpreted in this way, the notice in the present case was valid and I would therefore allow the appeal.

...

LORD CLYDE.    A23–003

...

Where a notice of termination complies precisely and unambiguously with the provision which empowers the sending of the notice then its validity should be unquestioned. Where the terms of the notice do not altogether accord with the provisions of the contract that may or may not render the notice unenforceable. The problem then may come to be one of finding a fair and reasonable construction of the notice. But there can be cases where the validity of the notice cannot be saved by any construction and will have to be regarded as bad.

In some cases it may be obvious from the notice by itself that an error has been made. In *Carradine Properties Ltd. v. Aslam* [1976] 1 W.L.R. 442 an expressed intention to determine the lease at a date in 1973 was obviously incorrect in a notice served in 1974. In other cases the discrepancy can only be seen from a study of the terms of the lease. One would need to be aware of the provisions of the lease in such a case to appreciate that the permitted date was inaccurately stated. I see no reason in principle why in each of these kinds of case, provided of course that the wording is not absolutely clear and unambiguous, a notice should not be equally open to construction with a view to its possible validity.

In the present case the two letters in my view satisfy the formal and technical requirements of clause 7(13). But they go further and call for a determination of each lease one day before the day which the sub-clause identified as the date for the determination of the notice and for the determination of the lease. As I have mentioned that was not a formal requisite of the notice. Each notice proclaims at the outset that it is given 'pursuant to clause 7 (13)'. This was a precise reference to the particular provision under which the notices were each being sent, as distinct from some general reference to the agreement between the parties. But it is evident from a consideration of that clause that there is a discrepancy between the date there indicated for the termination of the lease and the date stated in the notice. Whether that inaccuracy in the notice is fatal or not depends on the proper construction of the notices. The formulation propounded by Goulding J. in the *Carradine* case, at p. 444, was 'Is the notice quite clear to a reasonable tenant reading it? Is it plain that he cannot be misled by it?' *Delta Vale Properties Ltd. v. Mills* [1990] 1 W.L.R. 445 concerned a vendor's notice to complete which was in condition 23 of the conditions of sale, but I see no reason why any different principle of construction should apply. Slade L.J. observed, at p. 454:

'In my judgment, notices to complete served under condition 23, if they are to be valid, must be sufficiently clear and unambiguous to leave a reasonable recipient in no reasonable doubt as to how and when they are intended to operate.'

C The standard of reference is that of the reasonable man exercising his common sense in the context and in the circumstances of the particular case. It is not an absolute clarity or an absolute absence of any possible ambiguity which is desiderated. To demand a perfect precision in matters which are not within the formal requirements of the relevant power would in my view impose an unduly high standard in the framing of notices such as those in issue here. While careless drafting is certainly to be discouraged the evident intention of a notice should not in matters of
D this kind be rejected in preference for a technical precision.

The test is an objective one. In circumstances where an estoppel might arise the actual understanding of the recipient may be relevant, but in general the actual understanding of the parties is beside the point. That the test is an objective one was recognised in *Micrografix v. Woking 8*
E *Ltd.* [1995] 2 E.G.L.R. 32. It was held there that the landlords would not have been misled by the references to a wrong date both in the notice to terminate the lease and in the covering letter. Each document was expressly written pursuant to the particular break clause in the lease. The recipients would have observed the errors because they would be familiar with the terms of the lease and would have known that the only date of determination had to be 23 June 1995. They would know that there was
F no requirement to specify any date in the notice. They would see that the tenant wanted to leave. It was held that the notice was valid.

. . .

# Appendix 24

# *Barrett v Morgan* [2000] 2 A.C. 264 at 270–271

LORD MILLETT.

...

A lease or tenancy for a fixed term comes to an end by effluxion of time on the date fixed for its determination. A periodic tenancy comes to an end on the expiry of a notice to quit served by the landlord on the tenant or by the tenant on the landlord. As Lord Hoffmann explained in *Newlon Housing Trust v. Alsulaimen* [1999] 1 A.C. 313, 317, it also comes to an end by effluxion of time. In each case the tenancy is determined in accordance with its terms. By granting and accepting a periodic tenancy with provision, express or implied, for its determination by notice to quit, the parties have agreed at the outset on the manner of its termination. The parties and their successors in title, including those who derive title under them, are bound by their agreement.

A lease or tenancy may also be surrendered at any time by the tenant to his immediate landlord. A surrender is simply an assurance by which a lesser estate is yielded up to the greater, and the term is usually applied to the giving up of a lease or tenancy before its expiration. If a tenant surrenders his tenancy to his immediate landlord, who accepts the surrender, the tenancy is absorbed by the landlord's reversion and is extinguished by operation of law.

A surrender is ineffective unless the landlord consents to accept it, and is therefore consensual in the fullest sense of the term. In *Coke's Commentary upon Littleton* (1832), vol. II, s. 636, p. 337b the nature of a surrender is described as follows:

> 'Surrender, sursum redditio, properly is a yeelding up an estate for life or yeares to him that hath an immediate estate in reversion or remainder, wherein the estate for life or yeares may drowne by *mutuall agreement betweene them.*' (My emphasis.)

On its surrender the tenancy is brought to end prematurely at a time and in a manner not provided for by the terms of the tenancy agreement. In this respect it differs from the case where a tenancy is determined by notice to quit. It is because the landlord or his predecessor in title has not, by granting the tenancy, previously agreed that the tenant should have the right to surrender the tenancy prematurely that the landlord's consent is necessary.

The destruction of the tenancy by surrender reflects the principle that a person cannot at the same time be both landlord and tenant of the same premises. Nemo potest esse tenens et dominus: see *Rye v. Rye* [1962] A.C. 496, 513, *per* Lord Denning. Formerly the extinguishment of the tenancy by surrender also extinguished the reversion to any subtenancy, so that the remedy for the rent and the covenants attached to the reversion ceased with the reversion to which they were annexed. The subtenant held the property as tenant of the head landlord for the residue of the term of the extinguished tenancy but without privity of estate and accordingly without any obligation to pay the rent or perform the tenant's covenants: see *Webb v. Russell* (1789) 3 Durn. & E. 393. This unsatisfactory state of affairs was remedied by statute in two stages. Section 6 of the Landlord and Tenant Act 1730 (4 Geo. 2, c. 28) (now section 150 of the Law of Property Act 1925) effected a partial reversal of the common law rule. Section 9 of the Real Property Act 1845 (8 & 9 Vict. c. 106)(now section 139 of the Act of 1925) reversed it more generally. These provisions apply only where the head tenancy is surrendered.

Although a person such as a subtenant having a derivative interest may benefit by the surrender and consequent extinguishment of the estate out of which his interest is derived, he cannot be prejudiced by it. It is a general and salutary principle of law that a person cannot be adversely affected by an agreement or arrangement to which he is not a party. So far as he is concerned, it is res inter alios acta. It would conflict with this principle if the destruction of a tenancy by surrender carried with it the destruction of the interest of a subtenant under a subtenancy previously granted. It has been clear from the earliest times that it does not do so . . .

Appendix 25

# PW & Co v Milton Gate Investments Ltd [2004] Ch. 142 at 164

8 August. **NEUBERGER J** handed down the following judgment.     A25–001

...

72 As explained by Lord Millett, it appears to me that the principle is that the determination of a head tenancy in accordance with its terms will lead to the destruction of any subtenancy, but where the determination of the head tenancy arises from is some consensual arrangement between the landlord and the head tenant not provided for in the head tenancy, then the subtenancy will survive. This view seems consistent, in particular, with the observations which I have quoted of Lord Millett, at pp 270–271, at p 272a–b and at p 272c–e. As I have said, care must be taken lest one places too much weight on words in a judgment where the tribunal did not have in mind the point at issue in the instant case. None the less, in the last two passages I have referred to, Lord Millett did say that the subtenant 'cannot survive the natural termination of the head tenancy in accordance with its terms agreed before his subtenancy was created' and that 'when [the head tenancy] is determined by notice to quit, it has come to the end of its natural life. There is no further period remaining during which the tenancy can have continuance'. It appears to me that, in those observations, he was stating, or applying, a point of general principle.

73. I consider that this conclusion is supported by a number of further points. First, it is always important to remember in connection with this sort of issue that a tenancy is not merely a contract: it is and it creates an estate in land. When a tenant grants a subtenancy, he is granting a subsidiary estate out of the estate vested in him by the head tenancy. As a matter of principle, it would seem to follow ineluctably that, if and when the head tenancy determines, and the estate thereby created ceases to exist, any subsidiary estate carved out of it, including

any subtenancy, must also determine. It is, I suppose, an example of the maxim nemo dat quod non habet. Ultimately, that is the simple proposition upon which decisions such as *Pennell v Payne* [1995] QB 192 and *Barrett v Morgan* [2000] 2 AC 264 rest. If that is the right analysis, it is difficult to see how a subtenancy can survive a destruction of the head tenancy simply because the landlord and head tenant agree that it should.

. . .

Appendix 26

# Davy's Of London (Wine Merchants) Ltd v City Of London Corporation [2004] EWHC 2224 (Ch) at 22–25

**MR JUSTICE LEWISON:**   A26–001

...

22. In deciding whether a new tenancy should or should not include a break clause, the usual starting point is the statement of Stamp LJ in *Adams v. Green* [1978] 2 EGLR 46 that:

> 'It was no part of the policy ... of the 1954 Act to give security of tenure to a business tenant at the expense of preventing redevelopment.'

23. I emphasise the word 'preventing', which is not the same as 'delaying'. In that case the landlord had no plans for redevelopment but wished to have the flexibility to sell to a developer. The Court of Appeal, reversing the trial judge, ordered the inclusion in the new tenancy of a break clause operable on two years' notice. In other words, the tenant had guaranteed security of tenure of two years.

24. In *JH Edwards & Sons Ltd v. Central London Commercial Estates Ltd* [1984] 2 EGLR 103 the landlord again had no formulated plans for redevelopment. The Court of Appeal held that the trial judge had been wrong to have ordered the grant of a new lease for as long as ten years. In exercising their own discretion, Fox LJ said:

> 'In considering what would be proper leases in the circumstances of this case I think that the predominant considerations are two. First, that so far as reasonable the leases would not prevent the superior landlord from using the premises for the purposes of development.

Secondly, that a reasonable degree of security of tenure should be provided for the tenants. Those considerations are to some extent in conflict. The function of the court is to strike a reasonable balance between them in all the circumstances of the case."

25. Bearing in mind that the landlord had no formulated redevelopment plans, the Court of Appeal held that the break clause should be exercisable after the first five years of the new tenancy. There is no indication in the formulation of the legal test that the landlord's desire to redevelop necessarily trumps the tenant's desire for security of tenure. On the contrary, Fox LJ expressly says that the function of the court is to strike a fair balance between the two competing aspirations. This necessarily presupposes that the landlord may have to wait for some time (though not so long as to prevent redevelopment) before being able to regain possession. Moreover, the new lease should not prevent redevelopment 'so far as reasonable'. Mr Harper's submission that, in effect, the landlord can have a break clause for the asking, exercisable at a time of his choosing, seems to me to be inconsistent with this.

. . .

Appendix 27

# Fitzroy House Epworth Street (No.1) Ltd v Financial Times Ltd [2006] 1 W.L.R. 2207 at 24 and 35–36

**SIR ANDREW MORRITT C**  A27–001

24 . . . It cannot, I think, be seriously disputed that the issue of 'material compliance' whatever it involves must be determined on an objective basis. This was the view of the Court of Appeal in *Fortman Holdings Ltd v Modem Holdings Ltd* [2001] EWCA Civ 1235, per Judge LJ, at para 26, and Pill LJ, at para 7, when considering a similar provision in a loan note.

. . .

35 . . . Materiality must be assessed by reference to the ability of the landlord to relet or sell the property without delay or additional expenditure. Where the provision is absolute then any breach will preclude an exercise of the break clause. But I see no justification for attributing to the parties an intention that the insertion of the word 'material' was intended to permit only breaches which were trivial or trifling. Those words are of uncertain meaning also and are not the words used by the parties.

36 Nor is it, in my view, of any assistance to consider whether the word 'material' permits more or different breaches than the commonly used alternatives 'substantial' or 'reasonable'. The words 'substantial' and 'material', depending on the context, are interchangeable. The word 'reasonable' connotes a different test. The issue here is whether, notwithstanding the breaches found by the judge the tenant had, nevertheless, 'materially complied' with its obligations. The application of an ordinary English word to a set of primary facts is itself a question of fact: see *Cozens v Brutus* [1973] AC 854, 861 . . .

Appendix 28

# Extracts From 'The Code for Leasing Business Premises in England and Wales 2007'

"LEASING BUSINESS PREMISES: LANDLORD CODE          A28–001

. . .

**3 Length of term, Break Clauses and Renewal Rights**

The length of the term must be clear.

The only pre-conditions to tenants exercising any break clauses should be that they are up to date with the main rent, give up occupation and leave behind no continuing subleases. Disputes about the state of the premises, or what has been left behind or removed, should be settled later (like with normal lease expiry).

The fallback position under the Landlord and Tenant Act 1954 is that business tenants have rights to renew their leases. It is accepted that there are a number of circumstances in which that is not appropriate. In such cases landlords should state at the start of negotiations that the protection of the 1954 Act is to be excluded and encourage tenants to seek early advice as to the implications."

# Break Clauses Index

**Administration**
  break notices
    service on companies in
      administration, 6–011
**Administrators**
  exercise of break clauses, 5–027
**Agents**
  break notices
    general agency cases, 5–034—5–039
    service on, 6–009
  exercise of break clauses,
    5–029—5–039
  notices to quit
    general agency cases, 5–031—5–033
**Agricultural holdings**
  break notices
    compensation, 10–014, A14–007
    compliance, 10–010
    conditions, 10–011—10–013
    purpose, 10–009
    time limits, 10–006—10–008
    notices to quit, 10–004—10–005,
      A14–004—A14–006
  statutory provisions
    Agricultural Holdings Act 1986,
      A14–001—A14–008
    generally, 10–001
    termination of contracts,
      10–002—10–014
**Agricultural Holdings Act 1986**
  relevant provisions,
    A14–001—A14–008
**Agricultural tenancies**
  *see* **Agricultural holdings**
**Agricultural Tenancies Act 1995**
  relevant provisions,
    A17–001—A17–007
**Assignment**
  "all estate" clause, 3–005—3–007,
    A9–001
  benefits of covenants, 3–001—3–004,
    3–010—3–013, A16–001
  burdens of covenants, 3–001—3–004,
    3–010—3–013, A16–001

common law position
  effect on lease, 3–002
  generally, 3–001
  right to end tenancy, 3–003
  "touch and concern" test, 3–004
contracts
  best practice, 3–034—3–035
equitable assignees
  exercise of break clause,
    3–027—3–030
landlord assigning reversion
  post-January 1, 1996 leases, 3–020
  pre-January 1, 1996 leases, 3–021
  restrictions, 3–022
  service of break notice, 3–026
  severance of reversion,
    3–023—3–026
partial assignment
  break clauses, and, 3–019
  post-January 1, 1996 leases,
    3–010—3–013, 3–015, 3–020
  pre-January 1, 1996 leases,
    3–008—3–009, 3–014, 3–021
restrictions
  assignment of part, 3–019
  break clauses assignable to limited
    group, 3–016, 3–018
  landlord assigning, on, 3–022
  personal break clauses,
    3–016—3–017
side letters
  options contained in, 3–031—3–033
  statutory provisions, 3–005—3–013
tenant assigning term
  post-January 1, 1996 leases,
    3–015
  pre-January 1, 1996 leases, 3–014
  restrictions, 3–016—3–019
**Assured shorthold tenancies**
  recovery of possession, A15–002
  termination, 11–013—11–017
**Assured tenancies**
  security of tenure, A15–001
  termination, 11–007—11–012

**Benefits of covenants**
assignment, 3–001—3–004,
3–010—3–013, A16–001
**Breach of covenant**
material breach, 7–006—7–007,
7–033—7–034
non-payment of rent, 7–027—7–030
server's own breach, 7–063
spent breaches, 7–010—7–012
strict compliance principle,
7–001—7–005
time for compliance, 7–013—7–022
**Break clauses**
*see also* **Assignment; Business tenancies; Conditions; Residential tenancies**
acceptance of repudiatory breach distinguished, 1–009—1–010
agricultural holdings, 10–001—10–014
assignment and, 3–001—3–034
business tenancies, 9–001—9–014
conditions for validity
landlord's break clause,
7–059—7–062
tenant's break clause, 7–051—7–058
contents, 4–001—4–055
drafting, 12–001—12–005
effect of exercise of, 8–001—8–022
exercise of break clauses
administrators, and, 5–027
agents, use of, 5–029—5–039
assignees, 5–019
break clause personal to original tenant, 5–009—5–017
joint lessees, 5–020—5–023
joint lessors, 5–024
landlord, by, 13–011—13–019
lease silent or unclear, 5–018
liquidators, and, 5–028
practical advice, 13–001—13–023
service by wrong party,
5–001—5–008
survivors of joint lessees/lessors,
5–025
tenant, by, 13–001—13–010
trustees in bankruptcy, and, 5–026
farm business tenancies,
10–015—10–023
forfeiture distinguished, 1–009—1–010
form
generally, 1–013
standard clauses, 1–014
types of tenancies, 1–013
formalities, 2–001—2–004
landlords
incorporating rolling break,
A2–001—A2–002
specified dates, A1–001—A1–002
meaning, 1–001
notices to quit compared,
1–002—1–004, 9–003
option, as
generally, 1–011
inflexibility rule, 1–012
strict compliance rule, 1–012
*United Scientific Holdings Ltd v Burnley Borough Council*,
1–011, A19–001—A19–003
procedural requirements
generally, 4–001—4–002
recipients' consent, 1–005—1–006
registration, 2–005—2–007
residential tenancies, 11–001—11–020
subleases, and, 1–008
surrender, and, 1–006—1–007,
A24–001
tenants
incorporating rolling break,
A4–001—A4–002
specified dates, A3–001—A3–002
unilateral right to terminate,
1–005—1–008
**Break notices**
*see* **Notices; Service; Withdrawal**
**Burdens of covenants**
assignment, 3–001—3–004,
3–010—3–013, A16–001
**Business tenancies**
break clauses
*Davy's Of London (Wine Merchants) Ltd v City Of London Corporation*, A26–001
drafting, 12–005
generally, 9–01
new leases, 9–008—9–012, A26–001
tenant seeking new lease after break,
9–013
subtenants, position of, 9–014
Code for Leasing Business Premises in England and Wales 2007, 12–003,
A28–001
Landlord and Tenant Act 1994
landlord's break notice,
9–002—9–007
relevant provisions,
A10–001—A10–007

**Compensation**
agricultural holdings, 10–014, A14–007
farm business tenancies, 10–022
**Compliance**
compliance periods
language of break clauses,
7–013—7–022

material compliance
  *Fitzroy House Epworth Street (No.1) Ltd v Financial Times Ltd*, A27–001
  qualification of strict compliance principle
    "desire", 7–061
    "intention", 7–060
    "material", 7–032—7–033, A27–001
    "reasonable", 7–025—7–031
    "reasonably", 7–025—7–031
    "substantial", 7–034—7–035
  server's own breach, 7–065
  strict compliance principle
    fairness, and, 7–006—7–009
    generally, 7–001—7–005
    words qualifying principle, 7–032—7–035, 7–060—7–061
**Conditions**
  *see also* **Compliance; Estoppel; Waiver**
  non-compliance
    server's own breach, 7–063
  validity of break clauses
    fairness, 7–006—7–009
    landlord's break clause, 7–059—7–062
    payment of rent, 7–046—7–049
    reinstatement obligations, 7–044—7–045
    spent breaches, 7–010—7–011
    strict compliance principle, 7–001—7–005, 7–060
    subjectivity, 7–006—7–009
    time for compliance, 7–013—7–022
    vacant possession, 7–036—7–043
  waiver
    tenant's break clause, 7–051—7–058
**Conditions precedent**
  cases
    *Bass Holdings Ltd v Morton Music Ltd*, A20–001
    *Finch v Underwood*, A18–001—A18–002
    *United Scientific Holdings Ltd v Burnley Borough Council*, A19–001—A19–003
**Content of break clauses**
  *see* **Mistake; Notices; Termination; Validity**
**Contracts**
  assignment
    best practice, 3–034—3–035
**Covenants**
  *see also* **Assignment; Breach of covenant**
  benefits of covenants

assignment, 3–001—3–004, 3–010—3–013, A16–001
burdens of covenants
  assignment, 3–001—3–004, 3–010—3–013, A16–001
  equitable assignees, 3–027—3–030
  Landlord and Tenant (Covenants) Act 1995, 3–010—3–013
  landlord assigning reversion, 3–020—3–026
  landlord covenants
    meaning, 3–013
  Law of Property Act 1925, 3–005—3–009
  option not contained in lease, 3–031—3–033
  tenant assigning term, 3–014—3–019
  tenant covenants
    meaning, 3–013
    performance, 7–026—7–030
    reinstatement obligations, 7–044—7–045
**Crown**
  service of break notices on, 6–012
**Dates**
  "commencing on", 4–015
  "from", 4–014
  "month", 4–012
  "quarter", 4–011
**Distress for Rent Act 1737**
  relevant provisions, A8–001
**Drafting**
  break clauses
    business tenancies, 12–005
    Code for Leasing Business Premises, 12–003, A28–001
    generally, 12–001—12–004
    rent review provisions, 12–002
    specific matters, 12–005
    subtenancies, 12–005
  break notices, 13–004—13–005, 13–013—13–014
**Estoppel**
  break notices
    invalid notices, 4–051—4–056
    service of notice, 6–035
    conditions in tenant's break clause
      landlord's position, 7–056—7–058
      tenant's position, 7–051—7–055
**Estoppel by convention**
  break notices, and, 4–052—4–055
**Exercise of break clauses**
  *see* **Break clauses; Landlords; Notices; Tenants**

# BREAK CLAUSES INDEX

**Farm business tenancies**
  break clauses
    compensation, 10–022
    generally, 10–017
    service of notices, 10–021
    tenancy from year to year, 10–019
    tenancy of more than two years,
      10–018, 10–020
  meaning, A17–001
  restrictions, 10–023
  security of tenure, 10–017
  statutory provisions
    termination of farm business
      tenancies, 10–015—10–023,
      A17–001—A17–007
**Forfeiture**
  break clauses distinguished,
    1–009—1–010
**Formalities**
  break clauses
    desirability of formality, 2–003
    lease to be by deed, 2–004
    new leases, in, 2–001
    separate documents, in,
      2–001—2–002
**Forms**
  landlord's break notice
    rolling break incorporated, A2–002
    specified dates, with, A1–002
  tenant's break notice
    rolling break, incorporating, A4–002
    specified dates, on, A3–002

**Housing Act 1988**
  relevant provisions,
    A15–001—A15–002

**Joint tenancies**
  termination by one tenant
    *Hounslow London Borough Council v*
    *Pilling*, 5–022, A21–001

**Landlord and Tenant Act 1730**
  relevant provisions, A7–001
**Landlord and Tenant Act 1954**
  landlord's break notice, 9–002—9–007
  relevant provisions,
    A10–001—A10–007
**Landlord and Tenant (Covenants) Act 1995**
  assignment
    s.3 provisions, 3–010—3–013
  relevant provisions,
    A16–001—A16–002
**Landlords**
  *see also* **Agents; Assignment**
  assignment

    break clauses, and, 3–003—3–004,
      5–019
  break clauses
    conditions for validity,
      7–059—7–062
    incorporating rolling break,
      A2–001—A2–002
    specified dates, A1–001—A1–002
  effect of exercise of break clauses
    landlord's entitlement to double rent,
      8–012—8–014
    liability for existing breaches, 8–003
    parties relieved of need to fulfil
      covenant, 8–001—8–002
    rent review provisions,
      8–004—8–011
    subtenancies, on, 8–015—8–022
  landlord exercising break clause
    drafting break notice,
      13–013—13–014
    litigation tactics, 13–022—13–023
    preconditions, 13–011—13–012
    service of break notice,
      13–015—13–016
  landlord receiving tenant's break notice
    preconditions in tenant's break
      clause, 13–007—13–010
  notices to quit, 3–003, 5–031—5–033
  subtenancies
    landlord exercising break,
      8–021—8–022
  tenant exercising break clause
    drafting break notice,
      13–004—13–005
    litigation tactics, 13–020—13–021
    service of break notice, 13–006
    preconditions, 13–001—13–003
  tenant receiving landlord's break notice
    checking break notice,
      13–018—13–019
    preconditions in break clause, 13–017
**Land Registry**
  break clauses in registered leases, 2–006
**Language**
  break clauses, in, 4–010—4–026
  compliance periods, 7–012—7–021
  mistakes, 4–016—4–026
**Law of Property Act 1925**
  assignment
    s.63 provisions, 3–005—3–007,
      A9–001
    s.142 provisions, 3–008—3–009,
      A9–003
  relevant provisions, A9–001—A9–005
**Lessees**
  exercise of break clauses
    joint lessees, 5–020—5–023

survivors of joint lessees, 5–025
service of break notices on
concurrent lessees, 6–004—6–007
joint lessees, 6–003
**Lessors**
exercise of break clauses
joint lessors, 5–024
survivors of joint lessors, 5–025
service of break notices on
joint lessors, 6–003
**Liquidation**
break notices
service on companies in
liquidation, 6–012
**Liquidators**
exercise of break clauses, 5–028

**Mistake**
break clauses
language in, 4–016—4–026
break notices
date of termination, as to, 4–027
description of premises,
4–037—4–039
identity of landlord or tenant,
4–028—4–036
service on wrong party,
5–001—5–008

**Notices**
break notices
agricultural holdings,
10–006—10–014
drafting, 13–004—13–005,
13–013—13–014
estoppel, and, 4–050—4–055
*Mannai Investment Co Ltd v Eagle
Star Life Assurance Co Ltd*,
4–016—4–026, 4–046, 4–047,
A23–001— A23–004
reaction of receiving parties,
4–040—4–042
sequential, 4–049
subject to contract, 4–046—4–047
validity, 4–016—4–026
without prejudice communications,
4–043—4–047
mistakes
date of termination, as to, 4–027
description of premises,
4–037—4–039
identity of landlord or tenant,
4–028—4–036
regulations, A9–004
**Notices to quit**
agricultural holdings, 10–004—10–005,
A14–004—A14–006

break clauses compared,
1–002—1–004, 9–003
general agency cases, 5–033—5–033
purpose, 1–003
service, 1–003
unprotected tenancies, 11–019—11–020
use of, 1–002
validity, A13–001
withdrawal, 6–035—6–039

**Partial assignment**
break clauses, and, 3–019
**Particulars of claim**
defence and counterclaim,
A6–001— A6–003
landlord's claim for declaration,
A5–001—A5–003
**Periodic tenancies**
notices to quit, 1–002, 3–003
**Postal service**
break notices, 6–015, 6–017—6–020
Recorded Delivery Service Act 1962
relevant provisions, A11–001
**Professional liability**
break notices
invalid notices, 6–040—6–041
**Promissory estoppel**
break notices, and, 4–052—4–055
**Protection from Eviction Act 1977**
relevant provisions, A13–001

**Quarter days**
meaning, 4–011

**Registration**
records of "broken" leases, 2–007
generally, 2–005
term of lease, 2–006
transfer of unregistered lease, 2–006
**Rent**
landlord's entitlement to double rent,
8–012—8–014
payment condition in break clauses,
7–046—7–049
reviews
effect of exercise of break clauses,
8–004—8–011
provisions in break clauses, 12–002
**Rent Act 1977**
relevant provisions,
A12–001—A12–004
**Repudiation**
acceptance of
break clauses distinguished,
1–009—1–010
**Residential tenancies**
assured shorthold tenancies

recovery of possession, A15–002
termination, 11–013—11–017
assured tenancies
  security of tenure, A15–001
  termination, 11–007—11–012
  generally, 11–001
  possession
    grounds for, A12–004
  Rent Act protected tenancies
    meaning, A12–001
    termination, 11–002—11–006
  statutory tenancies
    meanings, A12–002
    terms and conditions, A12–003
  unprotected tenancies
    generally, 11–018
    notices to quit, 11–019—11–020

**Reversions**
assignment
  equitable assignees, 3–027—3–030
  post-January 1, 1996 leases, 3–020
  pre-January 1, 1996 leases, 3–021
  restrictions, 3–022
  service of break notice, 3–026
  severance of reversion,
    3–023—3–026
obligations under lessor's
  covenants, A9–003

**Security of tenure**
assured tenancies, A15–001
farm business tenancies, 10–017

**Service**
break notices
  agents, on, 6–009
  bankrupts, on, 6–010
  companies in administration,
    on, 6–011
  companies in liquidation, on, 6–012
  concurrent lessees, on,
    6–004—6–007
  Crown, on, 6–012
  drafting, 13–004—13–005
  estoppel, 6–035
  joint lessors/lessees, on, 6–003
  method of service, 6–013—6–021
  multiple parties, on, 6–008
  practical advice, 13–006,
    13–015—13–016
  service by whom, 6–001
  service on whom, 6–002—6–012
  tenant, by, 13–006
  timing, 6–022—6–033
  trustees in bankruptcy, on, 6–010
  waiver, 6–034
postal service, 6–015, 6–017—6–020
professional liability

invalid notices, 6–040—6–041
Recorded Delivery Service Act 1962
  relevant provisions, A11–001
timing
  late service, relief for, 6–029—6–032,
    A22–001
  occasion for exercise, 6–022—6–026
  short service, acceptance of, 6–033
  time expressed, 6–026—6–027
  time not expressed, 6–028
  *Union Eagle Ltd v Golden*
    *Achievement Ltd*, A22–001
withdrawal
  break notices, 6–035—6–039
  notices to quit, 6–035—6–039

**Subject to contract**
validity in break notices, 4–046—4–048

**Subtenancies**
break clauses
  drafting, 12–005
effect of exercise of break clauses
  business tenancies, 9–014
  landlord exercising break,
    8–021—8–022
  tenant exercising break,
    8–016—8–020
survival of
  *PW & Co v Milton Gate Investments*
    *Ltd*, A25–001

**Surrender**
*Barrett v Morgan*, A24–001
break clauses, and, 1–006—1–007
survival of sublease, 1–007

**Tenants**
*see also* **Assignment; Subtenancies**
assignment
  break clauses, and, 3–003—3–004,
    5–019
break clauses
  conditions for validity,
    7–051—7–058
  incorporating rolling break,
    A4–001—A4–002
  specified dates, A3–001—A3–002
break notices
  service by tenant, 13–006
effect of exercise of break clauses
  landlord's entitlement to double rent,
    8–012—8–014
  liability for existing breaches, 8–003
  parties relieved of need to fulfil
    covenant, 8–001—8–002
  rent review provisions,
    8–004—8–011
  subtenancies, on, 8–016—8–022
joint tenants

termination by one tenant, 5–022,
A21–001
subtenants
tenant exercising break,
8–015—8–020
tenant exercising break clause
drafting break notice,
13–004—13–005
litigation tactics, 13–020—13–021
service of break notice, 13–006
preconditions, 13–001—13–003
tenant receiving landlord's
break notice
checking break notice,
13–018—13–019
preconditions in break clause, 13–017
**Termination**
assured shorthold tenancies,
11–013—11–017
assured tenancies, 11–007—11–012
date
calculation of, 4–007
"commencing on", 4–015
corresponding date rule, 4–013
definition clauses, 4–006
"from", 4–014
generally, 4–003—4–009, 4–010
landlord's break clauses, 4–004

"month", 4–012
mutual break clauses, 4–005
"quarter", 4–011
specification of, 4–006, 4–008
tenant's break clauses, 4–003
Rent Act protected tenancies,
11–002—11–006
**Trustees in bankruptcy**
exercise of break clauses, 5–026
service of break notices on, 6–010

**Vacant possession**
condition in break clause,
7–036—7–043
**Validity**
break notices
mistakes in language, 4–016—4–026

**Waiver**
break notices
defects in notice, 6–034
conditions in tenant's break clause
landlord's position, 7–056—7–058
tenant's position, 7–051—7–055
**Withdrawal**
break notices, 6–035—6–039
**Without prejudice communications**
validity in break notices, 4–043—4–047